Practical D3.js

Tarek Amr

Rayna Stamboliyska

Practical D3.js

Tarek Amr
Amsterdam
The Netherlands

Rayna Stamboliyska
Issy-les-Moulineaux
Paris, France

ISBN 978-1-4842-1927-0
DOI 10.1007/978-1-4842-1928-7

ISBN 978-1-4842-1928-7 (eBook)

Library of Congress Control Number: 2016944319

Managing Director: Welmoed Spahr
Acquisitions Editor: Louise Corrigan
Development Editor: Michael Koch
Technical Reviewer: Kent Russell
Editorial Board: Steve Anglin, Pramila Balen, Louise Corrigan, Jonathan Gennick, Robert Hutchinson,
     Celestin Suresh John, Nikhil Karkal, James Markham, Susan McDermott, Matthew Moodie,
     Ben Renow-Clarke, Gwenan Spearing
Coordinating Editor: Nancy Chen
Copy Editor: Laura Lawrie
Compositor: SPi Global
Indexer: SPi Global

Distributed to the book trade worldwide by Springer Science+Business Media New York, 233 Spring Street, 6th Floor, New York, NY 10013. Phone 1-800-SPRINGER, fax (201) 348-4505, e-mail orders-ny@springer-sbm.com, or visit www.springer.com. Apress Media, LLC is a California LLC and the sole member (owner) is Springer Science + Business Media Finance Inc (SSBM Finance Inc). SSBM Finance Inc is a Delaware corporation.

For information on translations, please e-mail rights@apress.com, or visit www.apress.com.

Apress and friends of ED books may be purchased in bulk for academic, corporate, or promotional use. eBook versions and licenses are also available for most titles. For more information, reference our Special Bulk Sales–eBook Licensing web page at www.apress.com/bulk-sales.

Any source code or other supplementary materials referenced by the author in this text is available to readers at www.apress.com. For detailed information about how to locate your book's source code, go to www.apress.com/source-code/.

Printed on acid-free paper

Contents at a Glance

Contents

About the Authors

Tarek Amr achieved his postgraduate degree in data mining and machine learning from the University of East Anglia. He currently works as a data scientist in Amsterdam. He has more than 10 years' experience in software development. Tarek participates in training data journalists and he works on promoting open data. He can be reached at http://tarekamr.com.

Rayna Stamboliyska is a trained scientist whose professional journey has shifted into data-driven innovation and strategy. She consults for international organizations, businesses, media and nonprofits, and is a polylingual bookworm. She conducts risk and crisis management assessments using OSINT on a daily basis and frequently works in conflict and postconflict zones in MENA, Eastern Europe, and Africa. She is the founder of the first-ever action research and service consultancy around open knowledge in the MENA region, and the curator of Data Colada, the only French-speaking weekly resource on data. Crunching data is an integral part of her existence, and so is data visualization. She frequently trains curious individuals about open data and data journalism. She can be reached at http://about.me/raynast or @MaliciaRogue on Twitter.

About the Technical Reviewer

Kent Russell manages money on a professional basis and believes that D3 and R are essential tools for visual exploration of data and decision making. He resides in Birmingham, Alabama.

Acknowledgments

I'd like to dedicate this book to my late mother, Sherifa. I am also grateful to many people who taught me a lot. Some of these people I know in person, some I haven't met yet, but without them all this book wouldn't have been what it is now: my postgraduate supervisor, Dr. Beatriz De La Iglesia; Alberto Cairo, author of the book The Functional Art; Stoyan Stefanov, author of the book JavaScript Patterns; and last but not least, my friend and data journalist, Ramzi Jaber.

—Tarek Amr

Writing those chapters consumed a fair amount of dedication and work. Still, achievement would not have been possible if I did not have a support of many individuals: friends, family and like-minded nerds. Therefore, I would like to extend my sincere gratitude to all of them: my parents for their pride and trust in my abilities, from day 0; Benoît, for answering silly questions while troubleshooting Ansible scripts and bearing with me throughout the process; Pierre, for embarking on the joyful folie we call Data Colada, started out between two paragraphs of this book; Gabriel, for being the most sensitive and funkiest mentor in the world; Sylvain and the #DataGueule team for inspiration; and everyone who provided ideas and expressed keen interest (and kicked me to go to the gym, too).

Last but not least, special thanks go to the Apress team who provided us with this opportunity. Thanks, Louise and Nancy, for your support, and thanks Kent for the insightful and cool editorial suggestions.

—Rayna Stamboliyska

Introduction

Data visualization plays an essential role in communicating ideas and concepts on today's data-driven world. Not only your personal computer, but maybe your mobile phone, smart watch, and other sensors in your home are all producing enormous amount of data. Last month when they came to install Tarek's washing machine, they told him it needs access to the Internet, so he can track his washing habits. If someone told him such a thing few years ago, he'd have laughed at them. Away from them being buzz words, terms such as the Internet of Things (IoT) and Big Data reflect how our world is very much into producing, storing, and analyzing data. That's why data visualization is not limited to few data nerds any more; journalists, marketing people, researchers, teachers, and many others also need data visualization to be able to understand the data at their fingertips so that they can base their decisions on it, or be able to communicate the insights they find there to others.

D3 is one of the most powerful and flexible data visualization frameworks out there. If you have been paying attention to the data team in the *New York Times* or the *Guardian* you sure would have noticed how it enables them to create visualizations we never thought possible before. Nevertheless, such flexibility comes at a cost; its learning curve is some how steep. Furthermore, you aren't normally given some data and asked to visualize it. Most of the time, you will need to know where to find your data, how to clean it, explore it, and pick the best visualization to represent it.

In Practical D3 we will try to walk the whole journey together, and show you how to pose your story hypothesis, and then find data to prove or disprove this hypothesis. We will also show you how to prepare your data as well as how to use D3 to be able to present your data story in a visual manner.

Book Organization

In the first four chapters, Rayna will be your guide in your journey with data visualization. Then, Tarek will be your guide in the next five chapters. As you will see in a moment, although the chapters build on each other, they are also self-contained. In other words, you are free to read this book from cover to cover or you treat this book as a hop-on hop-off bus:

Chapter 1 answers the question "what is data visualization?" It also explains how good visualizations are meant to help you explore the data. Rather than dumbing down facts, we will discuss the design heuristics, the different chart types, and how to choose the best visual structure to represent your data.

Chapter 2 explains some of the basics of HTML, such as the DOM. The chapter also introduces you to vector graphics and their underlying mathematical concepts.

Chapter 3 should be data journalists' favorite. It starts with explaining what is a journalistic story, how to find it, and how to pose your story hypothesis. You will also learn how to explore and analyze the data you have. Some basic mathematics is always nice for data journalists to learn.

Chapter 4 will show you where to look for your data. We look at what kind of data formats are out there. Along the way, you will learn some concepts, such as data scraping, data cleaning, and user-generated data.

In Chapter 5 you learn to create some basic shapes and to plot your first chart using SVG, so you understand the underlying technology D3 uses. The chapter also details how to recreate your chart using D3 and introduces some D3 concepts, such as scales, event listeners, and animations in addition to shapes scaling and transformations.

Chapter 6 shows you how to create more complex shapes using paths and path generators. It also shows you how to create line and area charts and add axis to your charts.

Chapters 7 and 8 will focus on D3 layouts. Layouts are how D3 transforms data and help you create complex data visualization. Chapter 7 starts with a layout for creating something as basic as a pie chart, and then shows you how to play with your pie and turn it into a sunburst diagram. You also learn how to create visualizations using layouts such as treemaps, packs, partition, and stack. Chapter 8 covers the force layout and shows you how to create your own layouts.

Chapter 9 builds on Chapter 4 and explains how D3 can help you load external data, regardless of whether it is in CSV or JSON format. You will also learn how to combine data from different sources, and how to use D3 and JavaScript to sort, filter, and manipulate your data before plotting it.

At the time of writing, the stable version of D3 is 3.5.x. Thus, the examples and code here are all based on that version.

Preboarding Notes

This book assumes that you have basic knowledge of JavaScript, CSS, and related web technologies. In cases in which the required knowledge is beyond the basic knowledge, we are going to explain things in more detail and get you prepared. We try to keep the book useful to users who have minimal JavaScript experience as well as to those who are JavaScript experts but are not that experienced in D3.

PART I

Understanding Data Visualization

CHAPTER 1

■ ■ ■

Understanding Data Visualization

Created in 2007, D3.js is a powerful charting library best used for complex and nonstandard data visualizations. Thus, before we get into the fine details of how to use D3.js for data visualization, we need to talk about the basics: how to learn to 'see' data, how to transform data into a visual, and what is best suited for the human eye.

Everyone likes to snap photos and post them online. We enjoy it yet more when friends and strangers like it. And, well, pretty pictures are the best. Marketers who use visuals observe significant returns of readers, customers and leads—and, by extension, revenue. That is why web communication experts have recommended using visuals and, more specifically, well-designed and easy-to-digest infographics. After all, "a picture is worth a thousand words"; it works because it makes sense: 90 percent of the data transmitted to the brain is visual, and visuals are processed 60,000 times faster in the brain than text.[1] But there is even more to that: New York University psychologist Jerome Bruner has observed a significant difference in information retention depending on how it is introduced. He found that 80 percent was retained using visuals, as opposed to 10 percent from hearing and 20 percent from reading.

We are constantly faced with a data glut of infographics and data visualizations—static snapshots are not enough any longer. Different services exist, both for general and for more specific uses of companies, experts and journalists. "Big," "open," or "smart," data needs to be processed and visualized to make sense.

No matter the technology one chooses and adopts, though, visualizing data is not done at random. When infographics were the new black, we would stumble upon fulgurant heaps of colors and typographies aimed to send important visual messages. Most of these were pretty, but also difficult to process and, more often than not, provided a little depth. Web communication consultants and designers were fighting the data visualization fight with statisticians and data analysts, the former saying that conveying a message swiftly and to the widest possible audience was far more important than being exhaustive about facts and numbers, a stance supported by the latter.

It took those of us working with data visualization some time to comprehend that transmitting information can be both beautiful and functional. Interactive graphics and creative imagination provide with the opportunity to produce deep and rich explorations while stunning the audience with aesthetics. We are nowadays even more often stunning than not—with visualizations that are too complex to understand and that are oft-geared toward showcasing one's technical skills.

Electronic supplementary material The online version of this chapter (doi:10.1007/978-1-4842-1928-7_1) contains supplementary material, which is available to authorized users.

---

[1]For more details, see http://www.billiondollargraphics.com/infographics.html and http://www.webmarketinggroup.co.uk/Blog/why-every-seo-strategy-needs-infographics-1764.aspx.

T. Amr and R. Stamboliyska, *Practical D3.js*, DOI 10.1007/978-1-4842-1928-7_1

Visualising Raw Data

One of the primary goals of a data visualization is to explain complex matters. These can be answering a question, supporting a logistical decision, describing demography, communicating observations, or increasing efficiency. These are rather passive processes.

In these cases, the visualization is simple and straightforward; it answers one precise question or supports one given statement. There is a clear advantage to applying such a chart as looking through the raw data itself is much more time-consuming. Take Figure 1-1, for example; can you tell, in less than 10 seconds, which are the top three of the world's 20 dominant mobile operators in terms of mobile revenue? (Hint: Some are at the bottom.)

Rank	Operator-group	Connections (millions) [1]	YoY Growth, connections	YoY Growth, rank	Mobile Revenue (US$ billion)
1	China Mobile	683.08	11%	-	22.05
2	Vodafone Group	386.88	5%	-	13.92
3	América Móvil Group	251.83	7%	-	7.98
4	Bharti Airtel Group	250.04	13%	+1	3.04
5	Telefónica Group	243.51	7%	-1	11.40
6	China Unicom	219.25	21%	+1	4.95
7	VimpelCom Group [2]	205.05	7%	-1	4.58
8	Reliance Communications	154.60	8%	-	0.48
9	Telenor Group	152.74	24%	-	2.55
10	China Telecom	144.18	33%	+2	3.37
11	MTN Group	136.59	14%	-1	3.85
12	France Telecom Group	133.38	57%	+9	7.18
13	Telkomsel Group	117.24	15%	+2	1.43
14	Idea Cellular	117.16	23%	+3	1.00
15	Sistema Group [3]	114.51	3%	-4	2.54
16	Verizon Wireless	111.37	5%	-3	15.78
17	Deutsche Telekom Group	107.86	2%	-3	8.38
18	AT&T	105.21	7%	-2	14.77
19	Telecom Italia	101.10	16%	+1	4.10
20	BSNL	98.28	5%	-2	0.44

Mobile operator group global ranking by connections, Q2 2012

Figure 1-1. *The world's top 20 mobile carriers[2]*

---

[2]Source: GSMA Intelligence (https://gsmaintelligence.com/research/2012/10/the-top-20-global-operator-groups-by-mobile-connections-q2-2012/353/).

Now have a look at Figure 1-2. Can you tell in less than 10 seconds, which are the top three of the world's 20 dominant mobile operators in terms of mobile revenue?

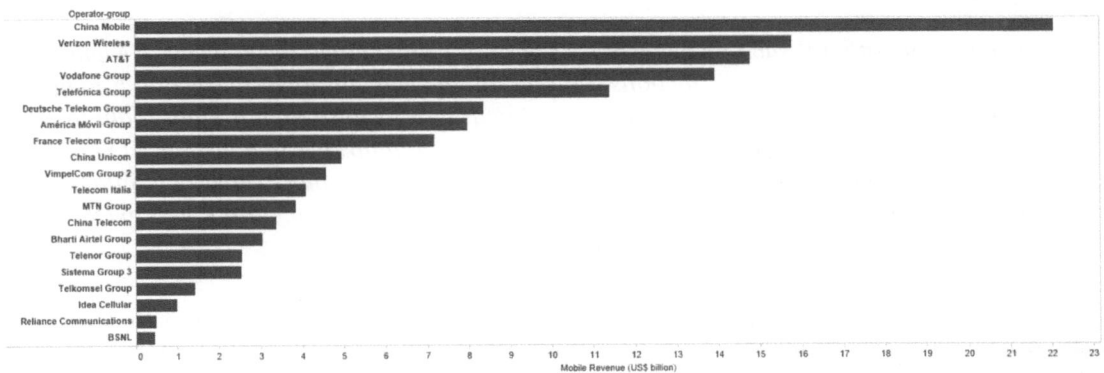

Figure 1-2. *The data from Figure 1-1, plotted*

Visualizing data enables fast understanding. But it can also allow to see what would otherwise go unnoticed or to bring forth questions one would not formulate otherwise. Good visualization enables anyone to browse, to research and to interact with data. Exploratory visuals offer multiple and layered dimensions to a dataset, that one can use to compare multiple datasets with each other or to fish for singularities across datasets from different natures. An interactive visualization gives the opportunity to not only observe and conclude about one fact but also to ask questions along the way—and find answers to those questions. Figure 1-3, for example, shows a playful visualization of data using D3.js.

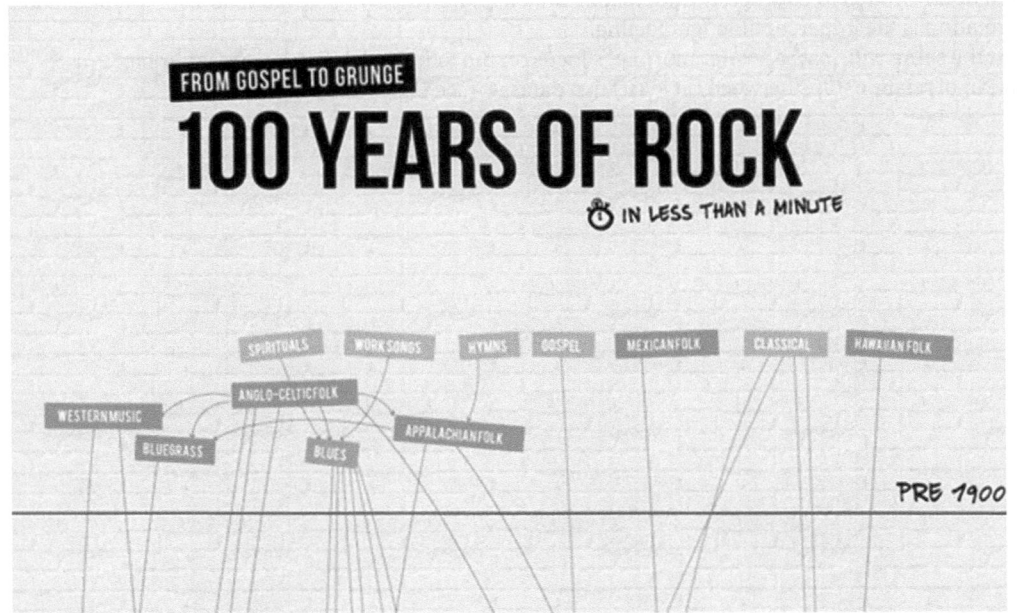

Figure 1-3. *100 Years of rock, by Brittany Klontz for ConcertHotels.com*[3]

---

[3]http://www.concerthotels.com/100-years-of-rock/.

Having a Good Eye for Data

In his *New York Times* article, "Learning to See Data" Benedict Carey explains:

> *Perceptual learning is such an elementary skill that people forget they have it. It's what we use as children to make distinctions between similar-looking letters, like U and V, long before we can read. It's the skill needed to distinguish an A sharp from a B flat (both the notation and the note), or between friendly insurgents and hostiles in a fast-paced video game. By the time we move on to sentences and melodies and more cerebral gaming— "chunking" the information into larger blocks—we've forgotten how hard it was to learn all those subtle distinctions in the first place.*

The *New York Times* piece centers on the reasons behind such reactions. Needless to dive in the realm of perceptual learning studies here: in a nutshell, we learn constantly, rather seamlessly and not that consciously, to distinguish patterns and shapes. Take a new language for example. If you are a native English speaker who decides to learn French, you will need to figure out which letters use diacritics and how to pronounce specific two-letter combinations. (And then, grammar, of course.) So, what to do when rules for placing such letters do not exist? With practice and time, you get the 'gut feeling' of where an "é" should stand rather than an "è". Nothing supernatural here: you just get to see trends of how words form which informs your spelling.

The same happens with data. A small table or a JSON file is a technical detail. What you get to learn— with practice—is how to look at the data rather than trying to see whether there is a zero somewhere. It is the same as with language: if you are a native English speaker, it is difficult to explain why you prefer to use "quick" rather than "swift." To any of us, it is uneasy and somewhat bizarre to explain how to read a bar chart, we just grasp the meaning of it in nanoseconds. This is because it has been there forever, our brains are thus exposed to it often enough to effortlessly understand what it is showing. We take bar charts for granted, and that interpretation is the imperceptible "gut feeling."

But is it the same with, say, a scatter plot? Let's focus on the following definition: a scatter plot is a representation of relationships between (at least) two datasets (see Figure 1-4).

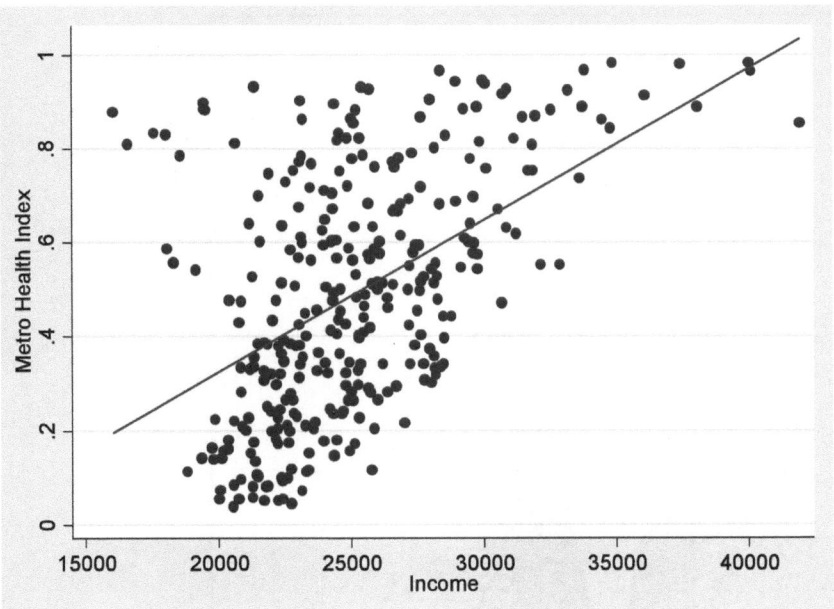

Figure 1-4. *This scatter plot is from The Atlantic Citylab (2012). It plots a city's "Metro Health Index," that is, a measure of the proportion of people who smoke or are obese as a factor that correlates to the city's median income.*[4]

Reading a scatter plot is not always straightforward. Figure 1-4 is quite simple: as one of its authors spells it out,[5] "Higher income metros have substantially lower levels of smoking and obesity, while poorer metros are plagued with considerably higher levels of both." By contrast, the scatter plot in Figure 1-5 shows data clearly grouped in two opposite directions of zero.

---

[4]Source: http://www.citylab.com/design/2012/01/why-some-cities-are-healthier-others/365/.
[5]http://www.citylab.com/design/2012/01/why-some-cities-are-healthier-others/365/

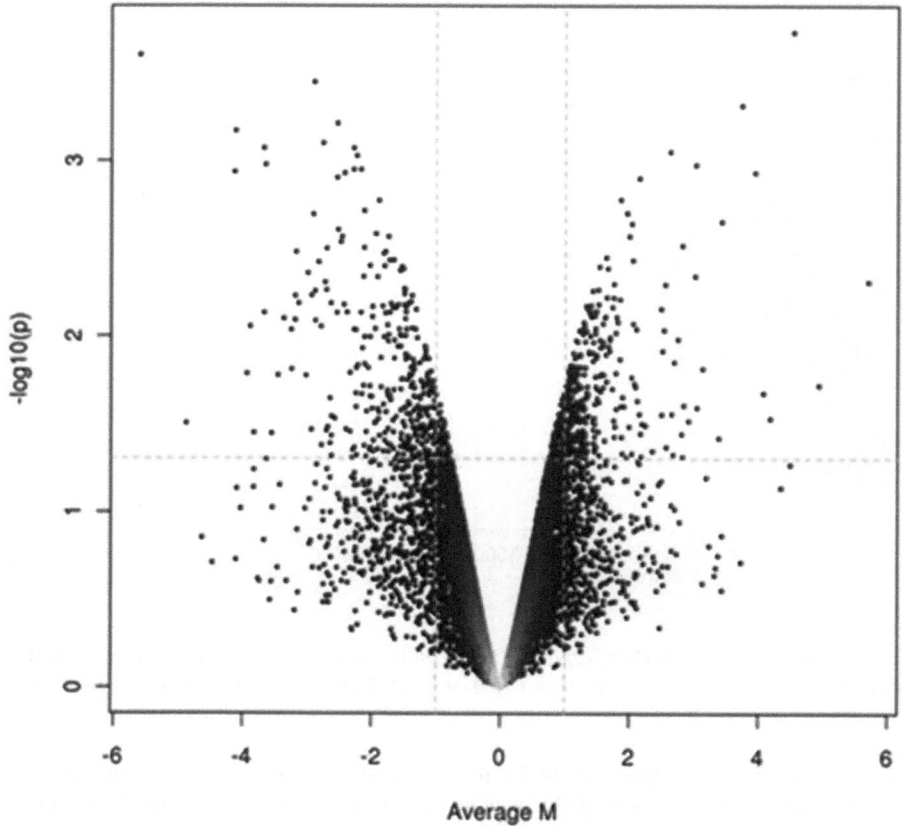

Figure 1-5. *A type of scatter plot named "volcano plot"*

Figure 1-6 is another routine check of data and another scatter plot. This particular plot made sense to the researcher, who knew exactly what she was plotting and seeing, but not to her colleagues for whom it represented an alien, hard-to-grasp visual.

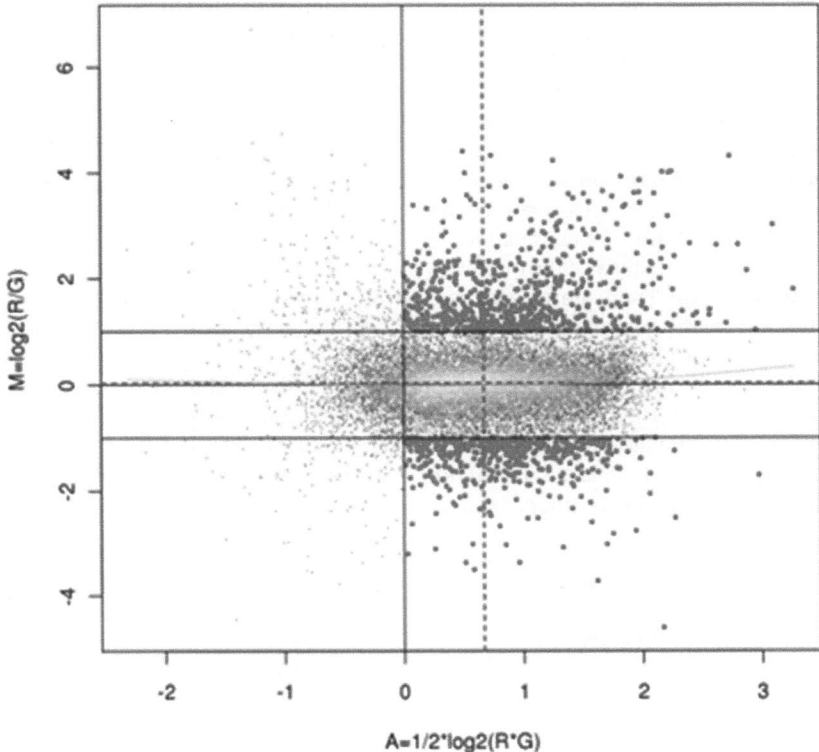

Figure 1-6. *Another type of scatter plot*

The bottom line is that reading visuals quite resembles reading words: you get better and better at it with practice. But shouldn't we choose a form that is adequate?

Choosing the Right Form

Any Evolution 101 course will teach you how the field evolved and that two main lines of thought left their mark on the way we think of the origin and evolution of living beings. One of these follows French scientist Jean-Baptiste Lamarck who was the first one to outline a theory of evolution at the beginning of the 19th century. It is the most famously illustrated with a giraffe, and it poses that acquired characters are passed to the offspring. So, the giraffe felt the need to reach higher branches and leaves, thus developed a long neck and all its children were born with long necks. More generally, the Lamarckian framework explains that the function appears first then a precise and fine-cut form appears.

Charles Darwin's *On The Origin of Species* came a few decades after Lamarck's death. His theoretical framework of natural selection and random appearance of variation provides quite an opposite vision of the relationship between form and function. Indeed, a giraffe developing a longer neck has nothing to do with a need to reach higher branches and leaves, but has to do with random variations which happen to give an advantage to the individuals that have them, in the precise environment where they live. Such variations are selected (by nobody in particular, just by the fact that the giraffes having them eat better and have potentially healthier offspring). With Darwin, the relationship between form and function turns out to be complicated.

Form indeed does not always follow function. In many situations in which we need to explore a dataset and thus provide an explanation, we may find the Lamarckian idea convenient. Then, we apply a kind of rule of thumb: for a comparison, pick a bar chart; for a correlation, pick a scatter plot. Designers also invent forms to suit a function. Or we just "hack" a preexisting form to fit a different, even unrelated function. Take the bubble wrap,[6] also known as the most dangerous drug ever, with addictions revealed from shippers to toddlers. (It is that dangerous that the company selling it has revamped it so it does not pop.[7] Keep calm, electronic devices exist to simulate the best procrastination activity.[8]) At its inception, the bubble wrap aimed to overtake the wallpaper market. After none of the then-hipsters bought "bubble wallpaper," its creators tried to sell it for greenhouse insulation, but that failed, too. Humanity would have been eternally exempt of bubble wrap if it were not for IBM. It had just launched the IBM 1401 computer and needed a proper packaging material to prevent the hardware in transport.

The function did not dictate form; neither was it the other way around here. But there is more to this complex relationship: functions force form. There are a few or even several forms that can visually fit a dataset, but generally few of them serve the goal you invest a visual with. Whether the form is pretty or you prefer another one to it is of little relevance here.

This is the right place to highlight the misuse of forms. One specific form is the bubble chart, or as Alberto Cairo calls it, "the bubble plague."[9] Using bubbles is fine in cases where you show proportions (remember the scatter plot in Figure 1-2) but is to be avoided for comparisons. Have a look at Figure 1-7 and find in less than 10 seconds which foreign nationals purchased how many hectares of land in New Zealand. Then, find how much more hectares did Americans bought compared to Malaysians.

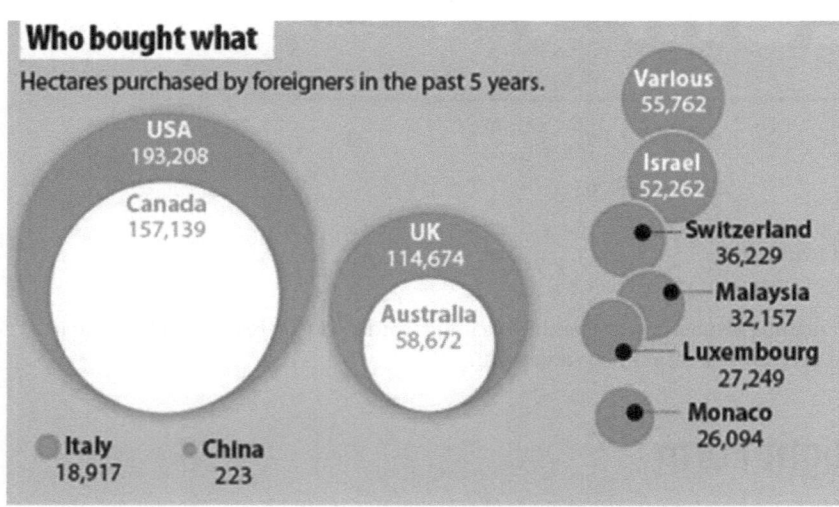

Figure 1-7. *An example of a bubble chart*[10]

---

[6]http://www.ehow.com/facts_7345549_history-bubblewrap.html
[7]http://www.wsj.com/articles/revamped-bubble-wrap-loses-its-pop-1435689665
[8]http://en.wikipedia.org/wiki/Mugen_Puchipuchi
[9]Alberto Cairo, "The Functional Art"
[10]Source: http://www.statschat.org.nz/2012/02/05/who-is-really-buying-new-zealand-and-its-not-what-they-plotted/

This chart does not enable an accurate comparison between the countries for everyone—some viewers will find this difficult to interpret. I can tell by the numbers who bought the most—but then, why do I need the bubbles? It would have been straightforward if the chart looked like the one on Figure 1-8.

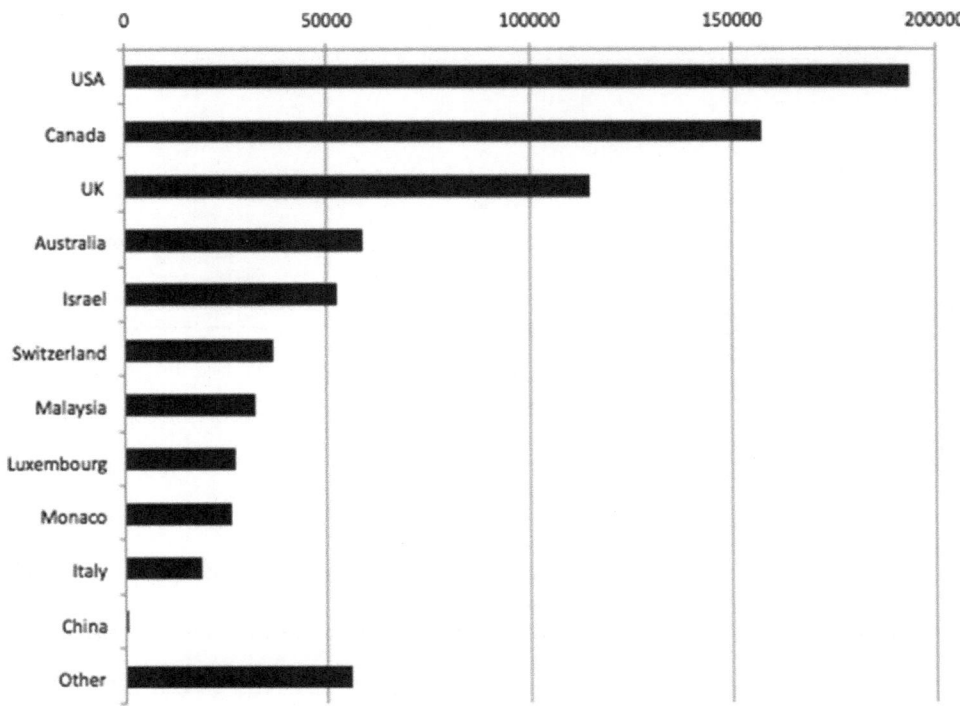

Figure 1-8. *A more efficient graph using bars rather than bubbles*[11]

So, why do some people find it more difficult to gauge numbers from bubbles? Our brain is wired to see volume: the intention of the person having plotted a bubble chart comparison is to represent radius. Mathematically speaking, you see r^2 while the comparison is between r^1 and r^2.

As mentioned earlier, bubbles are great when you want to show proportions. A scatter plot where correlation is illustrated by bubbles of different sizes enables to grasp quickly a big picture. With bubble charts, you plot data in terms of three distinct numeric parameters. Thus, a bubble chart allows a person to compare the different items with respect to their relative positions along each axis. The items' sizes serve to indicate and describe a value rather than compare across values (see Figure 1-9 for an example).

---

[11]Source: http://www.statschat.org.nz/2012/02/05/who-is-really-buying-new-zealand-and-its-not-what-they-plotted/

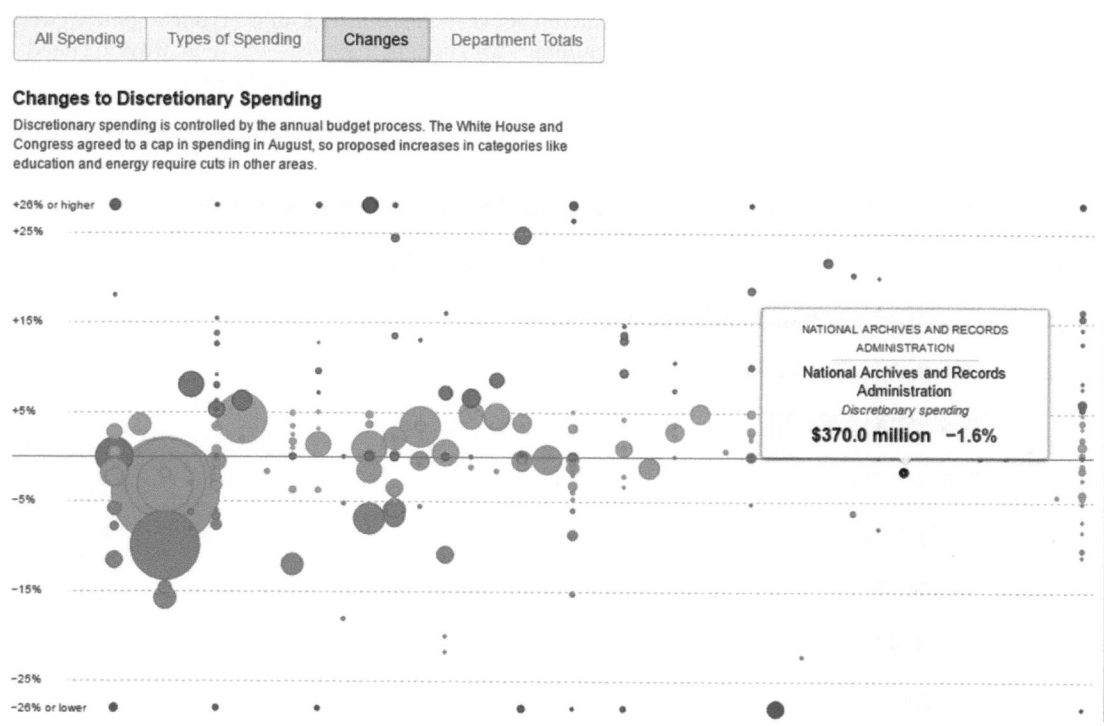

Figure 1-9. *An interactive visualization by the New York Times explaining President Obama's 2013 federal budget proposal*[12]

Designing Interactive Data Visualizations

We have already established that traditional static infographics or charts illustrating texts need to properly reflect the data and to be well-formed to enable understanding. This is not always straightforward as misconceptions or limited comprehension of datasets can impede on good visuals.

With interactive data visualization, this becomes a greater challenge as we add up to the viewer's cognitive involvement. This is even more so with D3.js which enables more than interactivity: it makes possible experimentation and increased visual complexity. With D3.js, a visualization is much more aimed to offer exploration, discovery and amazement than to support, for example, decision-making processes. A more thorough discussion on the opportunities that D3.js has to create new and outstanding visual metaphors is in the subsection entitled "Structuring an interactive data visualization" later in this chapter. For the time being, let's focus on the approaches one can adopt to take up on that challenge.

In his book *The Design of Everyday Things,* Don Norman introduced several basic user interface design principles and concepts which are of prime importance in the fields of industry design and human-computer interaction. But this is also why such principles are applicable to data visualization as they center on user's needs rather than on the designer's need for prettiness.

---

[12]Source: http://www.nytimes.com/interactive/2012/02/13/us/politics/2013-budget-proposal-graphic.html

Visibility: Design Indispensable Elements Well

Norman introduced the concept of "perceived affordance." As he explains it on his website,[13] "for in design, we care much more about what the user perceives than what is actually true. What the designer cares about is whether the user perceives that some action is possible (or in the case of perceived non-affordances, not possible)." In contrast with physical interfaces, screen-based ones allow much more clicking. But it is not necessarily meaningful as it rarely produces what the user expects or desires.

This is why one needs to make it visible when the ordinary action of clicking will result in a specific action. A functionality which has no dedicated visual representation is hard to identify. This is also valid for applications which have keyboard shortcuts: they still need visible buttons and menus. Take the example illustrated on Figure 1-10 above where clicking on specific tabs (upper left) provides you with a view of different aspects of the budget planning. Or see the timeline (Figure 1-11) where arrows indicate you can move along:

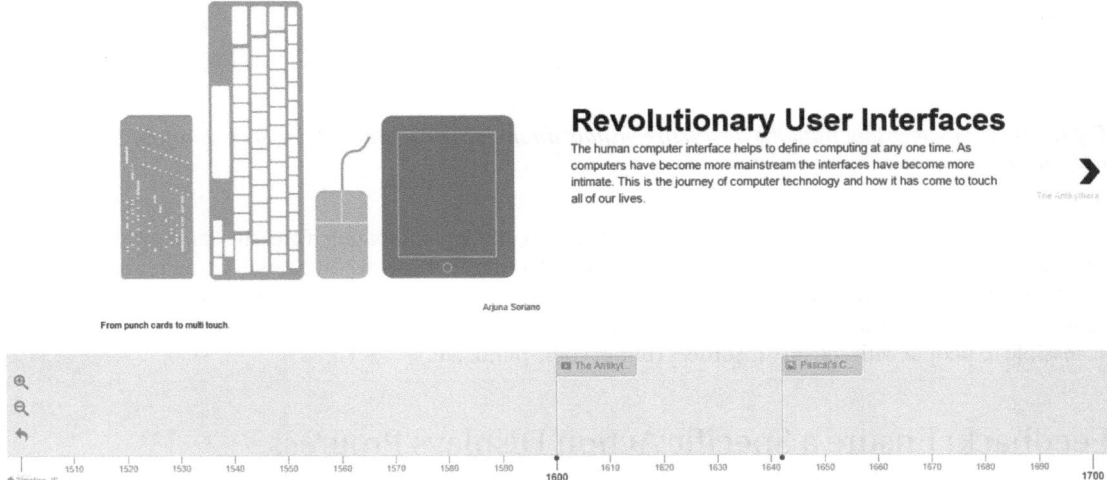

Figure 1-10. *"Revolutionary user interfaces", by the TimelineJS team*[14]

Alternatively, you can also indicate the navigation means before the use starts interacting with your visualization. The "History of Orange"[15] (the telco, not the fruit) does this elegantly in Figure 1-11.

---

[13]http://www.jnd.org/dn.mss/affordances_and.html
[14]Source: https://timeline.knightlab.com/examples/user-interface/index.html
[15]http://www.orange.com/sirius/histoire/en/history/

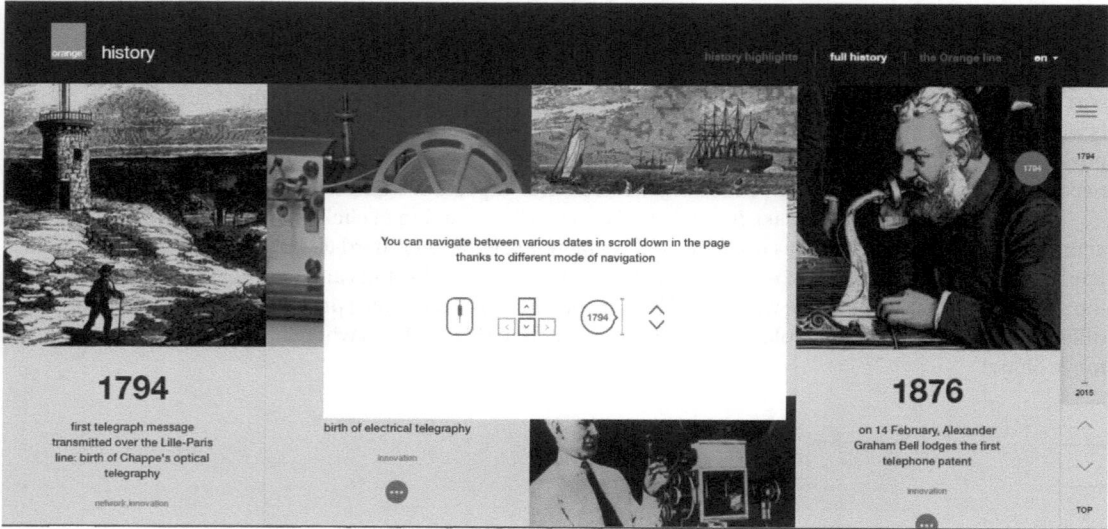

Figure 1-11. *A screenshot from the interactive visualization illustrating the history of the multinational telecommunications company Orange*

Thus, if you need, say, the viewer to scroll or zoom in, think of indicating it clearly. Same applies to any specific action that the user needs to perform in order to interact with your visualization for real. Even more so, such implementations are a must-do in a visualization where you as a data visualization architect experiment with forms and shapes. Last but not least, clear flags for navigating make your visualization accessible to people with sensory disorders (blind, color-blind, etc.).

Feedback: Ensure a Specific Action Displays Progress

The users should be aware of the system's current state. That is, every action requires a reaction. It does not need to be huge, but it needs to be clear enough for the viewer. Let's assume we are going to show a timeline for a series of events across history. Figure 1-12 is an example from a timeline produced with TimelineJS. There is an arrow button for them to travel in time as we saw in Figure 1-10, but also a highlight in a different color when the viewer is at a given moment of the timeline.

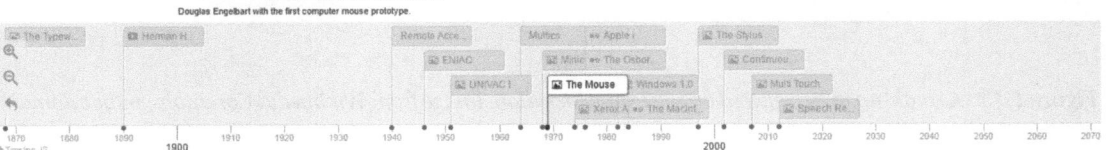

Figure 1-12. *"Revolutionary user interfaces," by the TimelineJS team*[16]

You should make sure to display the year they are on, whenever the scroll's position changes. As it often happens, the timeline may take some time to load. Make sure that you show that to the user with a loading button or similar.

Through using different music players we are used to the symbols used for play, pause, stop, and fast-forward. If you are designing an interactive visualization and want your users to press on a certain button for it to start playing and other button for it to stop, you better stick to buttons with the same symbols users are used to press on when dealing with their music players. It is also worth noting that arrows on the fast forward point to the right while the arrows on the backward button point to the left. The directions here are mapped to the sense of the direction the users have, especially those who have their languages written from left to right. You may need to redesign the arrows directions if your target audience speaks Arabic, or any similar language that is written from right to left.

We apply the same principles when illustrating high values vs. low values: the former are pictured with longer lengths than the latter. This is what we refer to as consistency. Renowned information architect and user experience professional Steve Krug pointed out that consistency makes your users think less about how to navigate than about the visualization itself.

Mapping: Mind Cultural Conventions

How does a new viewer grasp the possible interactions in your data visualization? Actionable items are visible and consistent, feedback is provided to inform on progress: we have said that above. But there is more to it. We use the word mapping here to refer to the ways people from different parts of the world, of different age groups, and so on can perceive actionable entities. In his fascinating "A History of the World in Twelve Maps," Jerry Brotton explains that what you see depends on where and when you are looking from (Figure 1-13). In other words, a given cultural group shares specific learned conventions.

---

[16]Source: https://timeline.knightlab.com/examples/user-interface/index.html

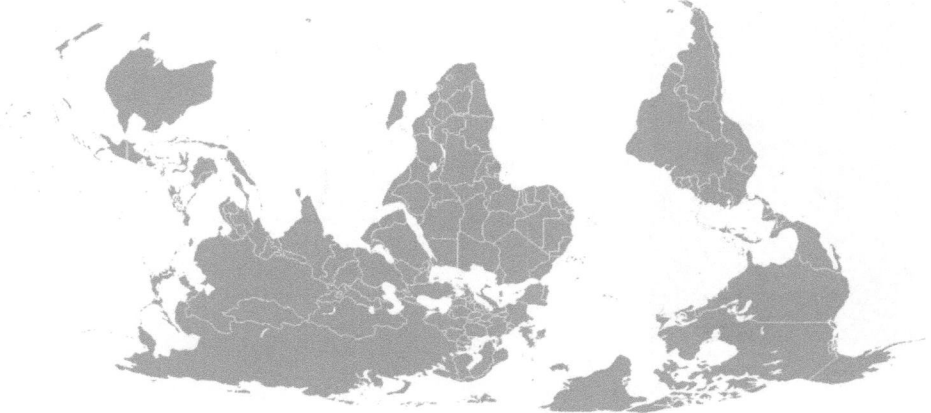

Figure 1-13. *A south-up map centered on the Prime Meridian. Image from Wikimedia Commons, public domain*

Constraints: We Can Do Nearly Everything

Don Norman links the conventions to "logical and cultural constraints." If you remember your first touch-screen device, you may remember how uneasy it could have been to discover how to highlight text, then to copy and paste it elsewhere. We barely remember this, but give such a device to an elderly who has never been exposed to it before, and you will witness the difficulties. It would not be too much of an overstretch to say that millennials have a shared learned convention in this case.

You need to pay specific attention to constraints. If you use a technology such as D3.js to explore and create new visual metaphors, your visualization may as well turn into a fail if you introduce new conventions for people to interact with. In plain English, keep the indispensable action items classical and known.

Structuring Interactive Data Visualizations

As Kathy O'Neil puts it in her book "Doing Data Science," the exploratory data analysis is "what happens between you and your data when you're not trying to prove anything to anyone yet." For this to happen, however, you first need to snatch the audience's attention.

As you will learn in detail in this book, D3.js operates through layers. An interactive visualization also operates through layers. This means that a complex, multilayered visual story has a structure and hierarchy of information. For the user to aptly interact with, applying straightforward items for navigation must be done along with making clear what hierarchical structure underlies the visualization.

In plain English, this means that the user needs to know quickly what stories we wish to tell and how each of them is part of the visual composition. The latter relates to the overall aesthetics of the visualization, that is its architecture and visual specifics, as these elements enable the user to engage at deeper levels.

Let's walk the walk down that road together.

The Concept of Image

A French cartographer and geographer, Jacques Bertin, published "Semiology of Graphics" in 1967. The book is like a unicorn: many have spoken about it, but few have read it, mainly because its availability in English is limited. This seminal work is the first theoretical framework for information visualization. There, he introduced the concept of image and identified levels of reading a representation: "Image is the meaningful visual form, perceptible in the minimum instant of vision."

To better understand the scope of Bertin's work, defining semiology is useful. Ferdinand de Saussure, "the father of linguistics," defined semiology as the science of signs we use in communication. Similarly, "Semiology of Graphics" explores the definition of visual signs with the rules that connect and govern them. These are what one needs to identify visual variables and the "grammar" that makes sense of them in a visualization.

Already for Bertin, graphic representation has a double function. It acts both as an artificial memory and as a tool for discovery. We will focus on the concrete visual variables in a future chapter. For now, let's look at the big picture: levels of reading. We have three of them: global, intermediate and elementary. A good visualization should answer these in a short to no time.

The Visual Mantra

These directly relate and lead to what Ben Shneiderman called the "visual information-seeking mantra." It goes like: "Overview first, zoom and filter, then details-on-demand." In other words, your visualization needs to present the big picture first: what is the take-away message and what are the most significant figures? Once this happens, your users can zoom, scroll, open, close, sort, rearrange, filter to explore and identify further details.

The mantra applies to both linear and nonlinear visualizations. Linear are these where you need to understand level 1 before moving to a more in-depth level 2, and so on. Other graphics are nonlinear, that is exploration does not depend on a given "entry" layer; the visualization of Doctor Who time travels (Figure 1-14) is a good example.

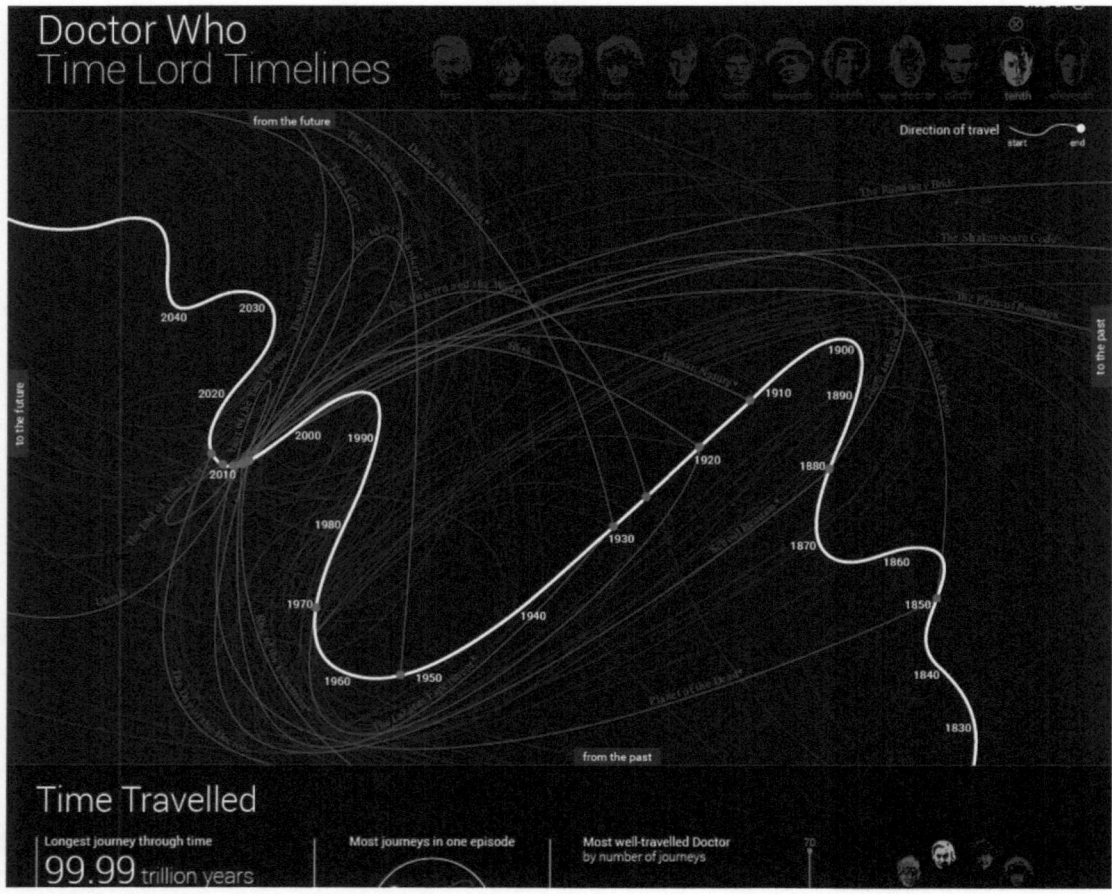

Figure 1-14. *"Doctor Who: 50 years of time travel in the TARDIS" is an interactive visualization by the BCC*[17]

Techniques for Exploration and Interaction

Let's focus on each of the techniques for exploration and interaction with examples.

Zoom

Zoom in visualizations is quite often used in visualizations that utilize maps. Take a look at Figure 1-15—a visual exploration of recovered guns produced by the Washington Post.[18] You can zoom in and obtain number and types of weapons recovered for a given timespan in the area. However, a zoom is not necessarily the action of seeing in bigger a part of one picture: it can also be a way of highlighting a given element. The interactive visualization "100 years of rock" shown earlier in Figure 1-3 is such an example: you see the connections and the timeline on the right but you can also zoom in by selecting a given style. The selection outputs an explanation and a sound excerpt.

---

[17]Source: http://www.bbc.com/future/story/20131119-doctor-who-travels-through-time
[18]http://www.washingtonpost.com/wp-srv/special/local/dc-recovered-guns/

Figure 1-15. *The welcome screen of the Washington Post's interactive visualization "Sea of Steel."*

Scroll

Scroll allows the viewer to move around and identify a zone of interest. More creative uses exist though: French online media Rue89 published a fascinating visual comparison between locations in Paris in 1914 compared to the same ones in 2013[19] (see Figure 1-16). Scrolling the red handle in the middle allows you to see different proportions of each "era."

---

[19]http://rue89.nouvelobs.com/rue89-culture/2013/03/24/paris-1914-2013-en-photos-grimpez-dans-notre-fabuleuse-machine-remonter-le-239913

Figure 1-16. *"Paris, 1914-2013" is an interactive visualization produced by the web media Rue89 showing a precise location in Paris dating back to the 1900s and its look in 2013*

Open, Close

The outstanding interactive visualization "Out of Sight, Out of Mind"[20] is an interesting example of "open, close." You can open and close different tabs ("Attacks," "Victims," etc.) but also open an info box for each victim (Figure 1-17).

---

[20]http://drones.pitchinteractive.com/

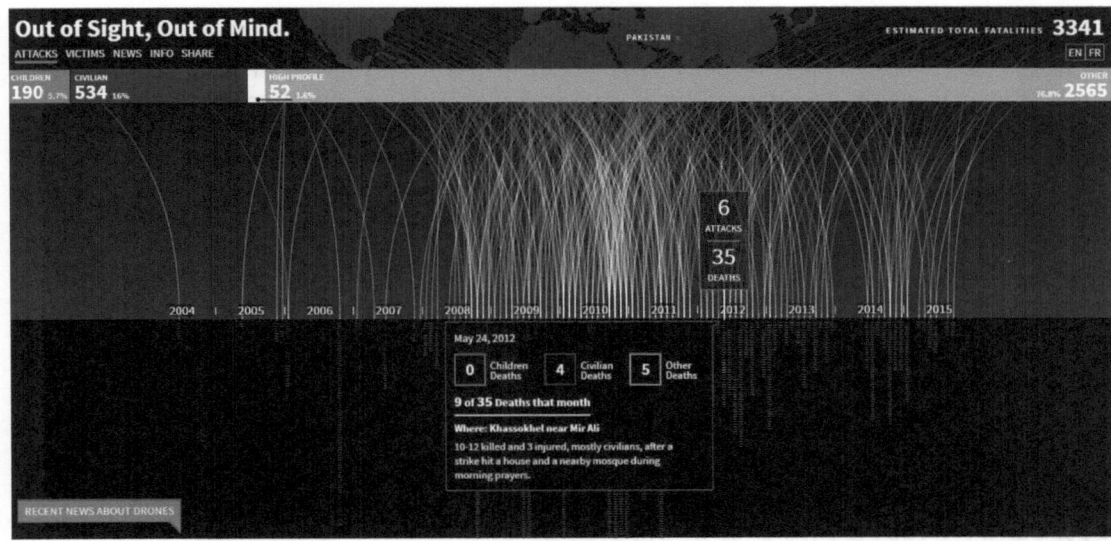

Figure 1-17. *Screenshots from the interactive visualization "Out of Sight, Out of Mind" documenting each drone strike in Pakistan and its casualties*

Sort and Rearrange

These two functions allow you to zoom in and more seamlessly explore complexity. For example, a visualization of the impact that vaccines have had would use a sorting or rearranging function to visualize the number of infected people. This could uncover different trends, for example, that infection rates for the same disease have decreased at significantly different paces in different U.S. states.

Filter

If a visualization is too overwhelming, filtering out particular data points helps better understand the whole. Consider, for example, the Oscar diversity problem visualization:[21] it is not possible to see it in its entirety in one view, so it would come handy to be able to filter specific years or category.

Search and Reconfigure

A search comes in handy to show specific details, for example, the *Washington Post* gun recovery visualization allows the user to search for information at a given address. Transparency International's EU Integrity Watch enables a lot of these as well.

Encode and Connect

You can encode time travel trajectories in colors (the Doctor Who visualization earlier) or with arrows of varying thickness to indicate cash flows in import-export. Arrows also serve to connect related entities.

Types of Interactive Experience

These actions underlie different kinds of interactive experience. In "The Functional Art," Alberto Cairo outlines four broad such types: instruction, conversation, manipulation and exploration. D3.js may be quite relevant as an enabler of these visual experiences:

- the exploration (a first-person player in a video game is a good analogy, but it could also be the volcano plot at Fig. 1-5 that's explored to highlight portions that "burst"),

- the instruction (the user tells the visualization to do something),

- the conversation (a dialogue between the user and the visualization),

- the manipulation (enables changes by the user to the structure and appearance of a visualization).

With all these technicalities in mind, we can outline a few major visualization patterns: maps, timelines, and networks. D3.js is quite difficult to include here precisely because of its inherent flexibility that enables an incredible amount of non-standard patterns. The aim of this brief overview is to outline the different kinds of interaction that you seek to instill in your visualization.

Let's have a few words on the three major visuals before discussing D3.js visualizations in further details.

Maps

Maps are amongst the most used visual patterns. You see geographic maps, cartograms, heat mapped maps, every day. In his book *A History of the World in Twelve Maps,* Jerry Brotton relies on the following definition: "maps are graphic representations that facilitate a spatial understanding of things, concepts, conditions, processes, or events in the human world." One reason maps are so popular is because they offer "a spatial understanding of events in the human world." However, there is more to maps: they can also integrate a time element, thus enabling the explorer to observe how events unfold sequentially.

Timelines

Speaking of time: timelines are another fundamental visual pattern. Be it for historical events or project management (remember Gantt charts?), timelines are a valuable visual that enables chunking, provides

---

[21]http://time.com/4185071/oscars-diversity/

structure and are an excellent source of interactions. The former characteristics is an important one as it allows to focus on individual events without missing out the big picture. Timelines provide structure as they streamline processes, from teaching to project management. The great thing about timelines is that you can shape them as you wish (see Figures 1-18 through 1-21) and even build them in the physical world (a widespread version of those are museums).

Figure 1-18. *Anne Frank timeline*[22]

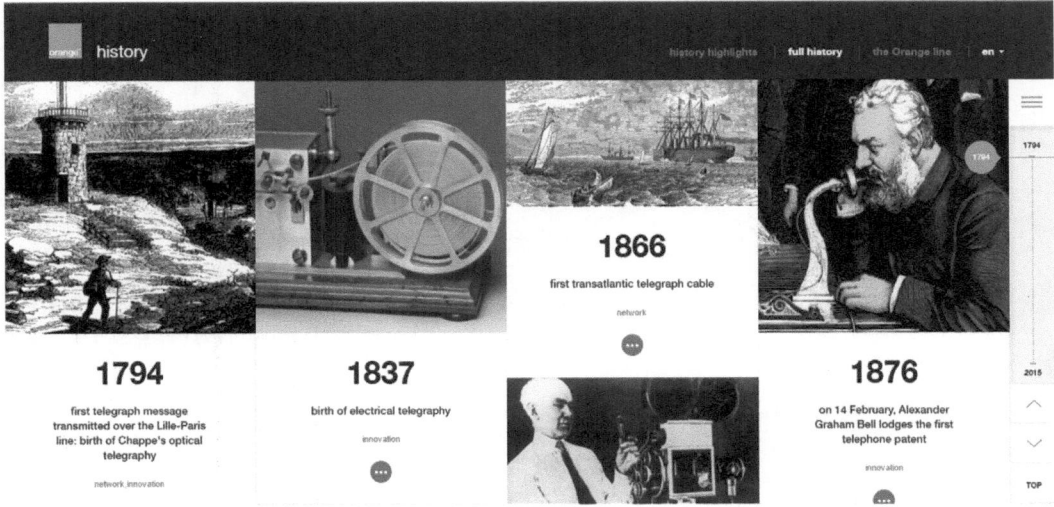

Figure 1-19. *A history of the telco Orange*[23]

---

[22]http://www.annefrank.org/timeline#!/en/Subsites/Timeline/Postwar-period-1945—present-day/ The-Anne-Frank-House-opens/

[23]http://www.orange.com/sirius/histoire/en/history/

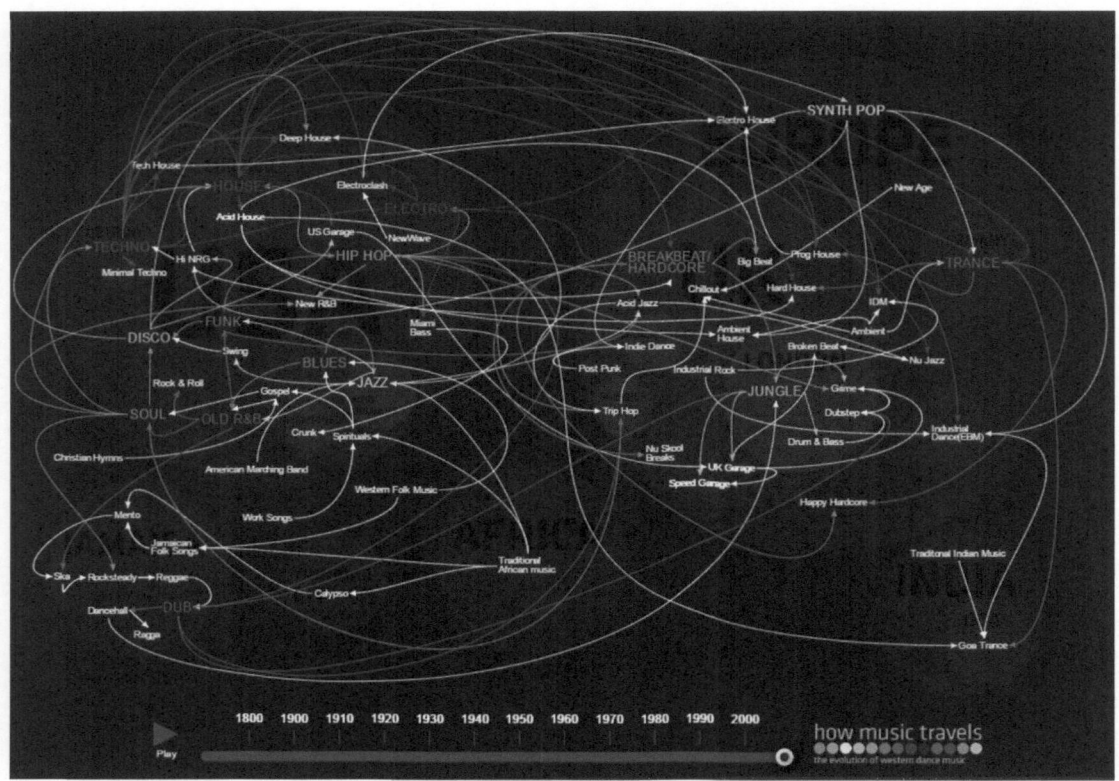

Figure 1-20. *How dance music evolved*[24]

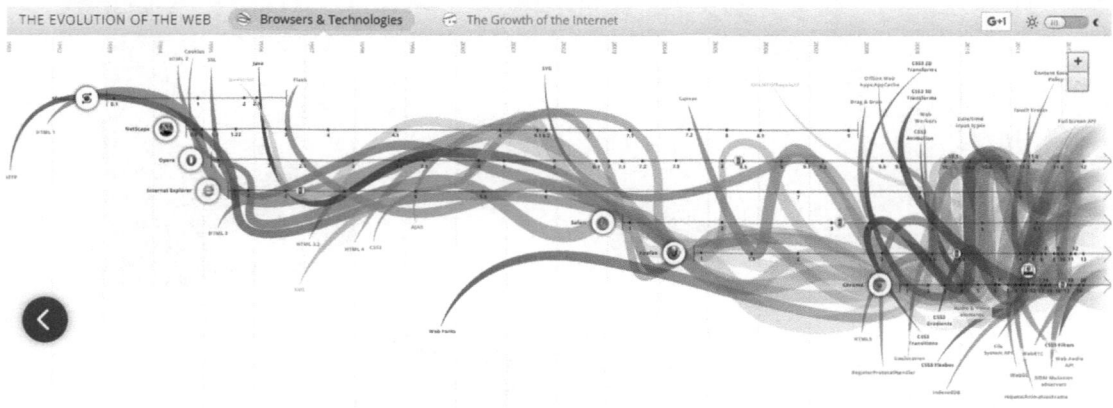

Figure 1-21. *The evolution of the web browsers*[25]

---

[24]http://www.thomson.co.uk/blog/wp-content/uploads/infographic/interactive-music-map/index.html
[25]http://evolutionofweb.appspot.com/?hl=en#/evolution/day

The final of the fundamental visual patterns identified earlier is a network. It allows to visualise connections, dependencies, and hierarchies altogether. Its basic structure is nodes and edges (lines, arrows) that connect the nodes highlighting the relevant relationship(s) between them. I have a soft spot for networks as, in my eyes, they constitute the level at which data, information, analysis and visualization become knowledge and lay the grounds for the next level of exploration. For an obsessively curious person like you, the reader, this makes sense, I believe. Networks are one of the most modular and flexible visual patterns that we have come across: you can map and explore transmission, internal structure, time, impact, topology, you name it. Interesting examples include gene interaction networks, Ask-Me-Anything (AMA) discussions on reddit,[26] cereal ingredient combinations,[27] and so on.

Why Use D3.js?

Now we've looked at examples of data visualization, let's return to D3. It stands for Data-Driven Documents. The name reflects the tools ability to connect data values to document elements. In doing so, D3 "drives" the document from data. It works with any browser, including mobile devices. What you may consider as a steep learning curve in the beginning is compensated for by its high flexibility and the fascinating ability to let you create a specific visual form. As a matter of fact, D3.js is not your regular graphics or data processing library: it does not come with a set of pre-built charts to pick from. There is more to the flexibility bit, though: as Drew Skau from Visual.ly points out,[28] D3.js "can manipulate any part of the document object model, it is [thus] as flexible as the client-side web technology stack (HTML, CSS, SVG). This gives it huge advantages over other tools because it can look like anything you want, and it isn't limited to small regions of a webpage like Processing.js, Paper.js, Raphael.js, or other canvas or SVG-only based libraries. It also takes advantage of built-in functionality that the browser has, simplifying the developer's job, especially for mouse interaction." On top of all these benefits, you also have a great community and carefully maintained documentation.

As we are starting the exciting endeavor of learning D3.js, it is the right moment to highlight what it is not.

It is not a charting library: I already mentioned it before, but here is to a useful reminder. Unlike Charts. js and other similar libraries, D3 does not come with a preset array of charts to which you pass your dataset, then get a fancy output. A few charting libraries that interface D3 exist (NVD3, dimple) in case you want to try out something higher level than D3 in the future.

D3 is also not a graphics layer: it provides a handy API to manipulate SVG (an XML-based markup) but it does not draw the graphics itself, which also means that your browser should properly support SVG.

It is not designed to work natively with Angular.js: both have their document object models (DOMs), thus for the two to work together, one DOM has to take over. It is feasible, but you risk wasting powerful opportunities provided by the other package. Other widely used libraries such as React.js have a similar issue. Shirley Wu, a javascript developer at California-based start-up Illumio, has shared different approaches to combining D3 and React, thus introducing interesting trade-offs to the realization that "both libraries solve the same problems and want to control the DOM."[29] Each compromise has an optimal use case. For example, if you used React for structure and rendering, but D3 for the data visualization part, you would lose out on D3's functions as they would not be able to access the DOM (controlled by React). Such a combination is best leveraged by a React app with a simple visualization.

---

[26]http://blog.embed.ly/post/57097477000/visualizing-discussions-on-reddit-with-a-d3
[27]http://moritz.stefaner.eu/projects/musli-ingredient-network/
[28]http://blog.visual.ly/why-d3-js-is-so-great-for-data-visualization/
[29]http://slides.com/shirleywu/deck#/2

D3.js does, however, enable beautiful exploration. Thus, understanding your data and 'dressing it up' in a relevant yet creative interactive visual is the point where you stop, but where your audience begins. In the following chapters, we will travel together to learn how to get a "good eye" about data, how to get the facts right and how to transform this abstract information into understandable vocabulary that our audience can use.

Summary

In this first chapter, we discussed the basics of data visualization and addressed fundamentals to account for when structuring such an object. In the next chapter, we will dive deeper in that discussion, a needed stepping stone before you go freehand with D3.

CHAPTER 2

■ ■ ■

Structuring and Designing Data Visualizations

In the previous chapter, we discussed the basics of data visualization and dressed up an overview of structuring and designing such an object. In this chapter, we will extend that discussion and dive deeper in those matters as they will be your lifeline when going freehand with D3.

Structuring and designing an interactive and complex data visualization can turn out to be a real challenge: it is not just a question of getting your audience to understand and engage, but to do it on different platforms. For example, how do you handle both complexity and interactivity on a smartphone screen? This chapter will prepare you for thinking about a modular and optimal approach to data visualization.

First Things First

It is also quite frequent to have people conflate operating system (the powerful software that ensures your hardware talks to you, the user) and a web browser or an app. With a growing number of tech actors promoting a specific app (*e.g.*, Facebook) to become a fully-fledged environment such as a web browser, these boundaries get blurred as we speak. Such concepts are, however, needed if you want to understand the key actors of your interactive data visualization.

As aforementioned, D3's strengths and challenges are contained in the same feature: versatility. As its creator, Michael Bostock writes:[1] "D3 allows you to bind arbitrary data to a Document Object Model (DOM), and then apply data-driven transformations to the document. [...] D3 is not a monolithic framework that seeks to provide every conceivable feature. Instead, D3 solves the crux of the problem: efficient manipulation of documents based on data. This avoids proprietary representation and affords extraordinary flexibility, exposing the full capabilities of web standards such as HTML, SVG, and CSS."

So, you have nothing to download, nothing to buy licenses for: if your browser gets new features tomorrow, D3's vocabulary naturally follows as it originates from web standards. Which also means that, when you write D3, you speak the same language as your browser.

This sounds cool and easy. Well, sorta. The only tricky part herein is understanding the Web. Because the Web has grown quite complicated. A recent opinion piece at Medium.com[2] composed by *"recovering magpie front-end developer"* Drew Hamlet stirred quite some controversy with its quite blunt honesty. Entitled "The Sad State of Web Development," the piece traces the evolution of JavaScript libraries used in web development and spits out frustration and disenchantment with the ever-growing amount of tools developers and big players can come up with. The bottom line is that web development could use simple tools fulfilling specific tasks rather than inventing a new JavaScript bazooka to shoot a tiny fly.

---

[1]http://d3js.org/
[2]https://medium.com/@wob/the-sad-state-of-web-development-1603a861d29f#.wxrrd13bi

© Tarek Amr and Rayna Stamboliyska 2016
T. Amr and R. Stamboliyska, *Practical D3.js*, DOI 10.1007/978-1-4842-1928-7_2

To use D3 requires some prior knowledge of the web technologies with which it interacts, but thankfully preserves you from the sufferings of actual front-end web developers such as Drew Hamlet. As Bostock defines it from the start, D3 interacts with HTML, CSS and SVG. Successfully using D3 requires a basic understanding of these technologies' fundamentals. Thus, we will go through these in a succinct fashion as the goal of this book is D3, not web literacy. If you need to, please refer to the end of the book for useful entry-level resources which will allow you to dive deeper into the Web world.

Organising Your Data Visualization

As a starting point, you need to decide what you want to achieve with your visualization. We already introduced you to the main rules of thumb: clarify, explore, mind the dialogue with your audience. But each of these is also a goal *per se*: do you want your visualization to enable personal discovery of complex data or should it instead tell a story or rather support and enhance an editorial perspective? Using D3 does not oblige you to create interactive visualizations, thus, you also need to decide whether to go for a static or an interactive one. All those are critical decisions to make and will reflect the clarity of concept you want to get to your audience.

While thinking and narrowing down the above answers and specifications, you should always mind the audience. As Alberto Cairo explained in his book "The Functional Art," you as a creator (journalist or otherwise) must respect your reader/viewer. A visualization transforms complicated matters into understandable subjects. Hence, my "clarify, but don't dumb down" from Chapter 1: your audience is composed of diverse individuals but the common feature among them is that they are smart and curious. Thus, clarity differs from reductionism and simplicity. Your visualization should not have the immediacy of interpretation as its primary goal. If your visuals are appealing enough, the audience will engage with—and put the effort it needs to comprehend the complexity you have attempted to clarify.

Look at the big picture: is your visualization a stand-alone piece of work or is it a part of a larger production? If it the latter, you need to think the visualization within the whole production, not as a mere colourful after-thought or a technical show-off. Such an integration requires rigour throughout the entire process for the visual to be aligned to the context and the questions it is answering.

The Connected China website (http://china.fathom.info/) helps illustrate the point we are trying to make (Figure 2-1). Connected China was built over a year and a half by a team of journalists and researchers at Hong Kong, and Ben Fry's *Fathom Design and presents a visual* exploration of China's social and institutional power. The visualization is an extraordinary tool kit for anyone wishing to understand the social and institutional power of China's elite: you can explore essential background on the country, compare careers for current and past leaders, read featured stories, and so on. Here, context is king and the driver behind such a unique effort to organise and transform with visuals Reuters' knowledge base of power in China. The production is radically different from news as we know it: the audience does not get either a story or a news item or a table, rather the entire visualization centers on narrating the structure of power in China.

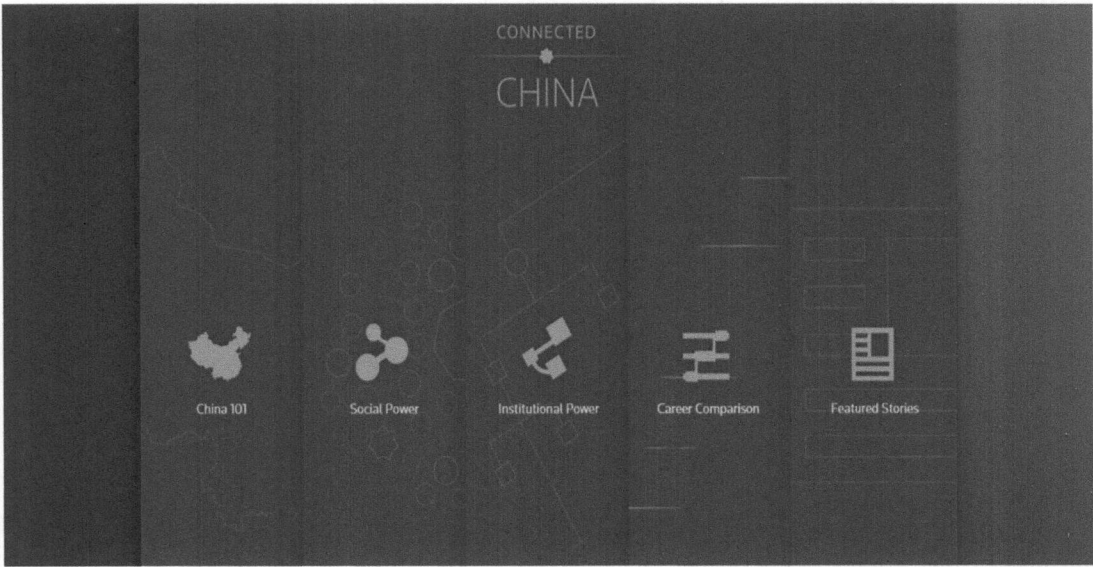

Figure 2-1. *A screenshot of the home page of "Connected China."*

Such a project is a huge one, indeed, but that is not its most important feature. Not much of the success of this visual exploration is technical. What's impressive is the team's commitment to maintain and update the database behind "Connected China." Reg Chua, Thomson Reuters' editor of data and innovation, wrote on his blog:[3]

> *[...] we updated the database (and hence the site) when the news was announced. That's not remarkable—right?*
>
> *That may seem like a strange question. After all, shouldn't data-driven apps offer the most up-to-date information to users? Certainly many do, especially those that take in regular feeds of government and publicly released data. But many data-driven projects— and especially heavily editorially curated projects such as Connected China—often don't; they're generally built to stand as a snapshot of a moment in time, not to be a constantly updated resource. [...] Most big projects analyzing reams of data and providing stories and analysis aren't designed to be updated. But shouldn't they be?*

Of course, not every newsroom can allow to build and maintain such a gigantic project. The bottom line here is, though: you are not in a vacuum, so strategically planning for the structure and the life of your visualization is crucial. A critique you could address to "Connected China" for example is on usability: how do I know when it was last updated since every time I visit the home page, it displays the same? If the plan was to have the underlying database updated as long as the visualization lives, then users should be given a way to know that this has happened and when.

If by now you think that this whole process is taking time, then wait for the data collection and preparation bit; we will spend more time on that in Chapter 3. For now, note that a compelling data visualization generally has a compelling data research and analysis behind. Whether it is on Doctor Who villains or casualties of drone strikes in Yemen, working with data and transforming it into visuals is time-consuming.

---

[3]https://structureofnews.wordpress.com/2013/03/27/current-connections/

Another reminder is to use visual restraint: you cannot show everything. If you want to use colours, do so, but ensure colour-blind could still see what you want to show. Furthermore, the diversity of forms needs to be carefully constructed to answer the primary question or enhance the main axes of a story. Your data visualization needs to amplify the impact of the content you are providing to the audience, not overwhelm it.

Finally, here comes a relatively overlooked element: the annotation. Going freehand with D3 is just that easy—but ensuring your audience follows you is a challenge. Thus, think of providing context and annotation for the key messages to be correctly interpreted. The *New York Times* is an outstanding example here, both regarding technical realisations and clarity of messages.

It's All About Gestalt

D3 transforms rather than represents data. In other words, D3 is a new set of metaphors with which to express hard-coded facts derived from one or more datasets.

Transform rather than represent has, however, nothing to do with lying about data. Regardless of the type of visual (a bar chart or a D3-powered data visualization), the outcome cannot alter the facts. You will learn about handling good and bad data, lying with visuals and the (not always) needed maths in Chapter 3. For now, we will focus on what visual forms tell.

Take, for example, the hoax game that spreads on Facebook where random letters are in a square grid: the first three words your eye catches define you (see Figures 2-2 and 2-3). Although this is suitable for preteens keeping busy on lazy afternoons, we are mentioning it here because of how it engages us: The human brain tries to detect anything meaningful by identifying patterns and, to do so, different "tools" are used sequentially. This is why we detect variations at different speeds: you spend some time figuring out which sequences of letters make sense (that is, make up a word).

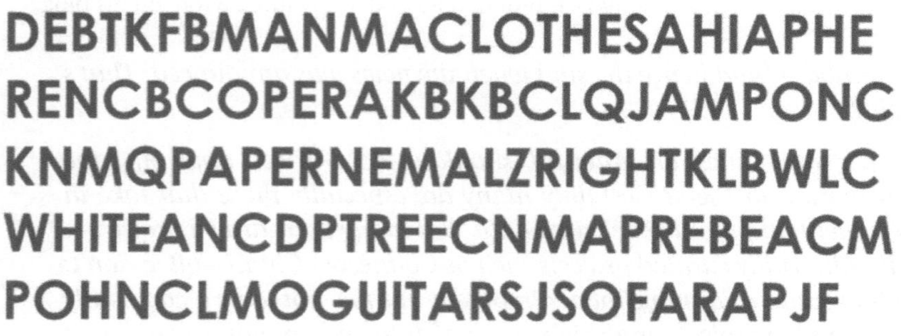

DEBTKFBMANMACLOTHESAHIAPHE
RENCBCOPERAKBKBCLQJAMPONC
KNMQPAPERNEMALZRIGHTKLBWLC
WHITEANCDPTREECNMAPREBEACM
POHNCLMOGUITARSJSOFARAPJF

Figure 2-2. A grid with seemingly random sequences of letters

DEBTKFBMANMACLOTHESAHIAPHE
RENCBCOPERAKBKBCLQJAMPONC
KNMQPAPERNEMALZRIGHTKLBWLC
WHITEANCDPTREECNMAPREBEACM
POHNCLMOGUITARSJSOFARAPJF

Figure 2-3. The same grid as in Figure 2-5 but the hidden words are highlighted in dark gray

Talking about perceptions brings about a different, complementary consideration. Don't search for words in such a grid, but for the letter R instead. Is it any easier to do? Probably not any easier. Still, you will figure them out much quicker than words (longer patterns). Naturally, one would object that a single word is easier to spot than a word, and this is true. You will need time and cognitive effort to achieve this task though, regardless of the length of the pattern.

Why are we discussing this? Because it is important to realise how your audience thinks visually for your production to not go through unnoticed (or worse: brushed off as too complicated).

In a nutshell, seeing patterns happens in an (utterly simplified) three-step process of visual perception:

- Step 1: rapid parallel processing to extract low-level properties of a visual scene. At this stage happens the detection of shape, spatial attributes, orientation, colour, texture, movement. This occurs automatically, that is, this computing step is independent of our cognitive focus. The resulting information is briefly held in a sort of visual buffer. This is what is often referred to as "preattentive" processing.

- Step 2: we "pull out" some structure thanks to pattern perception. Indeed, the outcome of step 1 is the division, in simple patterns, of our visual field. Those can be continuous contours, areas of the similar colour and so on. Object recognition happens here (is it an "R" or a "P"?). As you may have guessed it, this computing time is longer, that is, we deal with a slower serial processing.

- Step 3: here happens the sequential goal-directed processing. In other words, the information is further reduced to a few objects, which are buffered in a visual working memory. The latter is what we use to construct and answer visual queries. In contrast to step 1, this processing step is attention-driven, that is, visual thinking happens here.

When we asked you to identify a shape (a letter or a word), you first automatically and in parallel extracted colours, shapes, positions, then formed some organised pattern and ended up trying to spot only the shape you were asked to. If the grid is bigger, you will struggle more to remember where every occurrence of the shape is because your short visual memory is of small size, so the buffer cannot contain too many items at a time and removes some of them to make room for the newcomers.

You have certainly guessed the bottom line: keep it clear and help the brains understand the basics, so they have enough juice to process the really important stuff (your visual story).

How do we do that? Enter Gestalt theory. Dating back to the early twentieth century in Germany, Gestalt theory is mainly concerned with visual perception (for the German-impaired, *Gestalt* means pattern). The neurobiology behind the Gestalt is quite wrong, but the principles it posed still hold. The main idea is that the whole is greater than the sum of parts, that is, our brains do not see patches of colour or shape individually, but as groupings. Organisation FTW.[4] Let's explore these principles here.

We mentioned earlier in this chapter that a small number of basic visual properties are processed pre-attentively. It is like the information item just "popped out" (step 1 of our model). This is important for designing effective visuals as it directs you to the features which are perceived rapidly and distinctively. Our pre-teen-compliant word grid is a good example again, but look at it now keeping the same goal in mind: pick the "R"s (Figure 2-4).

---

[4]FTW: for the win.

DEBTKFBMANMACLOTHESAHIAPHE
RENCBCOPERAKBKBCLQJAMPONC
KNMQPAPERNEMALZRIGHTKLBWLC
WHITEANCDPTREECNMAPREBEACM
POHNCLMOGUITARSJSOFARAPJF

Figure 2-4. *The same grid as in Figure 2-2 but only the occurrences of the letter "R" are highlighted*

We are better at detecting variations in shades than in shapes. If the grid was a visual with a function—for example, how many R would appear in a 6×6 matrix with randomly picked letters—the visualization in Figure 2-4 is a much better tool: it complies with the way our brains function.

Shapes are also preattentively processed; just look at Figure 2-5.

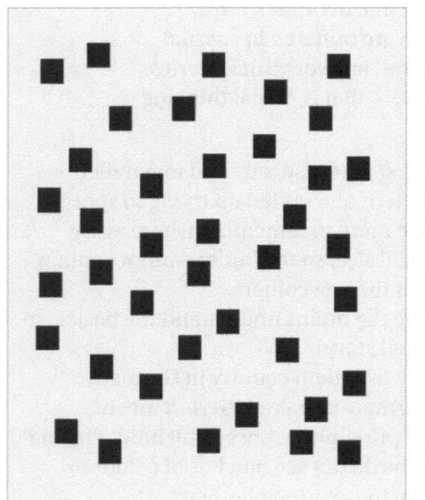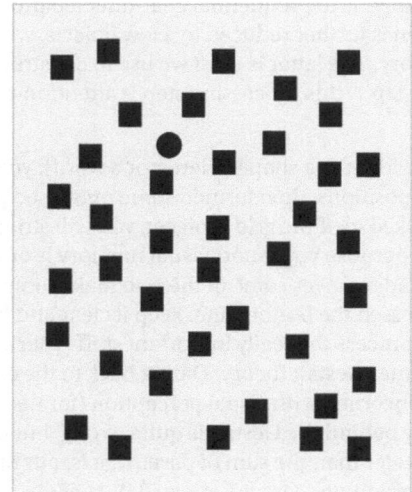

Figure 2-5. *Find the circle*

We are also better at detecting differences in size and orientation. When computing, our brains first sort similar vs. dissimilar, thus, for example, grouping together similarly sized items and singling out those that differ (see Figure 2-6).

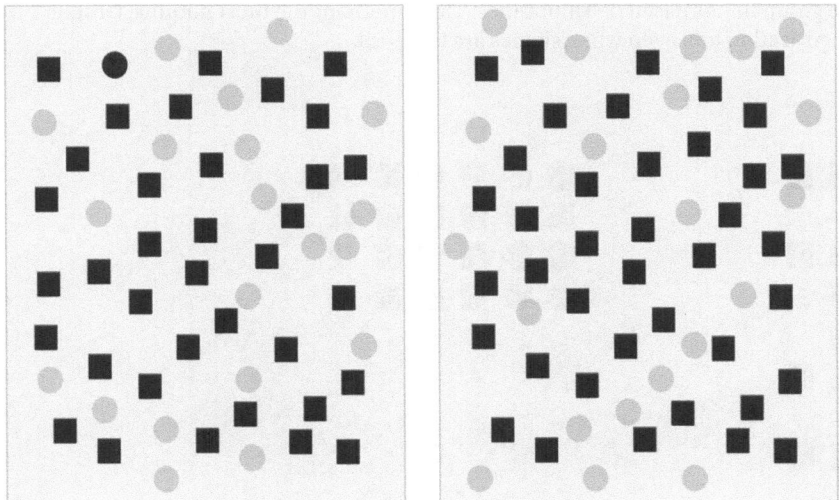

Figure 2-6. *Other ways of computing visually*

Beware, though: the conjunction of two properties (*e.g.*, color *and* shape) is not preattentively processed. Thus, do not ask your audience to figure out quickly messages encoded in both color and shape. An example of this difficulty is in the image Figure 2-7.

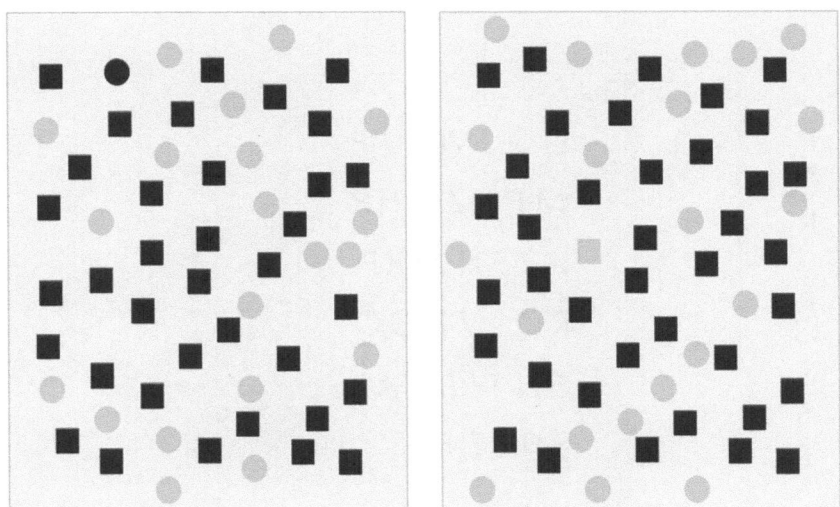

Figure 2-7. *Is there a yellow square anywhere? Or perhaps you noticed a dark colored circle somewhere? Was it easy to identify any of those?*

We mentioned that we group things based on similarities. This is perhaps the most intuitive Gestalt principle. It works as a categorization tool even when shapes are identical.

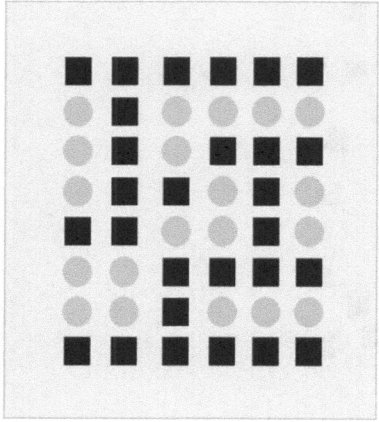 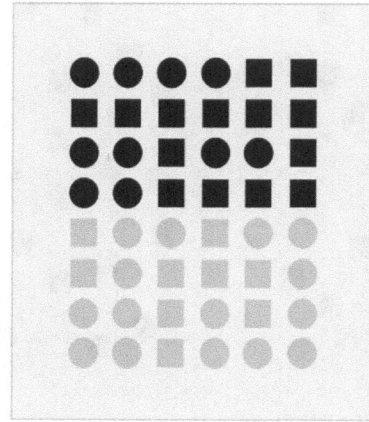

Figure 2-8. *An example of how we categorize items, here based on colors and shapes. Each item is equally spaced from its neighbors. The same is true for each range.*

And what happens then if some items are closer to each other than they are to other items in a group? We see them as belonging together although there might be no common element between them (see Figure 2-9).

Figure 2-9. *Those ranges of letters are spaced by line or column (left image and right image, respectively, so they appear "to belong together," albeit not sharing any common feature within each line or column.)*

The idea is that similar objects should be close to each other in your visualization following the spatial concentration principle: we group regions of similar element density. Some D3 tools (the Force layout for example, see Chapter 8 for how it works, or a sankey diagram) will do this natively.

Similarity between different elements can be graphically denoted with a container or a visible line that connects one element to another. It is a more powerful organizing principle than proximity, color, size, or shape (see Figure 2-10).

 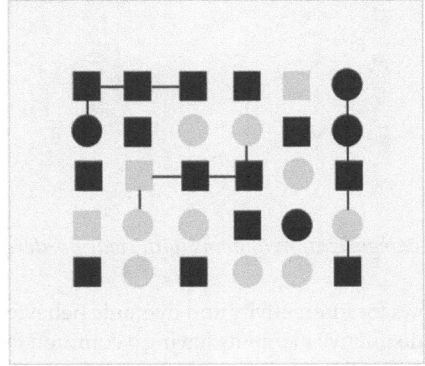

Figure 2-10. *An example of connectedness: (left) via a container; (right) via a visible line*

This spatial problem is difficult to solve, especially with complex datasets, so plan ahead for it.

The proximity feature is a really cool one, and a different way of thinking about it is in terms of boundary detection. In other words, you can wonder whether items form a boundary, and if so, based on which attribute(s). In Figure 2-11, the grouping in A happens based on color while the one in B is because of spacing.

Figure 2-11. *Grouping of items via A. shapes of two colours; and B. via spacing.*

But what happens to your items if you grouped them inside an area with clearly visible boundaries, as shown in Figure 2-12?

 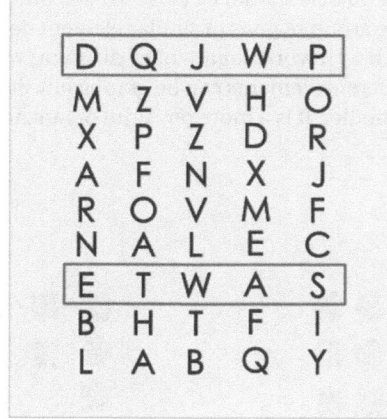

Figure 2-12. *Visual categorization of items with clear borders can overpower preexisting grouping*

Because D3 allows for interactivity and dynamic behavior, you can think of movement as indicating an entity. Think of it as distinctive elements having a common fate: if they all "move" in the same direction, you would most probably perceive them as a whole.

Revelation (as in animated transitions) is the last principle we will introduce here. Mike Bostock calls this "object constancy":[5]

> *Animated transitions are pretty, but they also serve a purpose: they make it easier to follow the data. This is known as object constancy: a graphical element that represents a particular data point (such as Ohio) can be tracked visually through the transition. This lessens the cognitive burden by using preattentive processing of motion rather than sequential scanning of labels.*

You may be thinking that this chapter is difficult and it's true that it requires some time to process and integrate. As Elijah Meeks put it:[6]

> *This "academic" approach to data visualization seems in opposition to a "pragmatic" approach that focuses on best practices and prior art demonstrated in the growing library of data visualization books and 2-day seminars.*
>
> *But let me suggest that gestalt is very much a pragmatic aspect of creating data visualization, in fact a necessary aspect if you plan to do more than simple bar and line charts (and perhaps even for those simple charts).*

The pragmatic Gestalt learnings are thus what will help you in applying D3. They are especially relevant when thinking visually with closure because you will be aware of the signals those graphics are sending. For instance, you may unintentionally produce a quite ... interesting Venn diagram[7] as shown in Figure 2-13.

---

[5]http://bost.ocks.org/mike/constancy/
[6]http://emeeks.github.io/gestaltdataviz/section1.html
[7]http://flowingdata.com/2014/08/19/unintentional-venn-diagram-suggests-opposite-meaning/

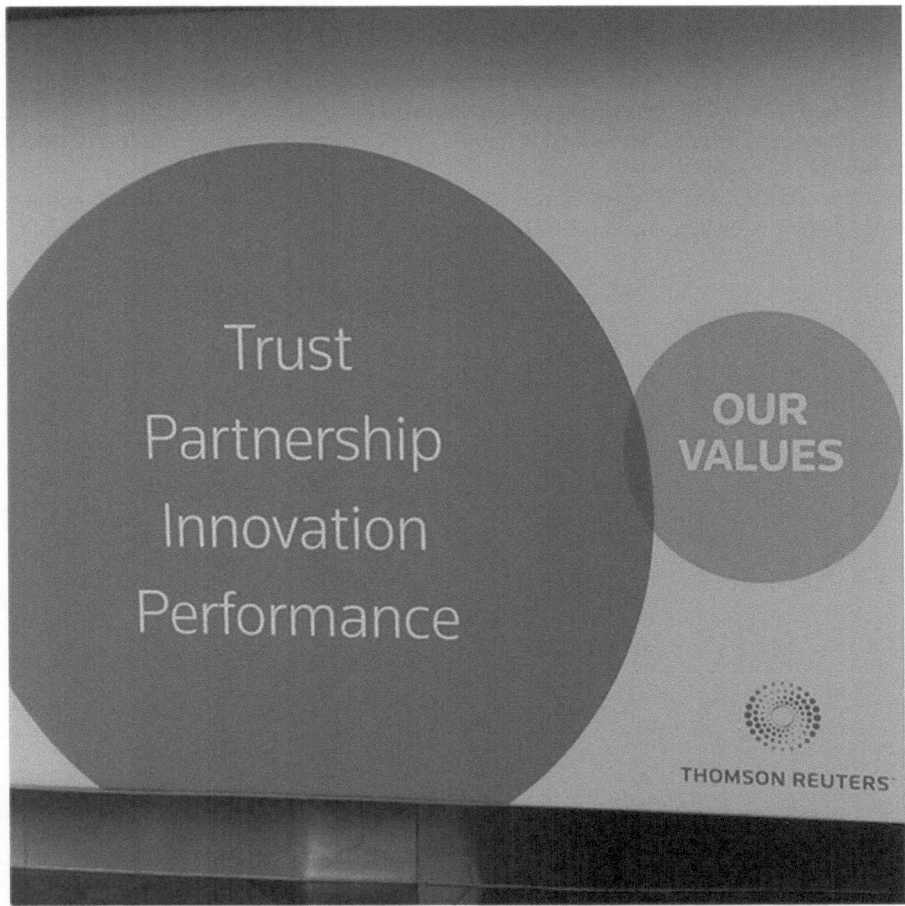

Figure 2-13. *An unintentional Venn diagram*[8]

We are thus talking about how to select the most optimal graphic form for encoding data, based on what function we want it to fulfill. Back in 1984, two statisticians, Cleveland and McGill, designed a list of 10 elementary perceptual tasks[9]. Each is a method to visually represent data and performs differently. In other words, one visual encoding of data will allow you to more accurately detect differences while another will enable generic judgments on, for example, the relationship between a variable and its geographical location.

---

[8]Image source: https://datavizblog.com/2014/08/20/thomson-reuters-unintentional-venn-diagram/
[9]https://web.cs.dal.ca/~sbrooks/csci4166-6406/seminars/readings/Cleveland_GraphicalPerception_Science85.pdf

Summary

Gestalt principles and carefully choosing the form to convey the data are important for producing effective visualizations. The principles explained in this chapter will guide you in the process of formalizing how to use graphical features to indicate a category, a quantity, or a topology—and help you avoid unintentionally conveying adverse meaning.

Now that we have addressed the basics of how to think visually, we are ready to proceed to understanding your data. In the following chapter, we will explore together how to get the facts right and how not to lie with data.

CHAPTER 3

■ ■ ■

Getting the Facts Right

So far, we discussed the best ways to visually think data. This chapter is a sort of a "data visualization FailCon." FailCon is a conference for startup founders to learn from their own and others' failures and prepare for success. And, indeed, we all can identify countless excellent data visualizations. They all look just perfect, so you need to be excellent at reverse-engineering to seamlessly learn how to achieve such quality. Thankfully, we can always call abysmal visuals to the rescue. The idea is not to bash on the people who have put those together but, rather, to learn from their errors in order not to repeat them.

What Is Your Story?

This is a frequent starting point: you have a question to answer or a theme to present from a fresh angle. One interesting way to go about narrowing down a story line is to decide why you want to tell that story. Do you simply wish to share something cool? Are you reporting on your latest research outcomes? Or did you uncover the mother of all corruption schemes?

Depending on the angle you take, you will need to collect relevant data. In today's big data glut, we are tempted to believe that, whatever the question, there will be data to answer it. This is hardly true, as John Tukey highlights it:

> *The data may not contain the answer. The combination of some data and an aching desire for an answer does not ensure that a reasonable answer can be extracted from a given body of data.*

Going further, it is also important to emphasise that some questions are easier to answer with data (and thus with a data visualization) than others. What you will do to the data determines to an extent how you will encode this in visuals next. I very much appreciate the decision-making chart shown in Figure 3-1, adapted from Jeff Leek's great book *The Elements of Data Analytic Style*. Although we briefly introduce the fundamentals here, we recommend that you read Jeff's book as it is an excellent resource for anyone who feels uneasy with data analysis. In Chapter 4, you will gain a better understanding of what a data format is and how to navigate the world of openly licensed, public, big, small, and all other types of data out there. For the time being, though, it is important to learn what you can do with the data and what it says. One of the best ways to figure out what the data means is to explore it using visuals, with or without an intermediate step of the analysis. We will thus discuss different approaches to analyze data.

T. Amr and R. Stamboliyska, *Practical D3.js*, DOI 10.1007/978-1-4842-1928-7_3

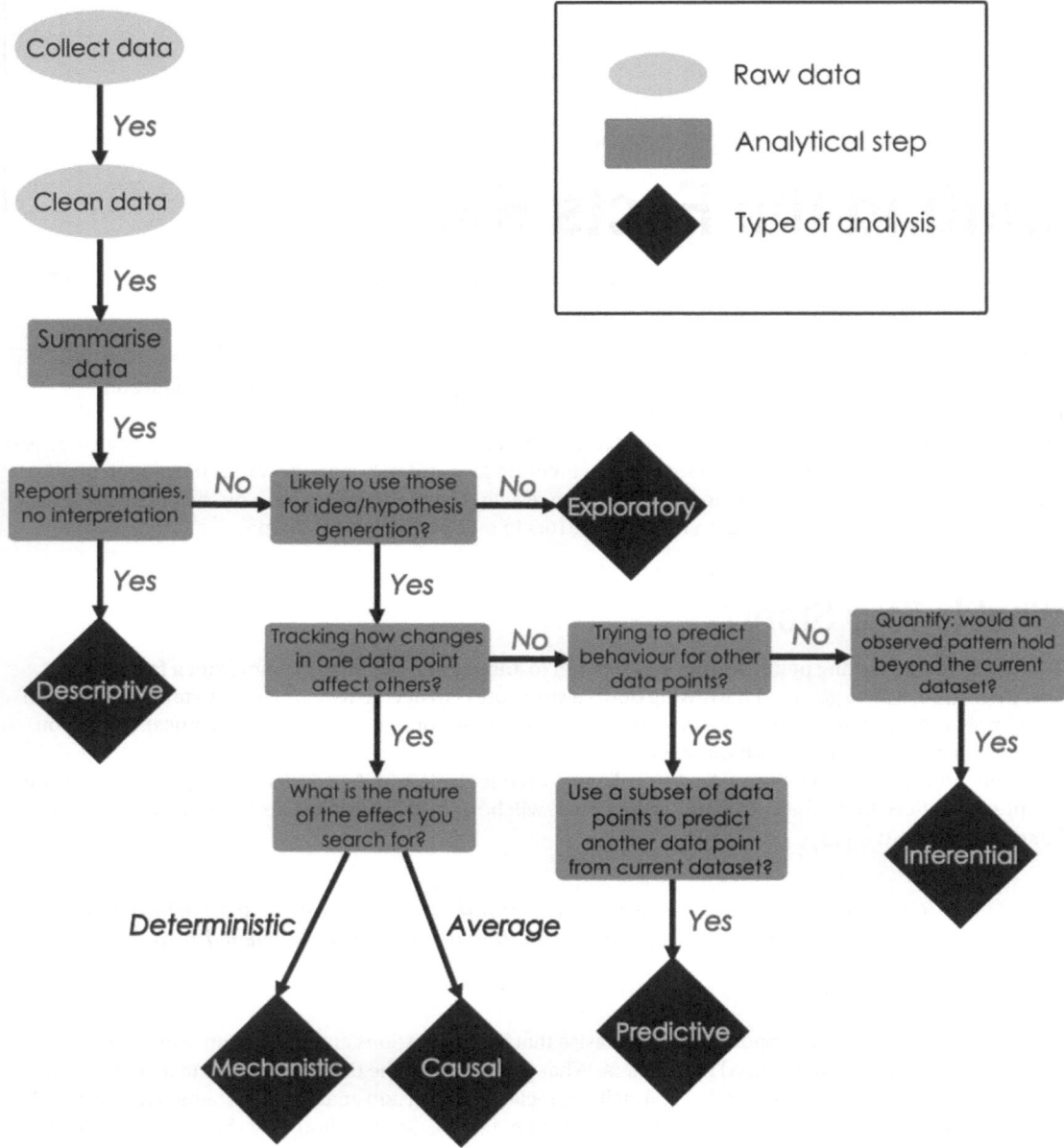

Figure 3-1. How to decide what type of analysis you should apply to your data

Perhaps the most general case we see online is a descriptive visualization. Such a production summarizes facts (data points, measurements, you name it) from a dataset but does not seek to interpret them further. The average snow coverage per year for the past 10 years, for a given city, is an example.

An exploratory analysis is more complex and in-depth than the descriptive because it seeks to build on datasets, for example, establishing relationships between them. You can make discoveries with exploration (but not necessarily confirm those, from a scientific point of view). The Google Consumer data ensemble enables exploratory analysis and visualization; you can, for example, compare obstacles to online shopping in the United States, the Czech Republic, and Saudi Arabia.

Making inferences is to go a step further from the exploration of trends and relationships. An inferential analysis will seek to quantify whether you can extrapolate a pattern or behaviour you observe beyond your current dataset. An example is inferring whether a pattern observed in fruit flies (eating less sugar prolongs life span) will hold for mice or rats. What you are seeking to identify with inferences is whether the relationship between the data and the behaviour or pattern is strong enough to occur in a different setup. You may have guessed it; this is challenging as the relationship may be reinforced or due to a factor unaccounted for in the current setup.

An inference is not to conflate with causality. When you search for causality, you are seeking to identify whether one measurement will change if you alter a parameter. With causality, you can identify both the relationship and the magnitude between variables.

Before we outline what predictive and mechanistic analyses are, let us emphasize that correlation does not imply causation. You may have heard that a lot, but we want to stress it again: a "cause" and its "effect" are a Grail to find. Interpreting an inference as causality is wrong. "While there are many approaches to establishing causality, everyone agrees that the cause must precede the effect," to quote Kaiser Fung.[1] Thus, two datasets may appear to have a converging or common behaviour, but in no case is this a reason to claim causality. That is the most familiar situation (see Figure 3-2).

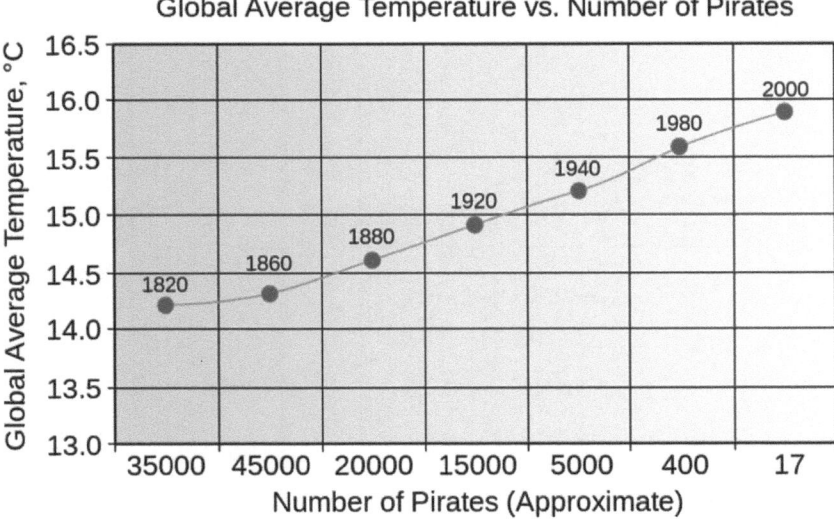

Figure 3-2. *Pirates vs. global warming*

The image was first used on venganza.org, the website of the Pastafarians (a parody religion movement that emerged to oppose the teaching of intelligent design and creationism in public schools in the United States that promotes critical thinking). The image is to denounce the too frequent confusion that correlation implies causation. (Image source: `https://commons.wikimedia.org/wiki/File:PiratesVsTemp(en).svg` CC-by-SA 2.5, Wikimedia Commons).

Back to our brief outline of types of analysis (Figure 3-1.) A predictive analysis takes a subdataset and uses its features to predict the outcome of another dataset. Think preelection polls. It is quite easy not to get causality in the way here as predictive analysis does not explain why a prediction works.

---

[1] `http://www.thedailybeast.com/articles/2015/12/07/does-standing-lead-to-weight-loss.html`. Greatly recommended is also Fung's blog, Junk Charts (`http://junkcharts.typepad.com/`).

Lastly, the mechanistic analysis only demonstrates that if you change one data point, it will always and exclusively lead to a particular pattern in another. This is referred to as deterministic behavior. In this case, the mechanistic analysis seeks to clarify how the causality effect operates.

Getting to Know Your Data (a bit)If someone gives you readily available results and tells you exactly what to do with the data, you only need to figure out the visual metaphors—no math required.

In real life, however, such a situation is not that frequent. If you are a journalist or a scientist, you will even refuse such an interaction with the facts you are provided with. Thus, if you want to stay truthful to the data—because numbers really do not speak for themselves—you need to be fully aware of the basics.

If you have plenty of values, you can check out how they are distributed (Figure 3-3).

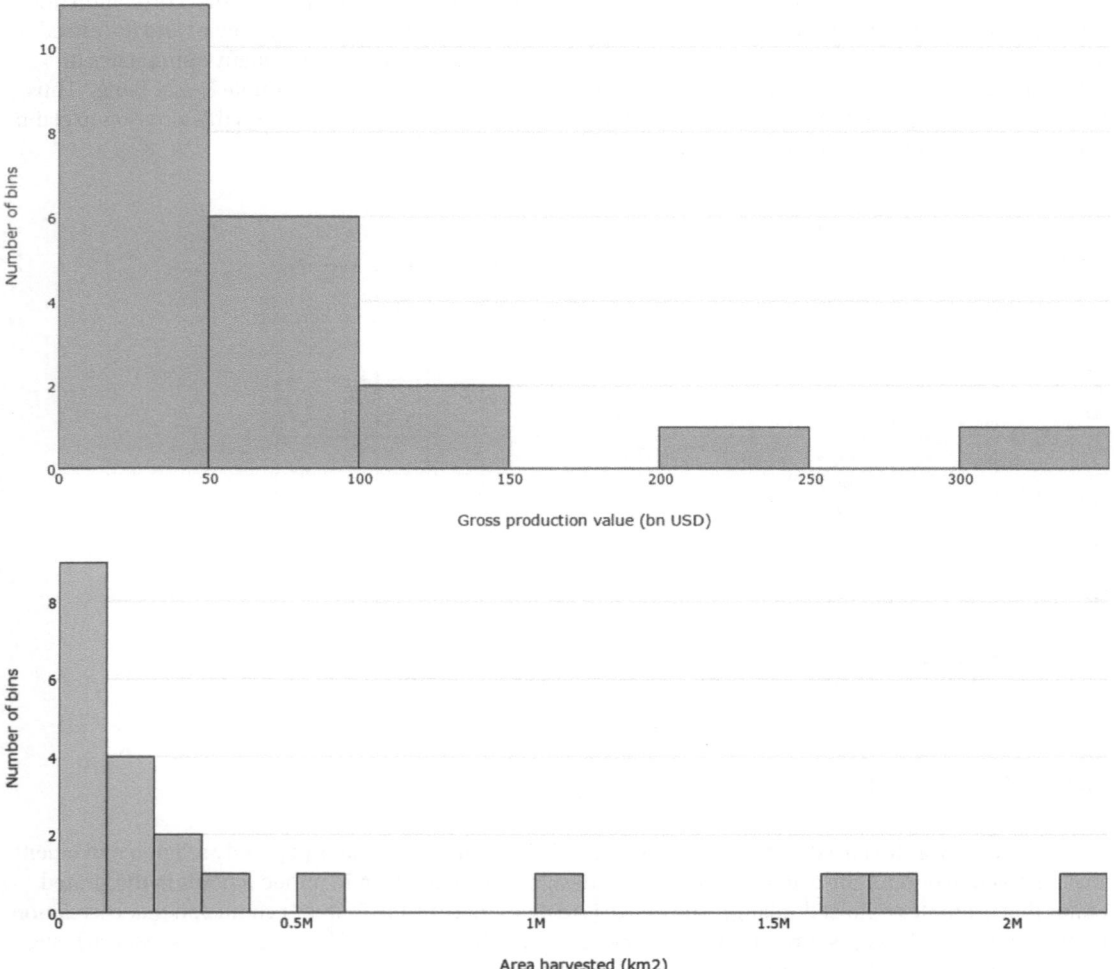

Figure 3-3. *Cash crops worldwide: (top) gross production value in billion USD; (bottom) area harvested in km². Data source: Information is Beautiful.*

The histograms (done with D3's Histogram Layout) shown in Figure 3-3 are the most straightforward way to assess data distribution. Each bar of the histogram gives you the count of each value, for example, we have 10 occurrences of 125, 1 occurrence of 500, and so on. This gives you insights about:

A. the range of the data: does it start with small or large numbers? Or does it stretch both negative and positive values? The range also provides you with hints about possibly erroneous data. For instance, you have school pupils' health data in front of you, and the heights range between 120 to 550 cm. I might get suspicious about the values indicating me that primary school kids can be 5 m tall. There are clearly errors in this dataset, so I will need to figure out what to do with them: double check is a must, but I may also choose to remove them.

B. the number of data points: this is important especially if you are going to perform statistical analysis on this dataset. Your data can be normally distributed (Figure 3-4), that is, there is one peak in the middle and the sides are equal. Alternatively, the distribution can be skewed. Those shapes indicate that you do not treat these datasets the same way when you are analyzing them.

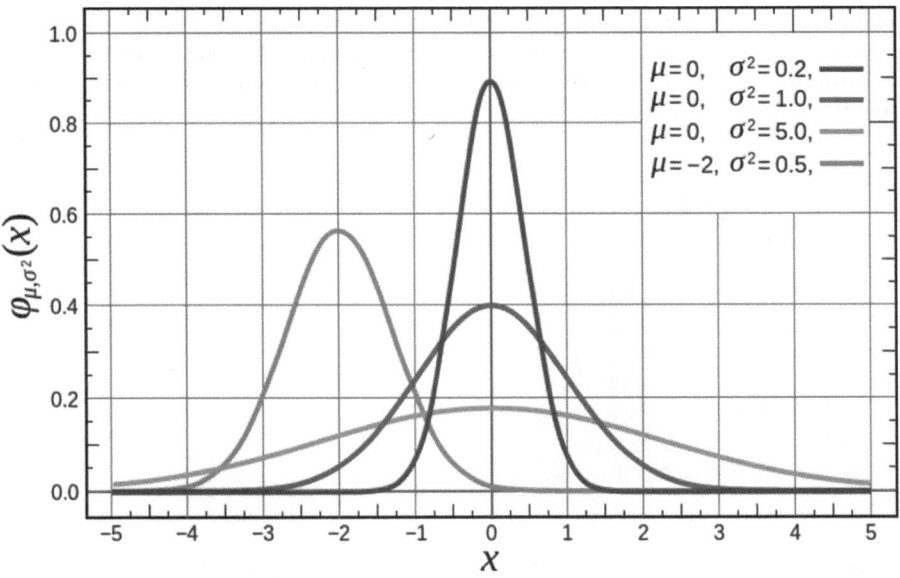

Figure 3-4. *Examples of different normally distributed datasets. Here, μ indicates the mean and σ² indicates the variance. See body of the text for explanations. Image in the public domain (Wikimedia Commons).*

Before we discuss normally distributed data in detail, it is important to highlight what benefits you get from plotting histograms. Quite often, we collect data with a question in mind. However, you may be in a situation where you get hold of data without a predefined question, for example, when visiting the National Statistics Bureau of your country. Thus, plotting those histograms can help you formulate the most interesting question(s) to ask the dataset you have at hand. Figure 3-3 (top) indicates a majority of crops occupy small harvested areas, but intriguing outliers also exist. The histograms in Figure 3-3 (bottom) show a similar pattern in terms of generated revenue. An interesting question you could ask such a dataset is: is the high revenue coming from large harvested areas? If not, how come that significantly lesser production generates more money? A second benefit from this histogram plotting could be to figure out whether you need additional data to answer your questions and to start hunting for their sources. In our case, it seems that cannabis occupies tiny harvested areas but produces immense revenues. This is an interesting question to investigate, especially in the light of different states and places moving to decriminalize it. Still, it can turn out a bit complicated to get hold of usable data on illicit substances,[2] which is a question you will need to explore in the next steps of your data collection.

Speaking of normally distributed data is a bit awkward: what is "normal data"? Normal distribution indicates a relationship of all values to a mean (as in average, indicated by μ on Figure 3-4). This value is calculated by summing all the values present in your dataset and dividing the sum by the number of values. For example, the mean of 1, 2, 3, 4, 6 is $(1+2+3+4+6)/5 = 16/5 = 3.2$. The variance (indicated by σ^2) represents how close or far the data clusters around the mean. You can observe these differences in Figure 3-4: the yellow curve has a huge variance; thus, the data spreads much wider away from the mean. By contrast, the blue curve has a small variance, the values clustering close around the mean.

The median is different from the mean and is often considered as more reliable in statistics. The median is obtained by sorting your data and selecting the value right in the middle. For our small dataset (1, 2, 3, 4, 6), 3 will be the median. The difference between the mean and the median is subtle here, so why is the median better than the mean? The median is more robust than the mean because its value does not depend on the extreme values in your dataset. Think of income inequalities: a few very wealthy people may make it look like the socioeconomic status of your sample is higher than it is. The median will not be impacted by these outliers because it is the number of data points that matters, not their value.

This discussion gets us to variation. From your normal distribution (Figure 3-4), you can see that the values on the sides are away from the mean. A measure called the standard deviation tells us how much the data points are spread out within the sample:

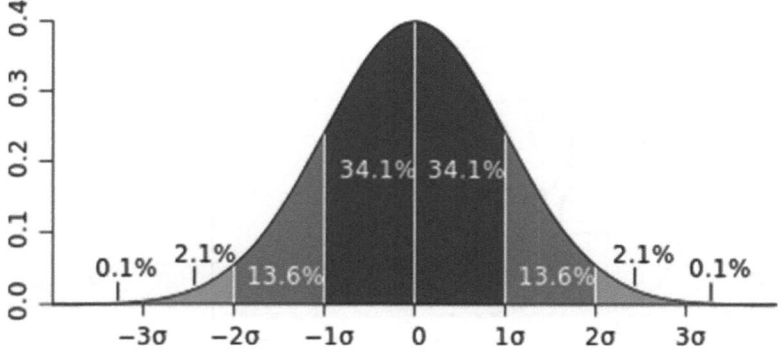

Figure 3-5. *Standard deviation illustrated. Image from Wikimedia Commons, CC-by 2.5.*[3]

What this figure tells us is that, if our data is normally distributed, then 68.27 percent of data points fall within one standard deviation from the mean, and 95.45 percent are within 2 standard deviations from the mean. So it gives us a good idea where most of our data is. To calculate the standard deviation, you can use any relevant tool in R or the formula in Excel/LibreOffice Calc. It is important not to confound variance and standard deviation. The latter is more useful to describe the variability of the data while the former is usually much more useful mathematically.

---

[2]The data visualization and the underlying data are from Information Is Beautiful http://www.informationisbeautiful.net/visualizations/what-is-the-worlds-biggest-cash-crop/.
[3]Source: https://en.wikipedia.org/wiki/File:Standard_deviation_diagram.svg.

For our earlier dataset, the standard deviation is of 1.92. Simply put, this means that 68.27 percent of our normally distributed data points will fall within this distance from the mean.

If you use the median, you will prefer the median absolute deviation. It is easier to calculate: you compute the difference between each value and the median, and then you identify the median of the differences. For example, our data is (1, 2, 3, 4, 6) and the median is 3. The differences are 2 1 0 1 3; you sort them: 0 1 1 2 3. The median absolute deviation is: 1.

Differences between Data Points

These descriptors are simple and straightforward. If you are using spreadsheets or the R language, you will compute these values in a simple way. If you are playful enough, you can also do it by hand.

How do we find differences between data points or datasets? By comparing them against a common baseline. You cannot compare apples and oranges, right. Let's take data on refugees to illustrate this.

Western countries retain a relatively small proportion of the rising numbers of refugees despite their wealth, whereas less developed countries welcome a majority of these. The UNHCR (United Nations High Commissariat for Refugees) highlights the structural problem in the refugee crisis that this imbalance constitutes:[4] poorer countries, that is, these in development, carry the burden of the crisis. As a measure of this discrepancy, the UNHCR uses the gross domestic product at purchasing power parity (GDP PPP) per capita:

> *In 2014, the 30 countries with the largest number of refugees per 1 USD GDP (ppp) per capita were all members of developing regions, and included 18 Least Developed Countries. More than 5.9 million refugees, representing 42% of the world's refugees, resided in countries whose GDP (ppp) per capita was below USD 5,000.*

Compare, for example, Italy, and Egypt. At the end of 2014, Italy hosted 93,000 refugees; when related to the country's GDP, this number of refugees indicates that Italy houses one refugee per 2.69 USD of GDP PPP per capita. Contrastingly, Egypt hosted nearly 240,000 refugees in 2014. More than Italy, for sure, but other MENA countries such as Jordan welcome much more. For Egypt, this means one refugee per 20.87 USD of the GDP PPP per capita. Thus, the financial requirement comes out as very low for Italy and quite important for Egypt. You can then visualize this financial burden for the countries of your choosing and select a form (e.g., a map, as in Figure 3-6) to encode this data visually.

---

[4]UNHCR Global Trends report 2014, http://unhcr.org/2014trends/.

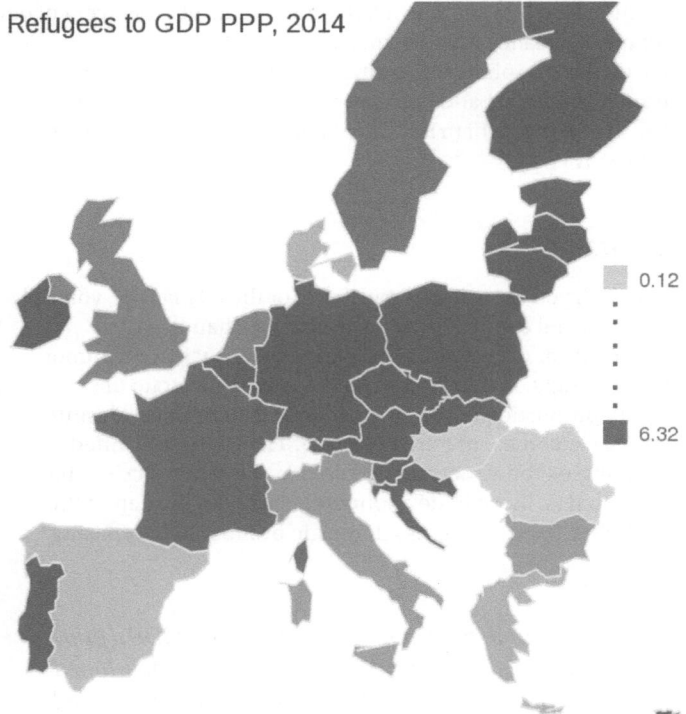

Figure 3-6. *The 'Refugees to GDP PPP' map is a snapshot of the 2014 dynamics in Europe. The measure is in USD of GDP PPP per capita. Data from the UNHCR.*

Transformation, Not Representation

As you know by now, D3 transforms rather than represents data. In other words, D3 is a new set of metaphors with which to express hard-coded facts derived from one or more datasets.

Transform rather than represent has, however, nothing to do with lying about data. If you have already crunched some data, you may have run into the challenge that your story is not that exciting after all. This is valid for investigations, scientific research and business KPIs alike. The options you have here is to either just tell the visual story as it is—that content has value as well—or add more data to identify a different angle or bridge missing gaps. Unfortunately, data visualization professionals around me have also encountered a third option: when the client asks you to "enhance" some of the visuals for the outcome to be less banal. Such a modification of reality may remind you student years when we were all taught about not cropping axes and using identical comparison basis.

It is the same with D3-powered data visualization: the outcome cannot alter the facts. Those are reflected in variables, which can be of different types.

A continuous variable is anything measured on a quantitative scale; it can be a fractional number. Think, for example, of height measured in cm or inches. By contrast, a discrete variable can solely take certain values from a finite set. For example, one or three people can be seated in a car, but it is impossible to have 1¼ or 3½ people therein. Thus, the number of people in a car is a discrete variable. It can sometimes be confusing to decide whether a variable is continuous or discrete. Here is an exercise: is shoe size a continuous or a discrete variable? And is the number of stars a continuous or a discrete variable? (Hint: answers are at the end of the chapter.)

Another type are nominal variables: they have two or more categories. For example, a real estate agent could classify their types of property into distinct categories, for example, house, bungalow, and flat. The ordinals are like the nominals, but are ordered, for instance survey responses where the choices are: poor, fair, excellent. These types are qualitative: you cannot attribute a value to neither of these two kinds of variable.

Think about all these things when reflecting on the analysis to apply to the data and, later on, when picking up a visual encoding.

The Importance of Telling a Story

The main purpose of a visualization is not entertainment but effective communication. This entire chapter follows on from the previous two ones in trying to explain how we should visually represent data without lying about it.

In December 2015, world leaders convened to an unprecedented gathering, the COP21, aiming to change how we treat our planet. The graph in Figure 3-7 was widely circulated.

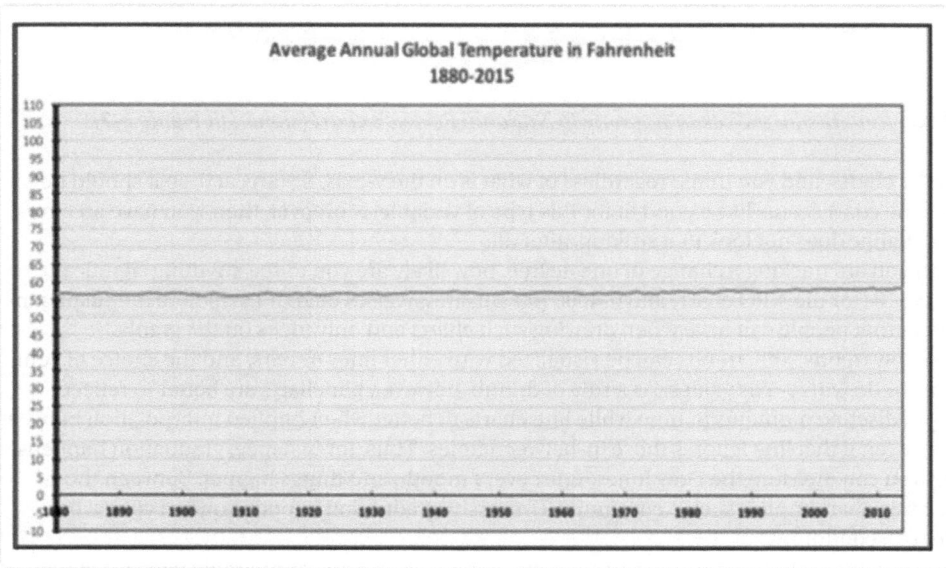

Figure 3-7. *A tweet from the National Review apparently holding that global warming has not happened*[5]

A COP21 Twitter controversy was born. *BusinessWeek* responded with the chart in Figure 3-8.

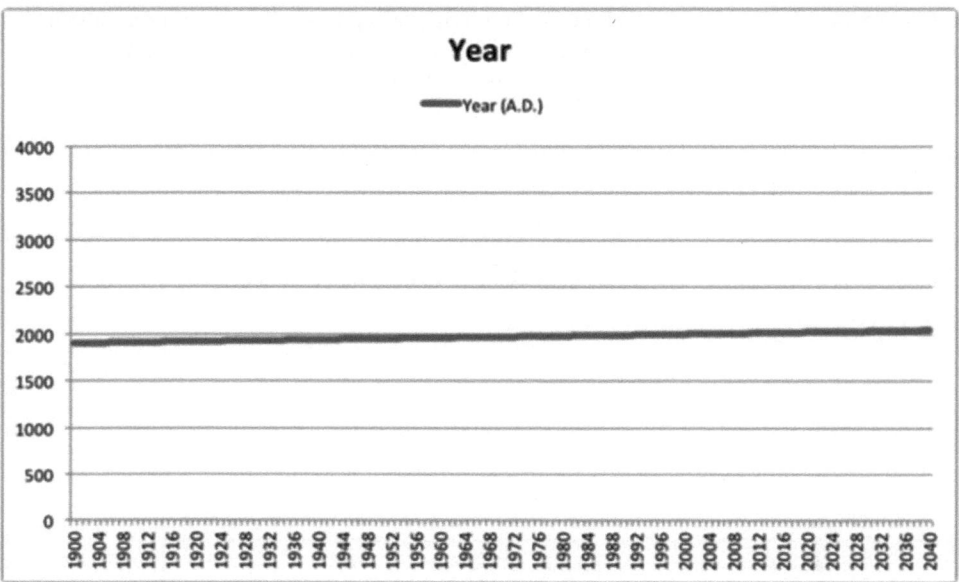

Figure 3-8. *A tweet from BusinessWeek in response to National Review's chart (shown in Figure 3-7)[6]*

You look at the charts, and you think: regardless of what is on the y-axis, it starts at 0, so it should be correct; also, the line chart seems like a good fit for this type of variable. Moreover, then, you have an after-thought: climate change does not look that striking, after all.

Yes, but no: if you are tracking a change of one degree, how likely are you to see anything significant when axes scale 0-110 (for the NRO chart) and 0-4000 (for BusinessWeek's chart)? I skip here the suspicion of fraudulent intent that people can have when drawing such charts and only focus on the graphs.

Both charts show trends. Still, trends can be visualized with either lines or bars, and the choice of your shape has nothing to do with y-axis values. As a rule of thumb, however, bar charts are better to reflect events occurring at discrete moments in time while line charts fit better when implied interpolation between points can matter, even if that line ignores those in-between times. Thus, for instance, graduation happens discontinuously. You can measure the Dow Jones index every month, and things happen between those measurements: a line chart implies such a continuity. University graduation happens once a year: a bar graph implies that discontinuity.

Back to the two climate change examples from earlier. First, they are not comparable because of the different scales. Second, if you want to reflect a one-degree change, does it make sense to zero the y-axis when your change is, say, between 59 and 60? If we decided to truncate the y-axis and start it off with a non-zero value, we would see significant changes, as shown in Figure 3-9.

---

[6]Source: https://twitter.com/bizweekgraphics/status/676533647567114240.

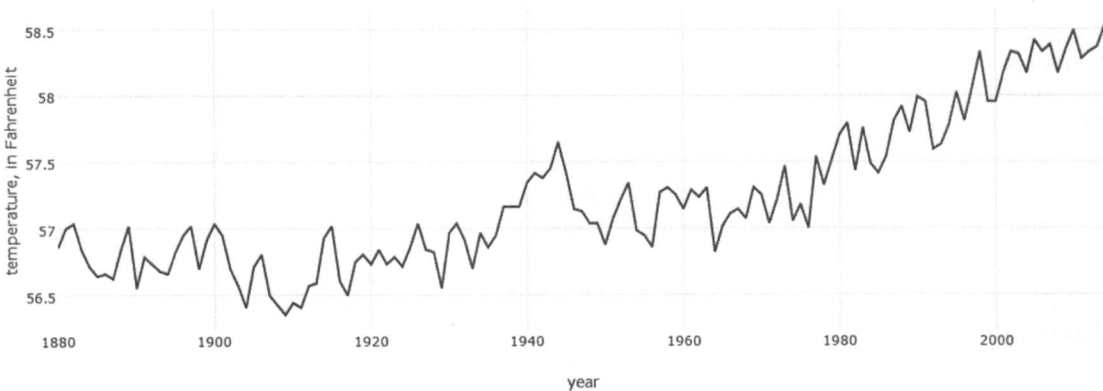

Figure 3-9. *A line chart showing the changes in average temperature (in degrees Fahrenheit) between 1880 and 2014. Evolutions in average values are visible after cropping the y axis and starting it at 56.5 degrees F rather than 0. Data from the NASA.*

Why did we truncate the y-axis? Isn't that like telling a lie? Not really; you should zero your y-axis if doing so does not alter the point your chart is trying to make, or muddle the information. In Figure 3-9, however, zeroing the y-axis causes the visuals to lie. One could object that this is how reality looks like and truncating the y-axis exaggerates what the data say.

Why do we insist on this example? After all, D3 is about doing anything else than a chart, and being creative with visuals. The examples in this chapter are, however, generic enough to serve as a lifeline when going freehand with complex visualization approaches. Moreover, talking about charts that everyone is familiar with achieves this modularity better than if I focused on one specific, complex visualization.

How then should we convey information by transforming the data but not lying with it? Back to line charts. The context of the climate change examples matters. In other words, our visuals illustrate ideas that have context beyond their x- and y-axes. In the examples, forcing the y-axis to start at zero does obscure and confuse the point. Also, remember my recommendation from the previous chapter: trust your audience, people are not idiots. This is the reason charts have scales. Thinking of the context here is important as well: the purpose of the charts in Figure 3-9 is to showcase small changes about when they have occurred, not about zero. Thus, small movements are necessary and if this is what you encode in a visual, you should "zoom in" and show it. Even if it means to nonzero the y-axis. Read Tufte:[7]

> *In general, in a time-series, use a baseline that shows the data not the zero point, don't spend a lot of empty vertical space trying to reach down to the zero point at the cost of hiding what is going on in the data line itself.*

If we look at our scale of elementary perceptual tasks (Chapter 2), we see that curvature tends to be more appropriate for allowing more generic judgements. Whenever possible (that is, nearly always[8]), column and bar charts should zero the y axis. That is because both bar and column charts rely on bars that stretch to zero to accurately mirror the ratios between data points. If you truncate the y-axis, then you break

---

[7]http://www.edwardtufte.com/bboard/q-and-a-fetch-msg?msg_id=00003q.
[8]https://twitter.com/_cingraham/status/478926885385424896/photo/1.

the relationship between the size of the rectangle and the value of the data. Simply put, you are lying. Oh, and a final note: Never use a zero y-axis on a log scale. A kind reminder: $\log(0) = -\infty$ (this is minus infinity). Thus, if you wanted to zero a y-axis on a log scale, it would be like asking to see $-\infty$ on a linear-scale graph … You are certainly aware, but it is always better to say it out loud: that makes no sense.

And this is how we come to a conclusion that a visual has to be fair and true to the data, not impartial.

As we are talking about misleading forms, consider pie charts. In Chapter 1, we spoke about what Alberto Cairo calls the "bubble plague"; here is another sarcastic quote, from Tufte again:[9]

> *Pie chart users deserve same suspicion + skepticism as those who mix up its/it's, there/their. To compare, use little table, sentence, not pies.*

He is quite right (as usual, in fact). Pie charts can be a valuable element to use when you have two data elements.

Just as with the "bubble plague," a "pie plague" exists and enjoys widespread credibility. However, as Tufte emphasises, pie charts are misleading when it boils down to comparisons between different sets of data. Because what you try to do with visuals is clarifying complexity and conveying facts, you should think twice when creating a pie chart because it does not do any of these. The current discussion applies to any form you choose to work with when you decide to go freehand with D3; we are only using pie charts as a starting point because of their widespread nature.

When using a pie chart, the intent is to show the relationship that a part has with a whole. Look at these three then:

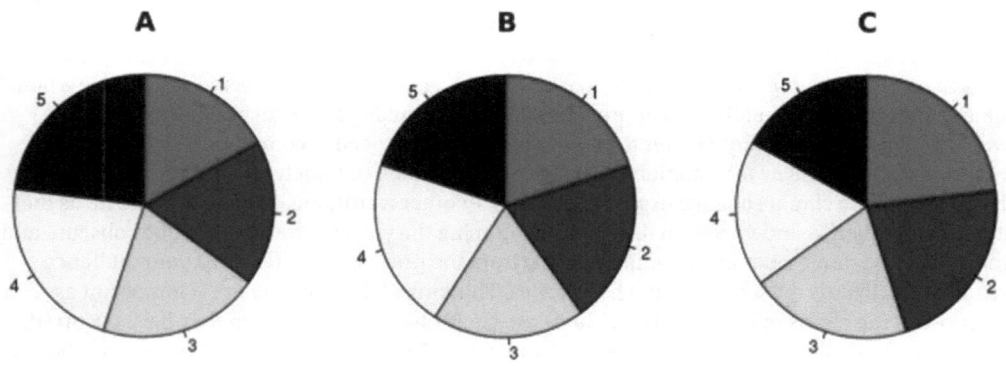

Figure 3-10. *Pie charts. Image from Wikimedia Commons, public domain.*[10]

Imagine that they represent the polling from a presidential election with five candidates at three different stations (A, B, C) during an election. What did you learn from this image? Who is doing better at which polling station? Who is winning? Not exactly making information more clearly understandable!

Indeed, as Tufte suggests, a table of the polling values would make it easier to understand the information that these pie charts are supposedly conveying. Presenting values as a table is, however, what we want to avoid as this gets cumbersome when you start dealing with bigger datasets. Thus, a bar chart works much better telling us what the pies above failed to tell.

---

[9]https://twitter.com/EdwardTufte/statuses/289208399621672960.
[10]Source: https://en.wikipedia.org/wiki/Pie_chart#/media/File:Piecharts.svg.

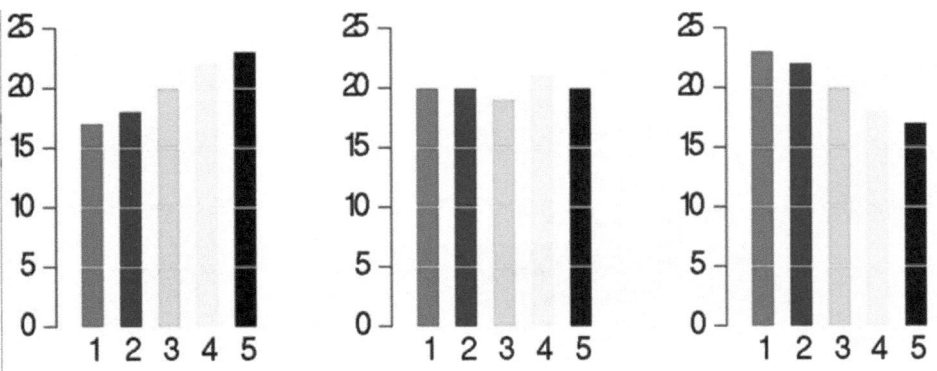

Figure 3-11. *Bar charts showing the same numbers as the pies in Figure 3-10. Image from Wikimedia Commons, public domain[11]*

Another caveat of a pie chart is that it does not allow to compare the slices and figure out distinctions in size between each and every pie slice. For example, the party breakdown of the current European Parliament only indicates that the PPE has more seats than the ECR. However, this same information can be transmitted by just providing the seat count. In this case, the chart is useless.

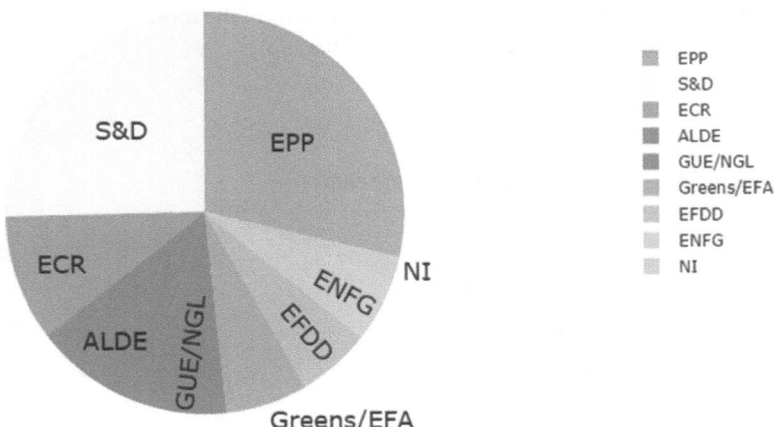

EPP
S&D
ECR
ALDE
GUE/NGL
Greens/EFA
EFDD
ENFG
NI

Figure 3-12. *European Parliament party breakdown. Data from the European Parliament website, current composition.*

Remember the scale from Chapter 2? Areas perform worse than bars or heights along a common scale regarding accurate comparison. Thus, it is not surprising that the same data encoded as a bar chart is clearer and enables precise comparisons, both pairwise and across all.

[11]Source: https://en.wikipedia.org/wiki/Pie_chart#/media/File:Piecharts.svg.

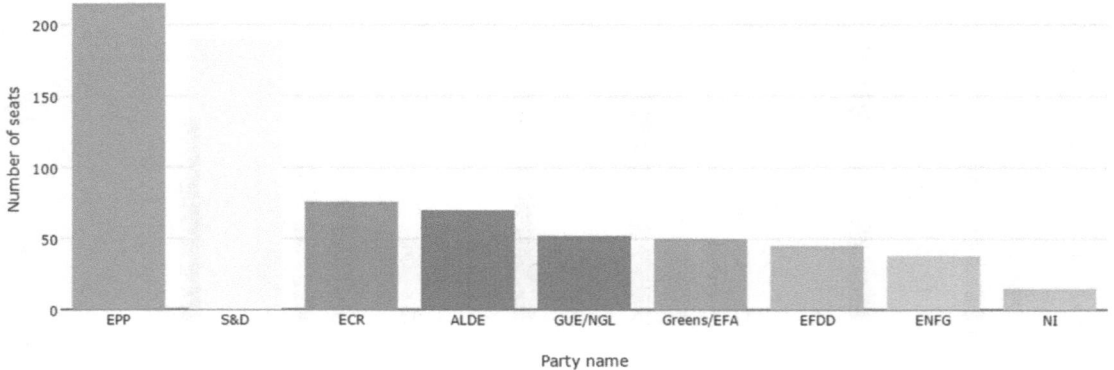

Figure 3-13. *European Parliament party breakdown. The numbers are the same as in Figure 3-12. Data from the European Parliament website, current composition.*

In brief:

- If your visualization wants to highlights similarity in the information available, think what form would be the most appropriate to use (hint: not a pie chart or area-based comparison).

- If there are multiple (three or more) different data points of data, think of the most appropriate analysis. Avoid charts and forms that are easy to abuse.

It Is D3, Not 3D

Figure 3-14 shows the same data as Figures 3-12 and 3-13 but in a 3D pie chart.

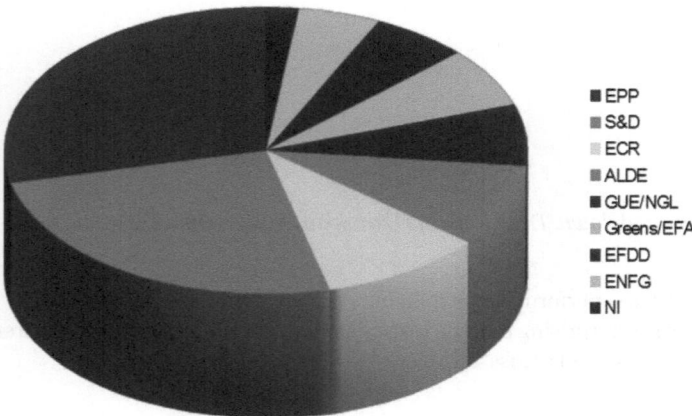

Figure 3-14. *European Parliament party breakdown, illustrated in a 3D pie chart. Data from the European Parliament website, current composition.*

Looking at this chart, the EPP appears to be roughly even with the S&D, the orange party. This is wrong (the EPP has 215 seats while the S&D has 190), but the misperception happens because the 3D element distorts your perspective by making the red part bigger.

If your data has a three-dimensional spatial component, then 3D visualizations can be an excellent tool. But for data that have no such characteristics, adding a third dimension to the visualization harms communication. Pie charts are the worst offenders (yes, again). A pie chart encodes data as angles of the slices. Regardless of pie charts' caveats mentioned earlier, a 2D pie chart represents such angles accurately. In a 3D pie chart, however, the angles are distorted to create the 3D effect. The problem is that our brains struggle to build a 3D mental representation of the graph that will then be rotated back to an oblique view. Worse: areas encode data the same way angles do in a pie chart. And areas are also distorted in a 3D pie chart. Thus, the only two features encoding data in a pie chart are twisted when applying a 3D transformation.

Things That Can Go Wrong

As we mentioned at the beginning: this chapter is a visualization FailCon. Pie and donut charts champion the competition of part-to-whole visuals that do not add up to 100 percent. In other words, if you decided to go with three data points showing percentages and use a donut chart (or a stacked bar graph), make sure that the total is 100. This consistency matters because of the nature of these forms: you show how parts relate to a whole, but this whole should be a logical one.

Poor labelling is another usual caveat. Scales and correctly named axes tend to disappear when the chart is included in a bigger composition. Sometimes, people even remove the axes. But those are key to understanding what your visual shows. We already said it in Chapter 2, but we are insisting on this again: labels are not decoration.

D3 enables you to create radial charts (e.g., radial treemap or bar chart). These look real cool but perform poorly in data readability. We read Cartesian charts (you know, rectangle-based forms such as a radar chart or a Coxcomb chart) much more quickly, perhaps because we live in Cartesian space.

A final note: colors. D3 provides representations for various color spaces (RGB and HSL are included) and allows specification, interpolation, conversion, and manipulation. Then, we all have our favorite colors. However, encoding data with colors needs care: rainbow color scales, for example, make for fresh and attention-grabbing choice. Their main disadvantage is that they can either hide data features or emphasize characteristics that do not exist. An excellent short outline on why rainbow colors are not welcome is discussed at the end of this chapter. You should keep in mind color-blindness in males when designing your visualizations, as any color scale with red and green components means nothing to this audience. A wonderful resource, mainly designed for maps but also applicable to other types of visualizations, is ColorBrewer. In addition to allowing you to choose color palettes with color-blindness in mind, it can also suggest the best colors to use if you will need to print on paper.

D3 in a Nutshell

D3's specifics are introduced starting in Chapter 5. We will thus not discuss them in detail here but will provide you with working definitions. Two features are significant here: SVG path generators and layouts. Each generator is a function of data; that is, it is The Shape to Draw Them All. To put it simply, imagine your pencil on a sheet of paper. If you do not move it, it only marks a point. If you need to draw a circle, you will need to mark many points and connect them. The connection lines can be anything: arcs or different Bézier curves. This is what the SVG path generator does.

Unlike SVG path generators, layouts facilitate the conversion of data to display form. To do so, layouts operate across a collection of data as a whole. Mike Bostock defines layouts as follows:[12]

> *A layout encapsulates a strategy for laying out data elements visually, relative to each other. It could be a simple as stacking bars in a chart (where the base of one bar depends on the height of any below it) or as complex as labeling a map (by shifting labels around until overlap with conflicting map features is minimized). Layouts take a set of input data, apply an algorithm or heuristic, and output the resulting positions/shapes for a cohesive display of the data.*

An important number of layouts are built in D3. This versatility and diversity can be confusing at first. So, here is your ultimate guide to D3 forms.

Maps

Think layout of the box: we may want to show refugees flows in particular countries. You can do that with bar charts in which each bar is the name of a country. It will allow the audience to compare, and so on. However, those do not depict flows. You can consider either producing highly customized map flows (with DataMaps,[13] a plugin for D3) or to use a Sankey flow (see Figures 3-15 and 3-16).

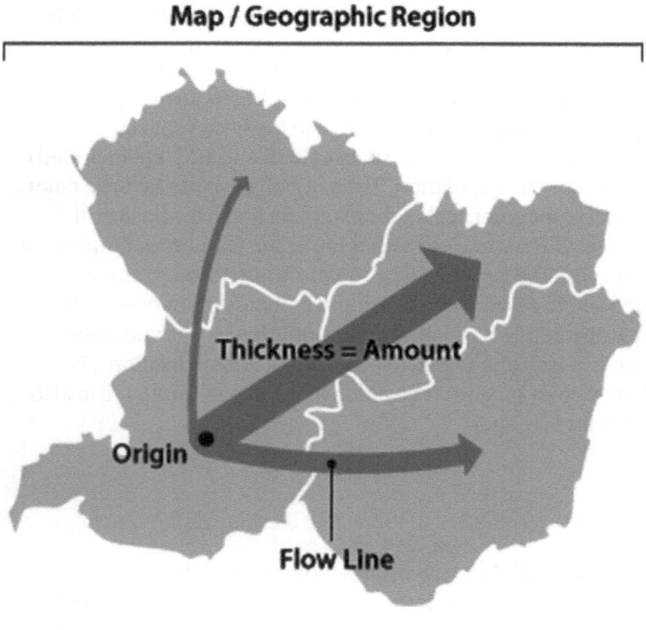

Figure 3-15. *With DataMaps*

---

[12]https://github.com/mbostock/d3/wiki/Layouts.
[13]http://datamaps.github.io/.

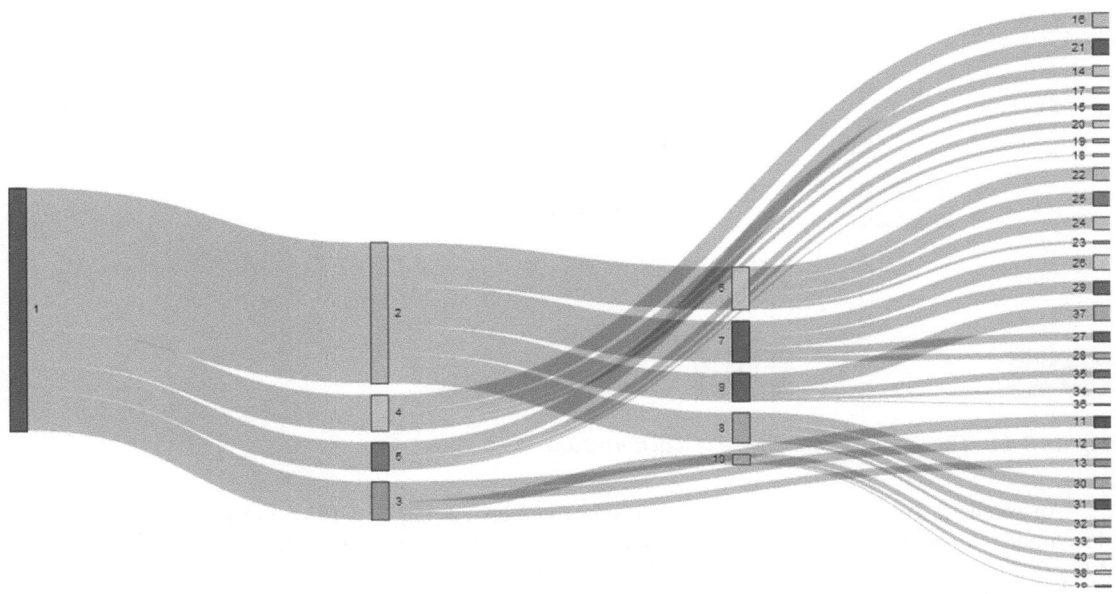

Figure 3-16. *With a Sankey diagram*

Another famous visual you can do using D3 and geo data is a choropleth map. My map in Figure 3-6 is an example. The countries are colored in relation to the data variable (number of refugees per GDP PPP). A choropleth map is an excellent way to visualize values over a geographical area. Thus, you can show variation or patterns across a country or a continent, for instance. You may already have figured out one significant caveat: the use of color does not allow you to compare values from the map; rather, it enables you to get an idea of tendency and a general pattern. Still, choropleth maps are useful when reflecting differences on a geographical dimension.

Hierarchies

A tree diagram or a dendrogram is what comes quickly to mind. Such a representation allows you to visualize hierarchy in a treelike structure. Just like a tree in real life, you will have a root node and "offspring" nodes that are linked together. Those connections or branches represent the relationships between the nodes. The end-nodes have no child nodes (Figure 3-17).

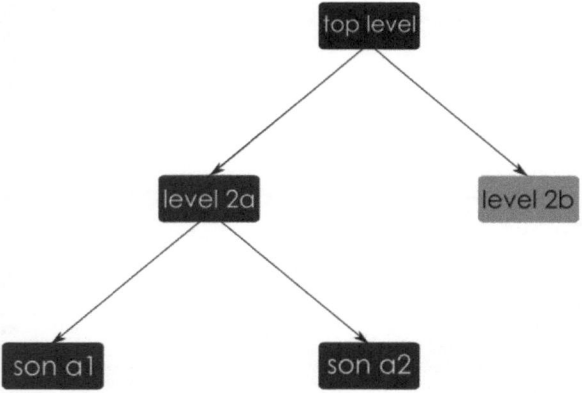

Figure 3-17. *The organization scheme of a dendrogram*

An excellent "spin-off" of the dendrogram is the treemap (see Figure 3-18). Ben Shneiderman developed it to visualize a vast file directory on a computer all by taking up limited space on the screen. A key feature of treemaps is to display both hierarchy and quantities. This characteristic makes treemaps an efficient tool for comparing the proportions between hierarchical categories. Treemaps are often used to visualize budgets.

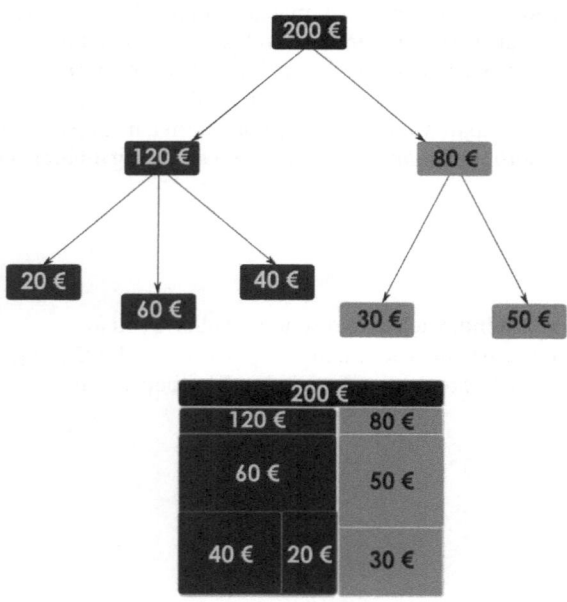

Figure 3-18. *A schematic overview of the treemap structure and its transformation into an actual treemap chart*

Circle packing is a variation of the treemap. It uses circles instead of rectangles; thus, the whole is less space-efficient than a treemap. However, circle packing is better at showing the hierarchical relations between entities. You can use colour to assign categories to represent another variable.

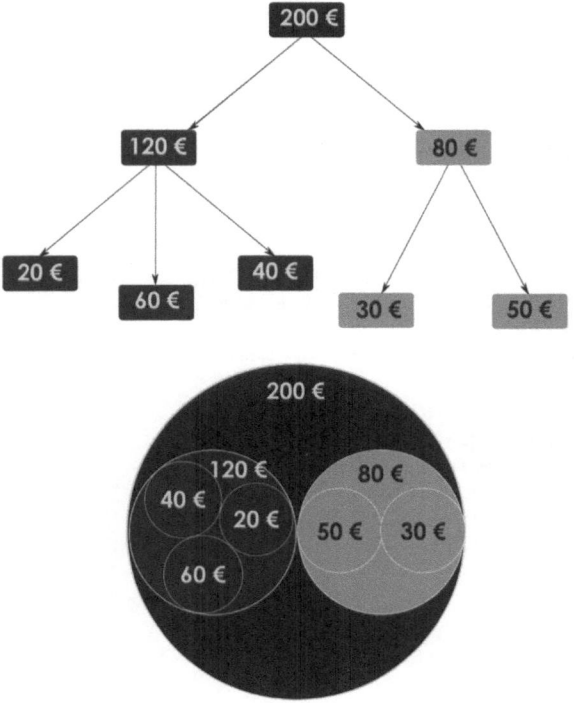

Figure 3-19. *A schematic overview of the circle-packing structure and its transformation into an actual circle-pack chart*

Related to dendrograms and treemaps are Marimekko charts.[14] Contrary to a treemap, those are used to visualize categorical data over a pair of variables. Thus, axes are both a variable with own scale, thus determining the width and height of each segment. Such a structure allows detecting relationships between categories and their subcategories via the two variables. I guess the explanation is already a bit of a headache to follow. This is the chart's greatest issue: it may come off as hard to read as well, let alone provide for accurate comparisons between segments (they are not plotted against a common baseline!). It is worth considering, though, in case the visuals do not correctly encode your data.

Spider and Chord Charts

Finally, we want to show the radar (or spider net) and the chord charts (Figures 3-20 and 3-21).

---

[14]http://bl.ocks.org/mbostock/1005090.

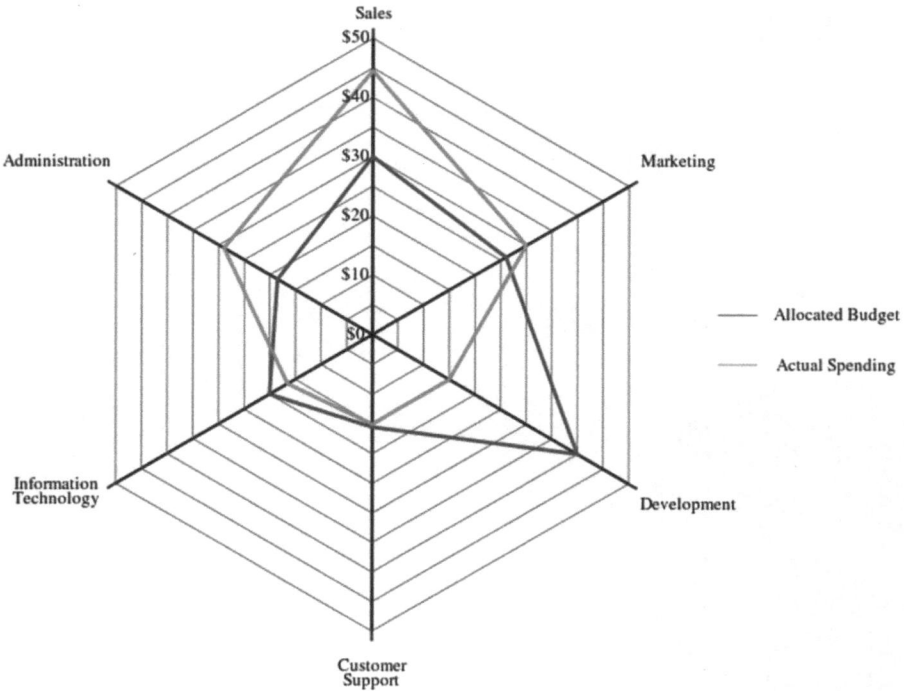

Figure 3-20. *An example of a radar chart in which two line series are compared*[15]

For many people in data visualization, the radar chart is a no-go. We like it, though, because it is a playful way to give your audience a glimpse of performance. Indeed, you can quickly show which axes score low or high for different questions. Of course, if you want people not to dub you names, you would avoid clutter your radar chart with multiple questions (i.e., what appears as a polygon on the graph). Similarly, having too many variables creates too many axes, which can make the chart hard to read. Thinking of the most optimal variables to show is a great exercise, though, especially provided that you are not aiming to enable accurate comparisons across variables but to give a more general overview.

Last but not least, there is the chord diagram (see Figure 3-21). This visualizes the interrelationships between entities. The connections between objects display that they share something in common. Remember the Doctor Who villains? Or gene-sharing among related species? Chord diagrams to the rescue (well, provided they are not overcluttered with too many connections). We chose to discuss chord diagrams because they are intimidating more often than they are intriguing. One reason for that is the temptation to use too many data at once instead of gradually introducing the different subdatasets. This creates an overcluttered diagram, so the cognitive demand for the audience is enormous. But, hey, we are talking about D3 here; that is, about interaction, movement and creativity. So there is no reason not to use chord diagram for telling stories.

---

[15]Image source: https://commons.wikimedia.org/wiki/File:Spider_Chart.svg.

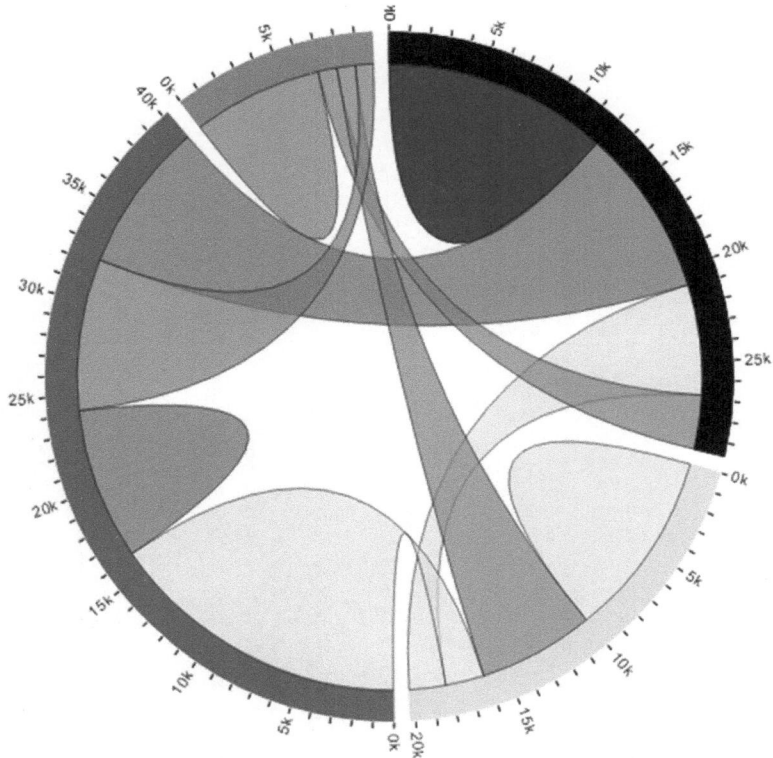

Figure 3-21. *An example of chord diagram*[16]

Summary

We explored the main steps of the data analysis process and provided you with a couple of useful tips and tricks to quickly decide what type of analysis you should apply. In addition, we explained the features and structures of several interesting charts that you can produce with D3. Feeling the ideas brewing? Great. Let's then get to collecting and understanding data.

And, in case you were wondering, here are the answers to the questions posed earlier:

> - Is shoe size a continuous or a discrete variable? Shoe size is a discrete variable as it can only take some values, for example, 39, 38½, and so on (or 4, 4½ for the United Kingdom and the United States). By contrast, the length of a foot is a continuous variable as it can take any value (measured in cm or inches).

> - Is the number of stars a continuous or a discrete variable? The number of stars is a discrete variable: we cannot have a fractional number of stars. This holds even if you cannot count them all.

---

[16]Image Source: `https://bl.ocks.org/mbostock/4062006`.

CHAPTER 4

Sourcing Data

The previous three chapters covered the basics of perception, how D3 talks to the web and how not to lie with your data visualizations. This chapter introduces you to the incredibly diverse world of data and aims to provide you with ways to navigate it.

Finding and Acquiring Data

Finding data is easy: we are drowning in it. Of course, obtaining *relevant* data is more complicated, but we will get there, too. First, we will explore the realm of readily available data online.

Open Data Portals

Open data is data released publicly online, in a machine-readable format and under permissive license allowing anyone to use, reuse, modify, and distribute it. We will talk about formats below, but for now, just think of the facility to use data as a .csv compared to a table in a .pdf file. A .csv file is much easier to work with because you do not need specific (often proprietary) software to process it. By contrast, a .pdf file is a nightmare: you cannot easily extract data from it, most often you need a particular software to read it, and so on. Right: .csv is machine-readable, not .pdf.

Regarding the permissive license bit: you may have heard about Creative Commons (CC) licenses. Those are legal frameworks complementing traditional copyright legislation. Contrary to copyright, CC licenses allow you to more freely and openly make use of content and data. Copyrighted materials require you to obtain prior permission for using them; you may also need to pay a fee to use those materials. By contrast, if a CC-by license exists for given content, it will mean that you can do whatever you like with the material provided you credit the original author. No payment, no waiting for approval. Copyright exploits rarity. But in an era of (digital) abundance, a permissive legal framework makes more sense.

In the past 10 years, the idea of opening up public sector data has gained a lot of traction. It is in fact a mainstream public policy in many countries worldwide. Data-specific open licenses have also been composed, to more adequately cover specificities. The most usual realization of such public policy is a portal where the released datasets are stored for anyone to access. French startup Open Data Soft counted more than 1,600 portals around the world (Figure 4-1).[1]

---

[1] http://opendatainception.io/.

© Tarek Amr and Rayna Stamboliyska 2016

T. Amr and R. Stamboliyska, *Practical D3.js*, DOI 10.1007/978-1-4842-1928-7_4

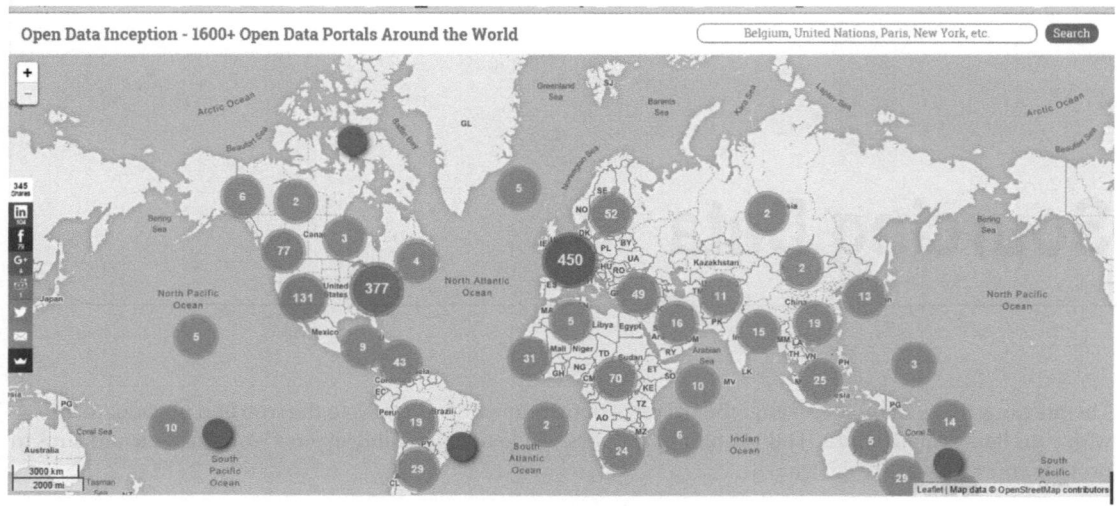

Figure 4-1. *A screenshot from OpenDataSoft's collection of open data portals worldwide*

So, go ahead and dig!

Reports by Institutions and Private Business Actors

The World Health Organization (WHO) will have data on health. The World Bank will provide insights on economic development. The UNHCR will publish data on refugees, asylum seekers, and other persons of concern worldwide. Remember the choropleth map on how much it costs a country to host refugees (see Figure 3-6 in Chapter 3)? This was all from UNHCR data (refugees per country) normalized to World Bank data (GDP PPP per country).

Big consultancy companies such as McKinsey, Capgemini, and Accenture will release reports on specific topics where a lot of data can be found. Scientists produce tons of data and it gets more and more publicly released at dedicated repositories. An example is these two visualizations on mobile patent lawsuits. Figures 4-2 and 4-3 show visualizations of patent-related suits in the mobile communications industry: different visual metaphors, same data.

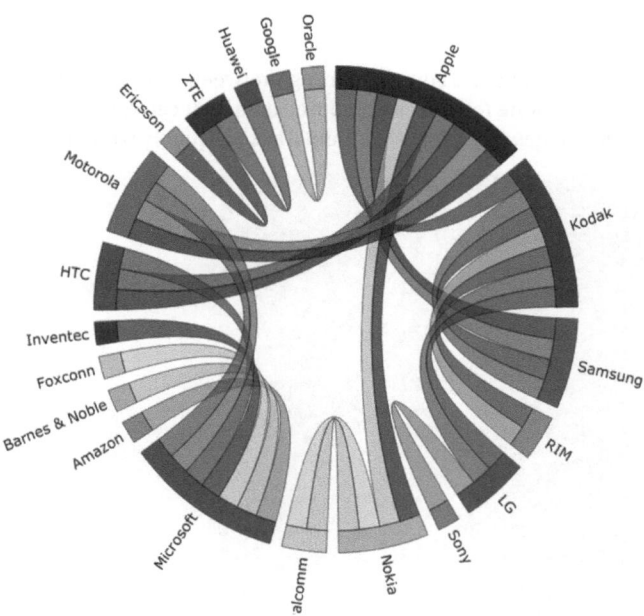

Figure 4-2. *Patent-related suits in the mobile communications industry; chords are colored by plaintiff* [2]

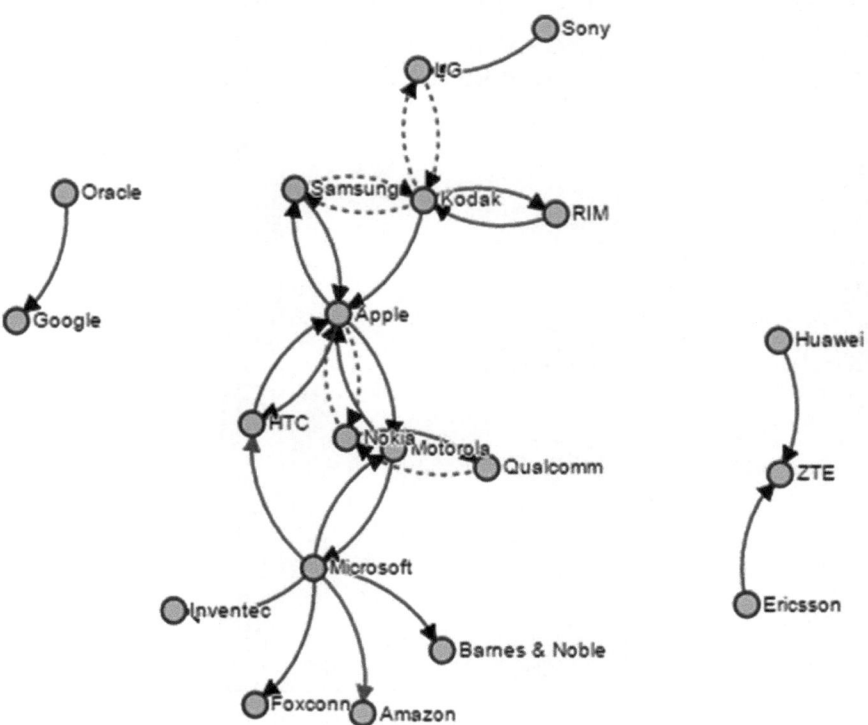

Figure 4-3. *Patent-related suits in the mobile communications industry: a different view* [3]

[2]Source: https://www.jasondavies.com/mobile-lawsuits/.
[3]Source: http://bl.ocks.org/mbostock/1153292.

User-Generated Data

We release data: our tweets are counted, their reach or impact is counted through retweets or citations or clicks on the links they contain. Platforms enable anyone to help crowdsource data. You can thus map election violations,[4] use tweets for crisis relief, rate movies (Figure 4-4), or help track air quality with lichens.[5]

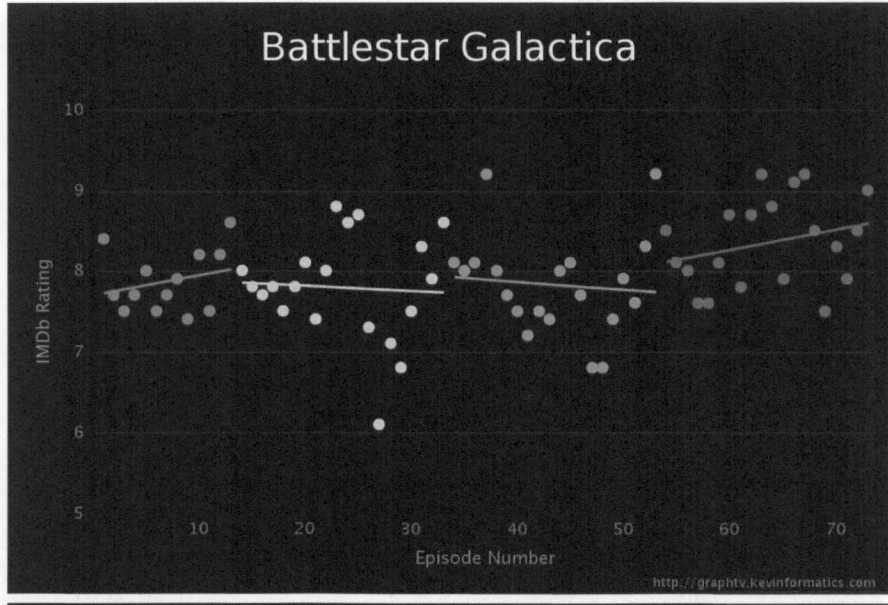

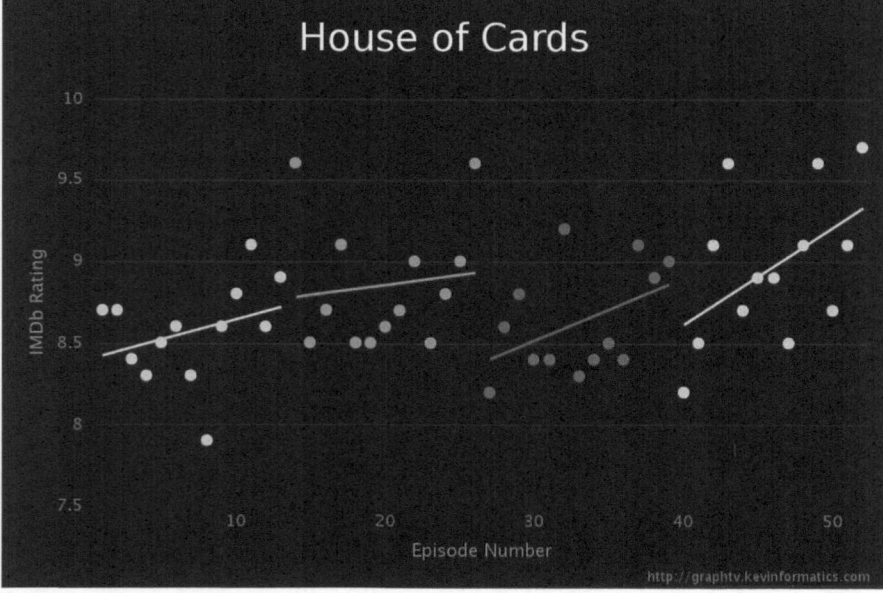

Figure 4-4. *An example of user-generated data as a substract for data visualization and insights: (top) how Battlestar Galactica performed; (bottom) how House of Cards performed*

[4]See, for example, https://www.ushahidi.com/blog/2015/05/21/beyond-voting-using-ushahidi-to-help-citizens-protect-their-elections and http://www.localinterventions.org.uk/programmes.php?post=22.
[5]http://crowdcrafting.org/project/airquality/.

Neat, right? Of course, one could swiftly object quality of user-generated data. We have indeed observed fake reports and images spread online. Verifying user-generated content can turn out to be tricky, but a number of high-quality resources exist to help you in this endeavor. Those are listed at the end of the chapter.

(Big) Data Professionals

You may as well work in a place that generates big data. A friend of mine, for example, is in charge of Booking.com's big data management. Realizing 1 million room rents a day is not a simple task. But you could think of providing your clients with data visualization dashboards where they could follow how their property performs, how to enhance its visibility, and so on. The opportunities are as big as the data.

Of course, it is legit to ask how D3 performs in fast-paced analysis situation or with huge amounts of data. It works in the browser, which is a limitation. As everything technical, you can find your way, and doing so depends on the available expertise. D3 allows you to iterate on different visualization forms once you have processed the data. In addition, many people have been writing in-house charting libraries based on D3. Thus, upon arriving in your company, preexisting D3 competency and tools may already be available. The clear advantage of such internally designed tools is that those solve specific problems fast. Finally, what you are trying to do will decide on the tool to use. It is unnecessary to brute force a tool to do what it is not natively aimed to do especially when other, decent tools exist.

Data Scraping

Enter the least obvious data acquisition procedure (to date, at least). Remember our short discussion about machine-readable formats? A .csv file is machine-readble, whereas a .pdf is human-readable.

So how do you deal with data contained in a .pdf file that you absolutely want to use? Copy-pasting each entry is an option, but do you really want to do that? The good news is that scraping can help overcome this problem.

If you are faced with a .pdf file, a process called optical-character recognition (OCR) can help. You can find such tools online, they are often used for free. For English and a proper document (even when scanned from paper), modern OCR can often be almost 100 percent accurate. For other languages (e.g., Arabic), OCR is just hopeless. However, even if OCR extracts the data well, you still need to validate that the results match the original.

Data scraping often ignores binary data (e.g., multimedia), and disregards display formatting, superfluous commentary, and, more generally, information that hinders automated processing. Sometimes the system you are keen to get data from has a convenient API (an interface that allows you to talk to the system and get data from it). A great example for a nice API is the Twitter API which provides you with all sorts of features: timestamp, included image links, geotags, and so on.

In other cases, a web page will have data of interest but no download available for a machine-readable equivalent. As discussed in Chapter 2, web pages are built using text-based markup languages (e.g., HTML), and as their design favors human end-users over machine end-users, the data a web page can contain is not appropriate for automated use. Many browser plugins and startup developed tools exist, both for free and commercial use, that allow you to scrape a web page. Thus, compared to the convenient API situation described above, you can think of the web scraper as an API to extract data from a website. Software products also exist that listen to data feeds from web servers. A format we will discover below, JSON, is a common "vehicle" to store and transport data between client and web servers.

Data scraping is an *ad hoc*, yet useful technique, a sort of "last resort" when no other mechanism for data interchange is available. More often than not, you need good programming skills (in Python, for example) to write scrapers. A useful resource to check out in any event is ScraperWiki. It is also important to keep in mind that scraping outputs data displays that are fit for human consumption. This modification alters data structure. We, humans, are fine by that, but your computer may as well produce nonsense. Indeed, your program expects a given format to work on; if you provide it with ill-structured or formatted data, your computer is unlikely to magically output meaningful and valid results. We have addressed the most interesting approaches to acquiring data. As you see it, this data is (perhaps never) just waiting for you to take it and plug it into an analysis-visualization process. In the following sections, we will briefly introduce D3 selections and then will explore ways that you can cocoon your data.

Understanding D3 Selections

Selections are a D3 core functionality. A selection refers to an array of elements pulled from the current document.[6] Let's have a closer look at selections.

Imagine that we have the following document and we want to produce a small bar chart:

```
<html>
  <body>
    <script src="http://d3js.org/d3.v3.min.js" charset="utf-8"></script>
    <script>
      // Our code goes here
    </script>
  </body>
</html>
```

The data is contained in the following array:

```
var nums = [10, 30, 50, 20, 80, 90];
```

A bar chart is in fact a collection of rectangles of different heights fitted against x- and y-axes. In D3, a rectangle is a SVG <rect> element. Thus, to render a bar (in the bar chart context), we need to first add an <svg> container element to the DOM (the "//" notation indicates a comment; those are not evaluated in the code):

```
d3.select('body').append('svg');
// d3 is the global object in D3: it enables selecting the elements in the DOM. In our case,
we use the d3 global object to select the <body> element.
```

And we just neatly defined D3 selections.

You have noticed the .append('svg') method. It is a method applied on a selection that creates an <svg> element. Besides, D3 returns a new selection after calling the method .append(). We use this new selection to "wrap" the newly created element:

```
var svg = d3.select('body').append('svg');
```

We just created a local variable whose name is svg. This formulation is equivalent to the declaration: d3.select('svg'). Since the SVG element will contain all other elements, we can set its width and height, and so on (you will see those details in the following chapters). The local variable svg will help us draw the bars of the bar chart. We need <rect> elements. Our local variable nums contains six values, so we may want to append them the same way we appended the svg element. That approach would mean that we should write the following six times:

```
svg.append('rect');
```

---

[6]https://github.com/mbostock/d3/wiki/Selections

Repeating such a declaration six times is tedious, cumbersome, would transform the code into a pile of repetitions, and would probably harbor errors: we can count six repetitions, but what about 106? Selections allow us to handle this correctly and seamlessly:

```
var bars = d3.selectAll('rect');
```

Voilà. Our local variable bars contains the a selection of rectangles. And here is another instance of D3 magic. You may think: "But wait, if I don't append the rectangles, using the selectAll will just produce nothing!". Well, no. Selections are arrays of elements and are higher-level than your current DOM elements themselves. Thus, selections enable you to both operate on preexisting elements and to use a 'representation' of the elements you need.

Understanding selections is a critical entry point to working with D3. Indeed, thanks to selections, you can "ask" D3 to bind different methods to the array which will in turn enable you to apply operators to the selected elements. A last remark on selections: these are grouped. In other words, a selection is not a one-dimensional array; rather, it constitutes *an array* of arrays of elements.

This grouping approach allows for the hierarchical structure of subselections to be maintained. Subselections are also very useful: they are a subset of the original selection and enable D3 to compare arrays. Three subselections exist in D3: *enter, update* and *exit*. To understand them, consider the data join first:

```
// A reminder of our values:
var nums = [10, 30, 50, 20, 80, 90];
var bars = svg.selectAll('rect')
            .data(nums);
// We join our values to what will be the bar chart
```

Thus, we produce a selection bound to data: an array of six elements (rectangles) each of which binds to a specific value. Subselections get into play here: *enter* concerns elements in the data that joined to our selection but absent from the current DOM. With *update* we refer to elements present in both the joined-in data and the current DOM. And, logically, *exit* concerns elements in the current DOM, but absent from the data that joined to the selection.

The best way to learn how selections work is to try selecting elements interactively using your browser's developer console. All of the fine details on selections are provided by Mike Bostock.[7] The following chapters will introduce you in greater detail to other data manipulation tools such as scales and layouts.

Reviewing Data Formats

Before getting to the specific formats D3 can process, let's see what data structures D3 works with. For those of you having some experience with programming, you may already know what a JavaScript array is. In a nutshell, an array is an enumerated list of variables. In other words, each element has an index number attached to it. The first element is numbered 0, not 1. For example:

```
var spaceCircles = [10, 20, 30];
spaceCircles[0]
// returns the number 10
spaceCircles[1]
// returns the number 20
spaceCircles[2]
// returns the number 30
```

---

[7]https://bost.ocks.org/mike/selection/.

As you may guess it, a JavaScript array can hold any type of information you want: numbers, objects, strings, other arrays, HTML elements, DOM elements, you name it. D3's canonical representation of data is an array.

There are two ways of feeding D3 with data. You can either provide it manually, hard-coded in the visualization code. Alternatively, you can have an external file that contains the data, and "feed" it to D3. The former option quickly gets tedious and is a really bad idea when you have dynamic data. Imagine loading 100 lines by hand? And doing that every time some of your data line changes? Thanks but no thanks. This is when you take advantage of D3's built-in functionality to load different external resources:

> –plain text. That can, for instance, be encoded in a particular way (see the D3 API) or constitute a more structured data body: be a comma-separated (.csv), a tab-separated (.tsv), or an unusual delimiter-separated (.dsv) file;

> –JSON. This abbreviation stands for JavaScript Object Notation. JSON is a great format because it makes it easy for both humans and machines to read the data. We will have a look at it later;

> –HTML document;

> –XML document. XML (eXtensible Markup Language) is from the HTML language family and is widely used for encoding documents in a human-readable form.

These are fed into D3 thanks to D3's Requests functions. They instruct the browser to go grab some data from somewhere, either locally (on the web server) or elsewhere online. Each of these Request functions return data in a structure that D3 can use, that is, an array. Different types of requests exist depending on the type of data you want to load. Consequently, each type of data is formatted following specific rules. The relevant request interprets those particular rules and ensures that the data is structured in a way that D3 can use. Be sure to read about requests in the D3 documentation.[8]

If this is the first time for you to see those technicalities, do not be scared. What you need to know is that data transfers between programs happen via data structures suited for automated processing by computers, not people. Such interchange formats and protocols are typically rigidly structured, easily parsed, thus keeping ambiguity to a minimum. Most often, data formats are not for humans to understand, but we need to know how they are structured to avoid erroneous analysis and visualization. The great news is that these formats are standards, thus they are well-documented and transparent for us. This is the reason we can have this little discussion on how to feed D3 with data.

CSV, TSV, and Other Data Files

As you know it by now, D3 provides built-in support for working with comma-separated, tab-separated values, and arbitrary delimiter-separated values. These tabular formats are popular with spreadsheet programs (e.g., LibreOffice Calc, Google Spreadsheets, Microsoft Excel). In addition, many open data portals provide their data as .csv files. Finally, tabular formats are often more space-efficient than JSON, which is useful when you need to load large datasets.

---

[8]https://github.com/mbostock/d3/wiki/Requests.

D3 provides you with d3.csv and d3.tsv to work with those.[9] The good news is that you also have d3.dsv to handle unusual delimiter-separated files. Imagine a file in which the separator is neither a comma, nor a tab, but a pipe ("|"). For example, you get a list of your kid's classmates attending a museum visit for which you will be in charge:

```
name|gender|parents phone
Annie|girl|00000000000
Bob|boy|11111111111
Steve|boy|22222222222
Lucy|girl|33333333333
```

Enter d3.dsv:

```
var psv = d3.dsv("|", "text/plain");
// PSV stands for pipe-separated values. Why not :-)
```

With this, you can proceed using this strangely formatted file normally in D3.

JSON

As mentioned earlier, JSON stands for JavaScript Object Notation. The format is a collection of name-values pairs. It comes out as this nested thingy:

```
pupils_museum.json:
[
 {"name":"Annie Bell",
  "gender":"girl",
  "age": 10,
  "attending": true
 },
 {"name":"Teddy Charles",
  "gender":"boy",
  "age": 10,
  "attending": false
 }
]
```

Feeding pupils_museum.json with d3.json is straightforward:

```
d3.json("/rawdata/pupils_museum.json", function(data) {
  console.log(data[0]);
});
=> {name:"Annie Bell", gender:"girl", age: 10, attending: true}
```

If you have a .csv and want to create a JSON out of it, you can use the d3.csv function. Have a look at Jerome Cukier's step-by-step guide and you will master format manipulation in D3 like a boss.[10]

---

[9]https://github.com/mbostock/d3/wiki/CSV.
[10]http://www.jeromecukier.net/blog/2012/05/28/manipulating-data-like-a-boss-with-d3/.

You certainly remember that I spoke about maps a bit and gave you examples of map-based visualizations that D3 lets you create. D3 is not able to directly read the usual GIS formats such as shapefiles .shp. The shapefile is a digital vector storage format that contains geometric location and associated attribute information. Shapefile formats do not, however, store topological information. D3 uses JSON (yes, again) to read geoformats: enter GeoJSON and TopoJSON. The latter is an extension of GeoJSON and encodes topology. Thanks to its data structuring rules, TopoJSON is more compact than GeoJSON which is a clear advantage. The documentation on those formats is well done and accessible online.[11]

Loading multiple files is the last technical mention for this chapter. With queue,[12] you can circumvent D3's basic one-by-one file loading and get as many files at once as needed. An excellent step-by-step guide about combining or merging files in D3 is available as well.[13]

It is now time to start looking at the data you have and prepare it for the subsequent analysis and visualization. We will see what can go wrong with data and how to fix those errors (if possible).

Cocooning the Data

As you may have guessed it so far, the data you acquire can be of heterogeneous quality and ill-formatted. When you get to know your data, you will face either of these issues or both of them. The good news is that most of those problems have solutions.

Problems with Data that You Can Solve

In my brief overview of data sources, data collected by other humans feature prominently. A frequent issue in this case is inconsistent spelling or names are not always formed the same way (e.g., surnames are misplaced). Confusing date formats are a usual problem as well. This happens when a European and an American write dates. But if you have no idea about the history of the data, how do you tell who entered this data? Alternatively, you may manually compose your dataset from individual datasets with diverging formatting. In this case, you should pay attention to the same details for everything to be consistent in your work data.

Character encoding is another issue. You know, it is when you see things like this: ◆◆◆. This happens because, for computers, all letters are represented as numbers. When you do not know what the number combination for a given character is, you get this ◆.

---

[11]https://github.com/mbostock/topojson/wiki.
[12]https://github.com/mbostock/queue.
[13]http://learnjsdata.com/combine_data.html.

Figure 4-5. *An unfortunate character encoding case*

If you are using a text editor or a spreadsheet application, they will take care of the correct encoding. If it does not, chances are that you still figure out what the actual word or name is because (with time) you will learn to read fluently things encoded in ISO-8859-1. A handy idea, if you are a Linux user, is to use command line tools such like *iconv* or *recode*. Here is a lovely and short Python script you can use if you are not feeling comfortable with the command line.[14] Do not forget to specify unicode in your own rendering either:

```
<meta charset="UTF-8">
```

Too often you will get data as .pdf or a table on a web page rather than easily usable format. I already discussed scraping and OCR above, so you should give those a try before completely losing hope.

An interesting situation arises when you get data that is too granular for what you need. For example, you are interested to work at the country-level but only find city-level data online. Contrary to the case in which data is provided to you aggregated (see later), there is a straightforward solution here: use the Pivot Table feature at Calc, Excel, or Google Docs. This works for most datasets (unless those are too large, so you will need some programming outside of the spreadsheet software to help the process). A final reminder: you need to always ensure that your data to aggregate does not contain empty or arbitrary values; I discuss this in the following section.

Before we continue with the things that can be blamed on someone else to solve, please remember to get back to Chapter 3 for all things sampling and strange margins of error.

Problems with Data that the Data Provider Can Solve

These issues are light-weight. More troubling situations exist, unfortunately: measure units or values can be missing, or worse even—missing values are replaced by zeroes. When units are missing, you need to carefully check the source and identify those; speaking of costs and price indices without knowing whether it is USD, GBP, EUR, or Russian roubles is impossible. If values are missing and you ignore why, then you need

---

[14]https://github.com/lovasoa/toutf8/tree/master.

to decide how to handle this. Whenever a blank or "null" or "N/A" is present where you expect a numeric value, you should ensure that you know what this indicates. Otherwise, you cannot say much about this variable since silence (or lack of value) is equivocal. The same critical gaze applies when you see zeroes: are those actual values or should they mean "null"? You can gauge this by checking how your data is distributed (see Chapter 3), with and without the zeroes.

Another problem you will face is with the granularity of data. You are interested at the city-level unemployment rates in a given province, for the past 10 years. However, the only data you get is high-level aggregates per year. There is not much you can do in this case, unfortunately. You can ask the authorities or the company or whomever your data source is, about more fine-grained data. They maybe have it, maybe not. They maybe are allowed to disseminate it, but maybe not. In France, ethnicity-based statistics for instance are prohibited by law. Thus, you will not obtain data on how many Algerians live in each district of Paris. Similarly, privacy legislation also requires that too granular data is not distributed to unauthorized entities and individuals. Thus, for example, you will never obtain housing data in France containing more than 11 features. This is the most detailed level you can get; if you continue adding features, it will be possible to identify people based on housing data.

Laws vary, of course, but aggregated data is not a problem you can solve. You are certainly aware, but a kind reminder never hurts: once the data has been put together, you cannot just disaggregate it together. Thus, you can never (as in never ever) divide the yearly data you have by 12 and call that the "average per month." That is always wrong (and from Chapter 3, you already can infer why).

More Bad Data (Science)

These examples are easy to detect and—sometimes—to handle and fix. For many things, you can have your own scripts or method, or use tools such as Open Refine.[15]

Many other things can go wrong with data, unfortunately.

Unless you know the machine that produced your data, be always careful with unusually precise values. Similarly, handle outliers with attention (we mentioned those at different occasions in the previous chapters). In addition, if you are computing means, then such values will be trouble. Depending on what pattern you are searching to discern, extreme values can be either a major red flag (something went wrong in the data production process) or a discovery. No matter your hopes, you need to be critical about what those values mean. Finally, a note about statistics. There is something I mentioned in Chapter 3 that's called a p-value. In a nutshell, a p-value (p for probability) tells you what are the odds that the pattern you are observing occurs by chance. A p-value is computed in a *post hoc* basis, after the data analysis is complete. In biology, a p-value equal or inferior of 0.05 is considered to indicate statistically significant results. Simply put, the chances of obtaining those results by chance are below 5 percent. You can get more stringent and go with a p-value below 0.01. Displaying such a significant p-value strongly supports claims for high-quality research and results. An outstanding article (with amazing interactive visualizations) at FiveThirtyEight.com[16] discussed hacking and misunderstanding the p-value in an accessible and critical way. Regardless of whether you are a journalist or a data scientist or a wanna-be such, this is recommended reading. Everyone needs to be able to make educated decisions on data-driven analysis and visualizations, especially if those involve statistics and claims of grandeur.

Summary

Now that you have learned all the good, hard, and tricky things you need to know, it is time to dive into D3!

---

[15]http://openrefine.org/.
[16]http://fivethirtyeight.com/features/science-isnt-broken/.

PART II

Using D3.js for Practical Data Visualization

CHAPTER 5

■ ■ ■

Getting Started with D3

This chapter introduces you to D3 and some of its underlying technologies and standards, such as JavaScript and SVG. You will start by creating basic shapes using SVG, then see how D3 can help you make this process easier and more flexible.

A Note on SVG

SVG (Scalable Vector Graphics) is a vector image format developed by the World Wide Web Consortium (W3C) in 1999. The SVG standard allows you to include shapes like circles, squares, and arbitrary polygons in your web pages.

Unlike raster images, where everything is explained in terms of pixels, vector graphics are expressed in terms of mathematical expressions. For example, when you want to draw a circle, you provide its radius and the coordinates of its centre, and maybe its background and border colors as well, and the computer will draw it for you. Vector graphics scale well, because no matter whether you are drawing your circle in a 10x10 pixels area or in a 1000x1000 pixels one, you can simply change the parameters of your circle on the fly and it will still be drawn perfectly with with smooth lines and no loss of resolution.

One additional benefit to this approach is that if you have a figure containing two squares and a circle, you have access to the three individual shapes in there separately. You, thus, can write JavaScript code to move, or scale any of the three shapes while keeping the other two as they are if you want. You can also listen to events fired for each shape separately. Think of all those things you can do with your DOM elements. Now, you can do the same to your shapes. You can even assign classes to them and style them using your CSS files.

Time to Plot Something

Your first drawing will be composed of a yellow circle and a red square on a white background. The shapes and their containing drawing area live inside an HTML file. Thus, the drawing area is defined as an <svg> tag.

In this example you will set the width and height of the drawing area to 200 pixels. By default, the background is white; however, just like any HTML element, you can change its background as you will see in the next example. The circle will be in the top left corner of the page, with its center located 50 pixels to the right and 50 pixels down, and with a radius of 40 pixels. The square will have its upper-left edge 100 pixels to the right and 100 pixels down. Actually, there are no square shapes here; you are just using a rectangle and setting both its width and height to 50 pixels. The two shapes will be surrounded by a 2-pixel-wide black border (see Figure 5-1).

© Tarek Amr and Rayna Stamboliyska 2016
T. Amr and R. Stamboliyska, *Practical D3.js*, DOI 10.1007/978-1-4842-1928-7_5

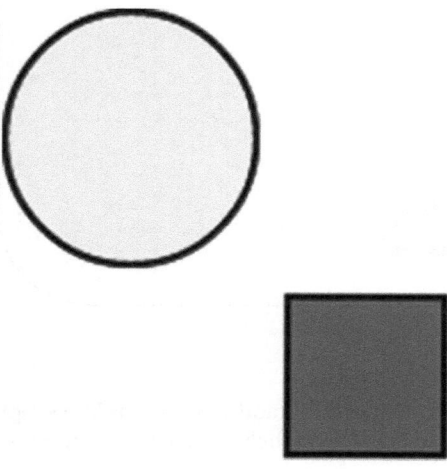

Figure 5-1. *Circle and square created using SVG*

To see the shapes in Figure 5-1, write the following in a new HTML file and open it into your browser and you will see the shapes shown in Figure 5-1.

```html
<html>
  <head>
    <title>My First SVG</title>
  </head>
  <body>
    <svg width="200" height="200">
        <circle cx="50" cy="50" r="40" stroke="black" stroke-width="2" fill="yellow" />
        <rect x="100" y="100" width="50" height="50" stroke="black" stroke-width="2" fill="red" />
    </svg>
  </body>
<html>
```

The tags for the shapes should be self-explanatory, especially because SVG is an XML-based format, hence its resemblance with HTML. The <circle> and <rect> tags identify the objects. The circle center coordinates are set using the cx and cy attributes for its position, and the r attribute is for its radius. The square has x and y attributes for specifying where to draw its top left corner, then comes its width and height. Note that the coordinates are handled here a bit differently than from what you may remember from your geometry class. The point of origin is in the top-left corner, so when you use x=30 you are telling the browser 30 from the left and using y=40 means 40 down from the upper border of our area and not upward from its bottom edge.

Your First Bar Chart

Can you create a bar chart representing the GDP (Gross Domestic Product) of the United States, China, Japan, and Germany using SVG? If you think about it, a bar chart is just a bunch of narrow rectangles, whose sizes are proportional to the data they represent (see Figure 5-2).

Figure 5-2. *Our first bar chart using SVG*

Suppose the GDPs for the United States, China, Japan, and Germany are 17, 9, 5 and 3 trillion USD, respectively. Furthermore, the size of your drawing area is 200x200 pixels. What you need to determine next are the placement, width, and height of the bars.

As for the width and height of the bars, it's easiest to represent the amount by a factor of 10; hence, the U.S. GDP of 17 trillion would be represented by a bar that is 170 pixels wide, China's 9 trillion would be 90 pixels wide, and so forth. As for the height, you can start with 20 pixels and see how they look.

Determining the placement of the bars—that is, their x and y values—is a bit trickier (although by no means rocket science). For example, for a cleaner presentation, you want to leave a margin, say 10 pixels, between the rectangles and the left side of the drawing area. Thus, set x=10 for the four rectangles. Additionally, you want the bars to be stacked on top of each other with some spacing in between, so they fill the whole drawing area. Here's the math: since the height of your drawing area is 200 pixels, and you have four bars with five spacings—one on top, one on the bottom and three between them—you can divide 200 by 5, to have the y values as multiples of 40. Thus, you set the y value to be 40, 80, 120 and 160.

Voilà! Replace the <svg> tag in the previous HTML file with the following one to get your first bar chart. To mix things up a little, give the drawing area a grey background, #EEE.

```
<svg width="200" height="200" style="background: #EEE">
        <rect x="10" y="40" width="170" height="20" stroke="black" stroke-width="2" fill="blue" />
        <rect x="10" y="80" width="90" height="20" stroke="black" stroke-width="2" fill="blue" />
        <rect x="10" y="120" width="50" height="20" stroke="black" stroke-width="2" fill="blue" />
        <rect x="10" y="160" width="30" height="20" stroke="black" stroke-width="2" fill="blue" />
</svg>
```

Finally, no self-respecting designer will create a chart without labels. Fortunately, SVG has you covered on this front as well, as it supports a text element. You can set your labels to 5 pixels above each rectangle, and have them all start 10 pixels to the right, just like the rectangles. As for the font size, try 12px.

```
<svg width="200" height="200" style="background: #EEE">
      <rect x="10" y="40" width="170" height="20" stroke="black" stroke-width="2" fill="blue" />
      <rect x="10" y="80" width="90" height="20" stroke="black" stroke-width="2" fill="blue" />
      <rect x="10" y="120" width="50" height="20" stroke="black" stroke-width="2" fill="blue" />
      <rect x="10" y="160" width="30" height="20" stroke="black" stroke-width="2" fill="blue" />
      <text x="10" y="35" fill="black" font-size="12">USA (17 Trillion USD)</text>
      <text x="10" y="75" fill="black" font-size="12">Chine (9 Trillion USD)</text>
      <text x="10" y="115" fill="black" font-size="12">Japan (5 Trillion USD)</text>
      <text x="10" y="155" fill="black" font-size="12">Germany (3 Trillion USD)</text>
</svg>
```

Check Figure 5-3 to see how the labels might look like here.

When to Use D3

Using SVG tags is easy when you are dealing with simple charts. However, suppose someone asked you to represent the GDPs of the top 20, 50, or 200 economies instead of just four. If you used the previous method, you would have to write 200 lines for 200 rect tags, each with the same x position, height and colors. And then you'd have to do the same for the 200 text labels. And then, just when you're finished, your client asks you to change the color of the bars from blue to red. That means you have edit the 200 lines of code you just wrote. And what if your client wants a thinner or thicker border? Or what if the client now wants to show only a fraction of the GDPs within the same drawing area? And what if the GDP of those economies differs only minimally, which means the scale you introduced before, based on the top four economies, no longer yields a noticeable difference (see Figure 5-3)? Would you start resizing your canvas and the dimensions of the bars? Clearly, coding charts by hand using SVG has its limitations: it makes it extremely difficult to modify charts dynamically because you cannot easily separate the data from the logical decisions you've made up front.

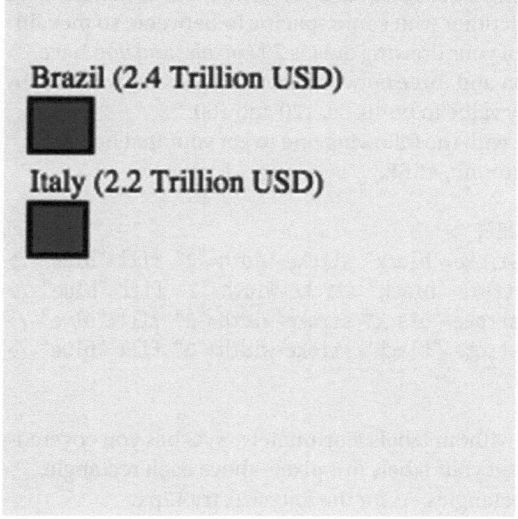

Figure 5-3. *Comparing Brazil's and Italy's GDP*

In conclusion, the D3 JavaScript library is designed to help decouple the data and the logic needed to represent the data, hence its name Data-Driven Documents (D3). D3 also offers you many additional capabilities. Throughout the remaining chapters of this book you will learn about the library's other capabilities, such as scales, layouts, animations, data handling, and so on.

Basic Shapes with D3

Perhaps the best way to understand how D3.js works is to redraw the yellow circle and red square from earlier in the chapter, with the help of d3 this time.

Start with a clean slate: an HTML page with just an empty SVG tag. Give the SVG tag an identifier, so that you can refer to it in your JavaScript/D3 code later on; for example, fun-drawing-area. Then in your page, include a <script> tag that points to the D3 library (either on the d3js.org website or locally in your site structure). This example uses version 3 of the library, which you can find at this http://d3js.org/d3.v3.min.js. Then comes our JavaScript tag, where we are going to write our super exciting code there. Here is what your starter page looks like:

```
<html>
  <head>
    <title>My First Chart with D3</title>
  </head>
  <body>
    <svg width="200" height="200" id="fun-drawing-area">
    </svg>
    <script src="http://d3js.org/d3.v3.min.js" charset="utf-8"></script>
    <script type="text/javascript">
      // ... Your super exciting code comes here! ...
    </script>
  </body>
<html>
```

HTML pages are composed of multiple elements or tags, including head, title, body, svg, and so on. D3 provides you with multiple selection methods, so that you can tell it, "Hey D3, go fetch that specific element of the page." You can select elements by their HTML tag names or CSS classes and identifiers, in addition to many other selection criteria. For this example, you are going to use d3.select() to select the SVG tag by its identifier. (If you've used jQuery before, you should feel at home here.) Then you are going to assign the result of the selection to a JavaScript variable, fda, short for fun-drawing-area:

```
// To tell D3 you are selecting an element by its id,
// you should use the # sign before the id.
// The result of the selection is assigned to the fds variable.
var fda = d3.select("#fun-drawing-area");
```

Next, append the yellow circle and the red square to that selection, and start setting their different attributes (e.g., cx, cy, r, x, y, width, height, etc.) as you did with the SVG elements before. D3 provides method chaining, which means that most of the time you will not need intermediate variables. In other words, rather than writing the following code:

```
var circle = fda.append("circle");
circle.attr("cx", 50);
circle.attr("cy", 50);
circle.attr("r",  40);
```

. . . you will more likely find it better to write more concise code like this:

```
var circle = fda.append("circle").attr("cx", 50).attr("cy", 50).attr("r",  40);
```

. . . or even more concise code as follows:

```
var circle = fda.append("circle").attr({"cx":50, "cy":50, "r":40})
```

Finally, here is the entire JavaScript code needed for the circle and the square using D3:

```
<script type="text/javascript">
    var fda = d3.select("#fun-drawing-area");
    var stroke_width = 2;
    var stroke_color = "black";

    // Drawing a Circle
    fda.append("circle")
        .attr("cx", 50)
        .attr("cy", 50)
        .attr("r",  40)
        .style("stroke", stroke_color)
        .style("stroke-width", stroke_width)
        .style("fill", "yellow");

    // Drawing a Square, i.e. rectangle with equal sides
    fda.append("rect")
        .attr("x", 100)
        .attr("y", 100)
        .attr("width", 50)
        .attr("height", 50)
        .style("stroke", stroke_color)
        .style("stroke-width", stroke_width)
        .style("fill", "red");
</script>
```

JavaScript, just like HTML, doesn't care about whitespace and line breaks. Lines starting with fda. append("circle") and fda.append("rect") are used to draw the circle and the square respectively. Up to the semicolon, these are actually just two lines of code from JavaScript's point of view. It is just nice to visually break chained methods into different lines, for better code readability.

The color and the size of the circle and square's border are the same, so we put them into two variables, stroke_width and stroke_color, respectively, and we referred to them later in our code like we normally do in any JavaScript code.

Your First D3 Chart

Now that you know how to draw basic shapes using D3, it's time to explore the real power of D3: its ability to decouple the charting logic from the data it represents. The key concept at work here is *data binding*.

You can think of data binding as a way you give d3 an array of data and ask it to tailor some elements (shapes) and match them with the data you have. For a better understanding, take a look at the following code:

```
d3.select("#fun-drawing-area")
      .selectAll("circle")
      .data([40, 80, 120, 160])
      .enter()
      .append("circle")
      .attr("cy", "40")
      .attr("cx", function (d) {
        return d;
      })
      .attr("r", "15")
      .style("fill", "red")
      .style("stroke", "black")
      .style("stroke-width", 2);
```

Assume that you have an empty SVG tag again, with #fun-drawing-area as its identifier. Thus, the first line tells d3 to select it. The second line tells it to select all circle elements that are in there. Wait a minute, didn't we say that this is an empty SVG tag? So, this second line is not going to select anything, right? That's correct, at least for now. Now, the third line will join the given array of numbers, [40, 80, 120, 160], with the empty selection we have just made in the previous line. Then, the enter() method in the following line is going to create placeholders tailored to your data so that you can use them later on. Thus, this example has four placeholders, as the data array is composed of four elements. From this moment, any method you are going to call in this chain, will be applied to each one of those four placeholders. Therefore, the append ("circle") in the fifth line is going to append four circles, and not only one. Similarly, the sixth line will set the cy attribute to 40 for all of them. The four circles are going to have their centre position 40 pixels below the upper border of our drawing area. More interestingly, rather that giving an attribute a fixed value, you can path a function to it, and d3 in turn, will give you the corresponding element of the data array as the first parameter of your function, that is, d will be set to 40 for the first circle, 80 for the second one, and so on. So, basically, what you are doing here, is giving each circle of the four circles a different value for cx, depending on the values in our array. The remaining lines just set same radius for the four circles and give them the same styling and color, so that we get the dots shown in Figure 5-4.

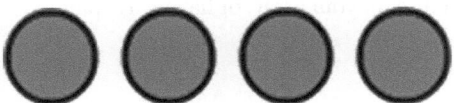

Figure 5-4. *Four red dots, using D3 data binding*

Applying what you have just learnt, you should be able to redraw the bar chart in Figure 5-2 using D3. Here's how:

```
// Array of GDP values.
var gdp_data = [17, 9, 5, 3];
// The drawing area's width and height.
var area_width  = 200;
var area_height = 200;
```

```
// Calculating the spacing between bars.
var spacing  = area_height / (gdp_data.length + 1);

// Select the drawing area and assign it to fda.
var fda = d3.select("#fun-drawing-area");
// Appending one rectangle for each item of gdp_data.
fda.selectAll("rect")
    .data(gdp_data)
    .enter()
    .append("rect")
    .attr("y", function (d, i) {
        // i is the order of this item in gdp_data.
        // Where first item is 0, second item is 1, etc.
        return spacing * (i+1);
    })
    .attr("x", "10")
    .attr("width", function (d, i) {
        // Widths are proportional to values in gdp_data.
        // d here is same as gdp_data[i]
        return 10 * d;
    })
    .attr("height", "20")
    .style("fill", "blue")
    .style("stroke", "black")
    .style("stroke-width", 2);
```

Recall the earlier bar chart: 4 bars, drawn in an area 200 pixels high; we divided 200 by 5 and set the y value of the bars to be 40, 80, 120 and 160. Similarly, we have done the calculations for the bars spacing in, spacing * (i+1). Note that D3 passes two values to your function and not only one. In addition to the corresponding element in the data array (d), it also gives you an index to which element you are dealing with at that moment (i), i.e., the value for i will be 0, 1, 2 and 3 for the first, second, third, and fourth bar, respectively. We ignored that second parameter (i) in the previous example, but this time you are going to use it. So, the y = spacing * (i+1) will result in 40 (40*1) for the first bar, 80 (40*2) for the second, etc.

Now, when you copy this code into your HTML file, you should get the same chart as shown in Figure 5-2. Remove the last element of the gdp_data array, and refresh your page. You should see three bars instead of four. Keep changing the values of your data and the number of values in the array and see what will happen.

Just for fun, try adding labels to the chart using the the same data binding approach. This time, you will need to append text and you may need to think of a different structure for your array, or having a separate array for labels if you want.

D3 Scales with Your Needs

So far, we have reached a good level of flexibility. You can change the data array, and the bar charts will adapt to those changes automatically. Now it's time to explore what happens when you are forced to leave the predetermined boundaries. For example, add a new number to the array, say 34. Now, when you refresh your graph you will notice that the new bar went outside your drawing area. That's because, you are setting the scale so that each trillion is represented by 10 pixels, and for the first four numbers, they never go beyond your graph's 200 pixels width, but for the 34, it should be represented by 340 pixels.

You have to do your calculations based on the given numbers and dynamically decide the scaling factor you are going to use based on the numbers you have. However, D3 offers you some help here, Scales. There are different types of Scales in D3, such as Quantitative and Ordinal Scales, but we will only focus on Quantitative Linear Scales now. The code looks like this.

```
d3.scale.linear().domain([0, 34]).range([0, 200]);
```

Here, you are telling D3 that the GDP values can go anywhere between 0 and 34, this is your domain. And you want to represent these numbers in a range between 0 and 200 pixels. You also want the relation between the domain and range to be linear. This means that for each value X in your domain, the output Y will be $Y = 200 * X / 34$. You may also have logarithmic or power scales, but let's not complicate stuff for now.

The code mentioned earlier returns a scale object, which also behaves as a function that you can call later on. Anyway, the following example should make things a bit clearer:

```
myScale = d3.scale.linear().domain([0, 10]).range([20, 30]);
myScale(0); // This will give 20
myScale(5); // You should get 25 this time
myScale(9); // 29, that's correct
```

In fact, this concept of creating an object, then using it later on as a function is something that you are going to see a lot in D3, so it is nice to get used to the library's logic. Now, it's time to use this new knowledge in the previous code:

```
// Defining the data and the drawing area size
var gdp_data = [17, 9, 5, 3, 34];
var area_width  = 200;
var area_height = 200;
var left_margin = right_margin = 10;

// Calculates the heightist GDP value
var max_gdp = Math.max.apply(Math, gdp_data);
// Then create a Scale, using max_gdp to define its domain.
// Its range goes between the left and right margins of the drawing area.
var myScale = d3.scale
                .linear()
                .domain([0, max_gdp])
                .range([0, area_width - left_margin - right_margin]);

// Calculate the spacings between bars
var spacing  = area_height / (gdp_data.length + 1);

// Draw the bars inside fun-drawing-area
var fda = d3.select("#fun-drawing-area");
fda.selectAll("rect")
   .data(gdp_data)
   .enter()
   .append("rect")
   .attr("y", function (d, i) {
     return spacing * (i+1);
   })
   .attr("x", left_margin)
   .attr("width", function (d, i) {
```

```
      return myScale(d);
  })
.attr("height", "20")
.style("fill", "blue")
.style("stroke", "black")
.style("stroke-width", 2);
```

To use your scale, you first need to find the biggest number within your list, max_gdp. Courtesy of JavaScript, you can use Math.max.apply() here. You better leave some margin so that your bars don't occupy the whole drawing area. These spaces can be useful in the future to add some labels or axis. Thus, you set the domain to go between 0 and max_gdp and the range should go between the graph width excluding the 10-pixel margin on the right and that on the left as well. In short, the width of the longest bar will be 180 pixels in this example. You can see now how we used the new scaling function myScale() in setting the rectangle's widths, rather than the old-fashioned calculation 10 * d we used earlier.

Can you also use D3 Scales to set the vertical spacing between the bars? Maybe, you can try setting one other scale for that instead of the spacing * (i+1) calculations we've used here.

In the previous two examples, we created an array, gdp_data, which was handed over to D3 later on. This was a simple array of numbers, [17, 9, 5, 3, 34], and d3 tied each element of that array to one rectangle. Nevertheless, you can use any kind of arrays you want.

For example, you can have an array of objects, and in such case, each rectangle will be assigned one of those objects. Here is an example of such array.

```
var gdp_data = [
  {
    'value': 17,
    'currency': 'dollars'
  },
  {
    'value': 15,
    'currency': 'dollars'
  },
  {
    'value': 25,
    'currency': 'dollars'
  }
];
```

In such cases, the first element of the array will be {'value': 17, 'currency': 'dollars'}, and the second element will be {'value': 15, 'currency': 'dollars'}, and so on. Now, when you need to set the rectangles' widths based on the value field, you should replace the myScale(d) part of the previous code with myScale(d.value). You also will need to alter the code finding the max_gdp to suit this new array. Similarly, you can have multidimensional arrays, that is, arrays of arrays, as we will see in our next example.

Web Development Tools

In case you already know how to use the web development tools in your browser, you can skip to the next section. Modern browser come with built in tools for web authoring and debugging. In Chrome it is called Chrome Developer Tools (DevTools for short). In Safari they have their web development tools under the name, Web Inspector. First, you have to enable the Develop menu in Safari's Advanced preferences. Firefox has extensions that you can use for debugging, too, such as Firebug.

To access the Chrome DevTools, click Ctrl+Shift+I (or Cmd+Opt+I if you are on Mac). As you can see in Figure 5-5, it has multiple tabs such as Elements, Sources, Network, Timeline, and so on.

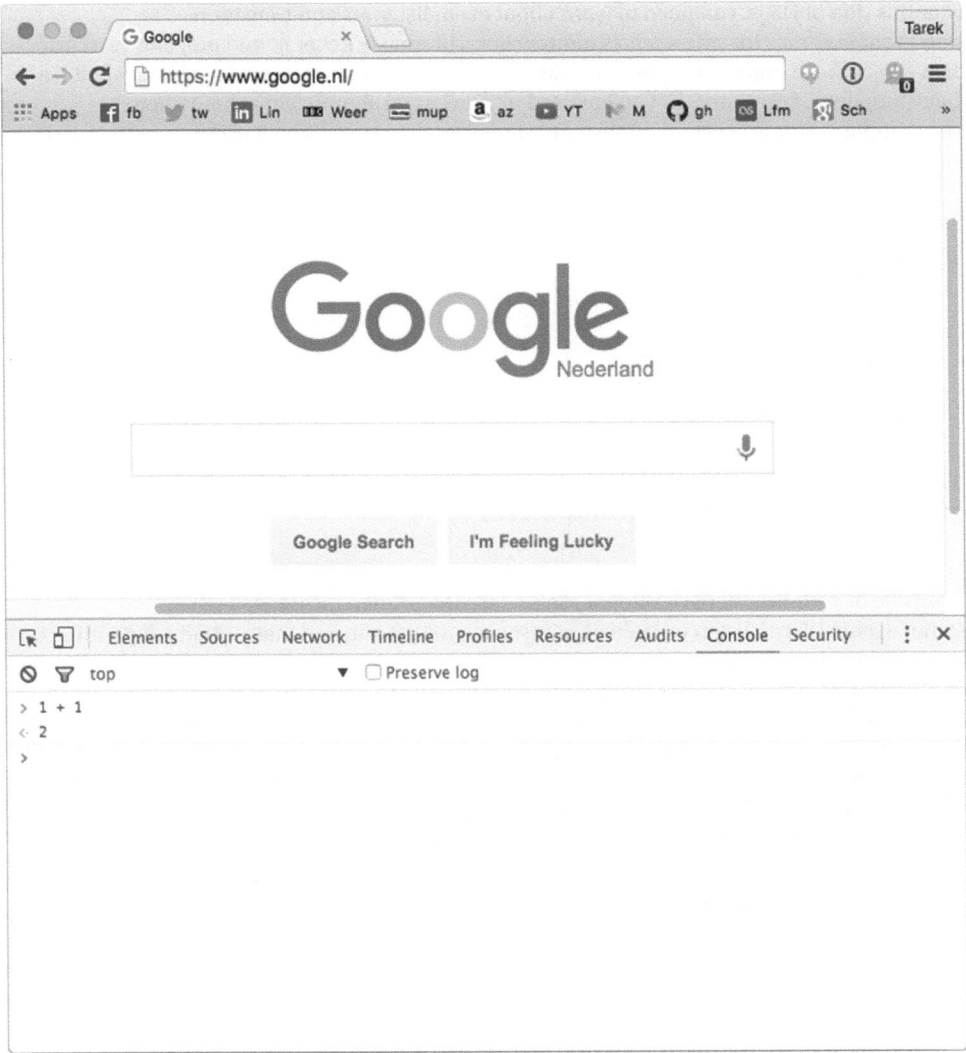

Figure 5-5. *Chrome DevTools*

The two main tabs we are going to use in this books are Elements and Console. The Elements tab shows you the source of your web page. Additionally, it allows you to see the CSS styles applied to each element. You can also edit any element of your page from within the tab and see the effect on that edit right away in your browser. The Console tab allows you to write JavaScript code, and also see its effect right away in your browser. By contrast, the JavaScript you already have in your page can print messages to the console, using the console.log() command. This is useful for debugging.

Your First Animated D3 Chart

Unless, your chart will be printed only in newspapers, why not have some interactivity and animations? In order to master this side of D3.js, you need to learn about event listeners and transitions.

D3 can listen to some events for you, such as mouse clicks, or mouse hover in and out, and you can set it so that when any of those events take place, it calls a function you already passed to it. We call those functions, callback functions. Once more, if you are used to jQuery you should feel at home here.

Here is a very simple example; a yellow circle that, when someone clicks it, will print a message saying that someone has clicked the yellow circle!

```
var circle = d3.select("#fun-drawing-area")
                .append("circle")
                .attr("cx", 50)
                .attr("cy", 50)
                .attr("r",  40)
                .style("stroke", "black")
                .style("stroke-width", 1)
                .style("fill", "yellow");

circle.on('click', function(d, i){
  console.log('Someone has clicked the yellow circle!');
});
```

Check the console in your browser's developer tools to see the printed message.

There are other events D3 can listen to, such as mouseover, mouseout, and many others depending on the DOM events supported by your browser.

Transitions, by contrast, are D3's way to make animation happen in a smooth way, you can set your animation to start few milliseconds after an event takes place, using delay(). Additionally, you can control how quick or slow you want your animation to be, using duration(). We better show this in the next example.

Next, we will show you how to rewrite the previous bar chart example, but this time, each bar will have an initial length, and when you click it, it will expand to its final length. Remember, the bars' lengths are actually the rectangles widths, since you are drawing horizontal bars here:

```
// Define the gdp data as an array of arrays

var gdp_data = [
  [10,15],
  [15,25],
  [25,30],
  [10,25]
];
```

```
// Then set the variables defining the drawing area's.
var area_width  = 200;
var area_height = 200;
var left_margin = right_margin = 10;

// Calculate the heightist gdp value, and create a scale using it.
var max_gdp = Math.max.apply(Math, gdp_data.map(
  function(d){
    return Math.max(d[0], d[1]);
  })
);
var myScale = d3.scale
                .linear()
                .domain([0, max_gdp])
                .range([0, area_width - left_margin - right_margin]);

// Scale for bars vertical positions.
var vScale  = d3.scale
                .linear()
                .domain([0, gdp_data.length + 1])
                .range([0, area_height]);
// Calculate the spacings between bars.
var spacing  = area_height / (gdp_data.length + 1);

// Draw the GDP bars.
var fda = d3.select("#fun-drawing-area");
fda.selectAll("rect")
 .data(gdp_data)
 .enter()
 .append("rect")
 .attr("y", function (d, i) {
    return vScale(i+1);
  })
 .attr("x", left_margin)
 .attr("width", function (d, i) {
     return myScale(d[0]);
 })
.attr("height", "20")
.style("fill", "grey")
.style("stroke", "black")
.style("stroke-width", 1)
.on('click', function(d, i){
  d3.select(this)
    .style("stroke-width", 1)
    .style("fill", "blue")
    .transition()
    .delay(100)
    .duration(500)
    .attr("width", function (d, i) {
     return myScale(d[1]);
    });
});
```

In this example, we replaced the gdp_data array with a new multidimensional array. Each subarray contains two elements, the initial and final values of the bar assigned to it. Consequently, we altered the max_gdp calculation using JavaScript array map to be able to calculate the maximum value among all the elements in our new multidimensional array.

Now, here comes the animation fun. We created an event listener for mouse clicks. The on('click', function(d, i){ ... }) part is how we tell the browser to call a function whenever someone clicks on that element. Inside the function we define the animation. Since the JavaScript keyword this refers to the object the function (method) belongs to, we can use it to refer to the object we have just clicked on. Thus, by using select(this), we are actually selecting the rect we have just clicked on. Then we apply the required animations to it. First, we change the color of the rect from grey to blue. This happens right after the click, without any delays. Then we want to wait for for 100 milliseconds and slowly change the widths of the rect after that. We want the width expansion to happen in 500 milliseconds. Hence these three function calls in our code:

```
.transition()
.delay(100)
.duration(500)
```

After that you call the attribute changing function to change its width to the value specified by the second element of the corresponding subarray. Notice how we are using d[0] and d[1] this time to access elements of the sub-arrays. That's it, copy and paste the above code and refresh your page, you should now see the bars changing their widths and colors once you click on them.

Moving and Rotating Objects

After drawing shapes, you can decide to move them within your drawing area. You can also group shapes together so you can move them as a single group. Here is the code needed to create a blue square and red circle, where both of them are members of a group:

```
<html>
  <head>
    <title>Grouped Shapes</title>
  </head>
  <body>
    <svg width="200" height="200" id="fun-drawing-area">
    </svg>
    <script src="http://d3js.org/d3.v3.min.js" charset="utf-8"></script>
    <script type="text/javascript">

    var fda = d3.select("#fun-drawing-area");
    var g = fda.append("g");

    g.append("rect")
      .attr("y", 0)
      .attr("x", 0)
      .attr("width", 40)
      .attr("height", 40)
      .style("fill", "blue");
```

```
    g.append("circle")
     .attr("cx", 40)
     .attr("cy", 40)
     .attr("r", 20)
     .style("fill", "red");

    </script>
  </body>
<html>
```

In this example, you first appended a group, g, to your area. Then rather than appending the shapes to your area, as you used to do earlier, you now appended the shapes to the newly created group.

The SVG transform attribute applies a list of transformation to shapes or group of shapes. Translate, rotate, and scale are three kinds of transformation that we are going to try now. Here is the command to translate, that is, move our shapes, 50 pixels to the right, and the same number of pixels down:

```
g.attr("transform", "translate(50,50)");
```

To move and rotate the figure, you can use the following command instead. Notice that the rotation angle is given in degrees, 30 degrees in our example here:

```
g.attr("transform", "translate(50, 50) rotate(30)");
```

And here is how to double the size of your shapes. You may use values less than one to reduce the size of your shapes:

```
g.attr("transform", "scale(2)");
```

You can combine these transformations with the earlier animations (transition, delay, and duration) to have smooth transformations if you want.

Notice that you are applying all your transformation to the group here. Obviously, you can still apply them to separate shapes if you want.

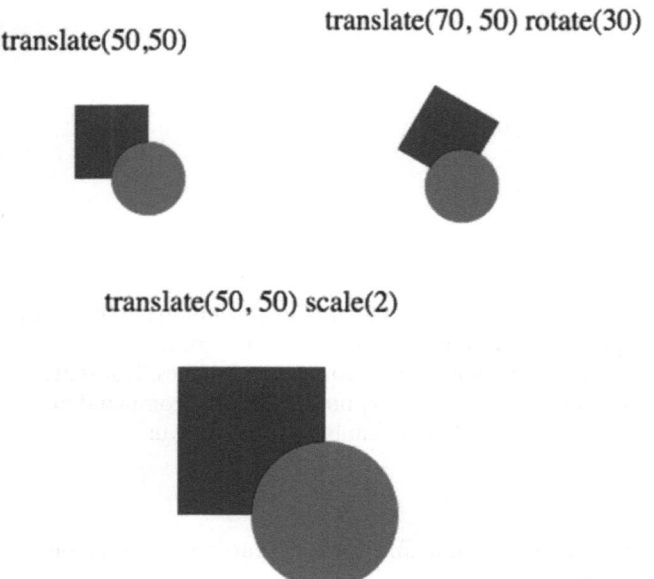

Figure 5-6. *Applying different transformations to our group*

There also exist matrix, skewX, and skewY as other transformation types. You may like to read about these yourself, although they are not as commonly used as the aforementioned ones.

Summary

In this chapter, we started with an introduction to SVG, then moved to the D3 library. You have learned how to create basic bar charts, dynamically assigning data to your chart and making it adaptable to the data you provide to it. You have also seen D3 scales and animations.

If you still want to experiment more, you can try creating vertical bars this time, column chart. Then you can add labels to the bars and make them only appear when someone hovers over the bars. Rather than GDP, let's say you want to represent some negative value such as deficiency. May be this time, you might like your columns to go downwards rather than upwards. Bars and columns are boring? Maybe rather than bars you can have a list of circles next each other, where their sizes are proportional to the data they represent. What about putting those circles inside each other?

See, with D3 the sky is the limit. You can always come with your own charts. You are not limited to the conventional charts you see all over the place any more.

CHAPTER 6

■ ■ ■

Creating Complex Shapes

This chapter introduces SVG Paths, and explains how you can use them in D3 to create any shapes you want. You will also learn about D3 Path Generators and how to use them to make the creation of paths easier.

Forget Rectangles, Go Freehand

Unless you are Piet Mondrian[1], you cannot limit yourself to drawing only rectangles, and eventually circles. SVG provides a path element that allows you to draw anything, from line charts to the world map. D3, in turn, makes use of the path element to draw interesting and complex shapes.

For the following example, start with the underlying SVG commands and its way of defining the path. In a 200x200 SVG area (see Figure 6-1), draw a line from the bottom left corner, that is, (x=0, y=200) up to (x=50, y=100), then draw a horizontal line of 100 pixels to the right, then go up to the upper right left corner, that is, (x=200, y=0).

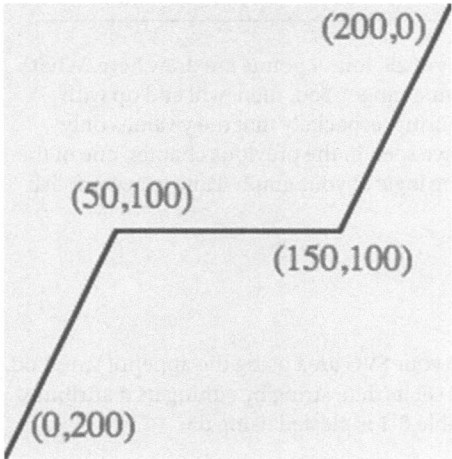

Figure 6-1. *Your first SVG path*

---

[1]Piet Mondrian was one of the founders of the Dutch modern art movement, De Stijl. He is best known for reducing his shapes to lines and rectangles.

T. Amr and R. Stamboliyska, *Practical D3.js*, DOI 10.1007/978-1-4842-1928-7_6

To draw the path shown in Figure 6-1, you have to specify its path data string as follows: M 0 200 L 50 100 L 150 100 L 200 0. The M means move to a specific point without drawing anything, whereas L means draw a line along your way from the current point to the next one. The numbers after the letter specify the x and y absolute values in pixels. The HTML for this page is as follows:

```
<html>
  <head>
    <title>My First SVG Path</title>
  </head>
  <body>
    <svg width="200" height="200" style="background: #EEE">
        <path d="M 0 200 L 50 100 L 150 100 L 200 0" stroke="blue" stroke-width="2"
        fill="#EEE" />
    </svg>
  </body>
<html>
```

If you add a lowercase z at the end of your path data (i.e., M 0 200 L 50 100 L 150 100 L 200 0 z), it will connect the first and last point. If you'd like to skip the horizontal line, all you have to do is to replace L 150, 100 with M 150 100. Thus, your path data becomes: M 0 200 L 50 100 M 150 100 L 200 0. You can separate the x and y values with commas, although they are normally eliminated for more compact path data.

The path element is suitable for line charts, where you need to plot values of y versus those of x. Looking at the data values in Table 6-1, can you think of the path data string to represent those vales?

Table 6-1. *Data points for an oscillating wave*

x	0	25	50	75	100	125	150	175	200
y	50	150	50	150	50	150	50	150	50

The x takes values between 0 and 200, and they are multiples of 25, thus 9 points are draw here. What if you decided to have the x values as multiples of 5, within the same range? You, then, will end up with 41 points. Writing a data string for all these points will be really boring, especially that the y values only alternate between 50 and 150, with some clear pattern. As you have seen in the previous chapter, one of the main values of using D3, is that you can separate the data from the logic of your graph. How to accomplish this for this chart is the topic of the following two sections.

A Simple Freehand Chart in D3

As mentioned in the previous chapter, you can append shapes to your SVG area using the append() method. Similarly, to append a path use the append("path") method, and set its data string by editing its d attribute. In the following code, an oscillating wave similar to the one in Table 6-1 is plotted using d3:

```
<html>
  <head>
    <title>My First SVG Path using D3</title>
  </head>
  <body>
    <svg width="200" height="200" id="fun-drawing-area" style="background: #EEE">
    </svg>
  </body>
```

```
<script src="http://d3js.org/d3.v3.min.js" charset="utf-8"></script>
<script type="text/javascript">
  var fda = d3.select("#fun-drawing-area");
  var lineGraph = fda.append("path")
                    .attr("d", "M 0,150 L 25,50 L 50,150 L 75,50 L 100,150")
                    .attr("stroke", "black")
                    .attr("stroke-width", 2)
                    .attr("fill", "#EEE");
</script>
<html>
```

Simple enough; but let's see if D3 provides a better way for setting paths.

Introducing D3 Path Generators

D3 provides Path Data Generators. The logic is as follows: You create the generator object—it also acts as a function—and define how it will convert the data given to it into x and y values. Picking up on the previous example, put the data in Table 6-1 in the following format, and then write a generator for that:

```
data = [
  [  0, 150],
  [ 25,  50],
  [ 50, 150],
  [ 75,  50],
  [100, 150],
  [125,  50],
  [150, 150],
  [175,  50],
  [200, 150]
]

// This creates a generator function, and assigns it to gen.
// Yan can then apply gen() to your data to create a path string.
var gen = d3.svg.line()
              .x(function(d){
                return d[0];
              })
              .y(function(d){
                return d[1];
              });
```

Now, if you call the generator function you just created, and pass it your two-dimensional array of data, gen(data), it we will return the following path data string:

```
"M0,150L25,50L50,150L75,50L100,150L125,50L150,150L175,50L200,150"
```

That's exactly what is needed to draw the line chart. As you have seen, when creating the line generator, we define two methods, x() and y(). These are used to specify how each element within the data array will be converted into x and y values, respectively. The data variable is an array of arrays, thus, you specify the first element of each sub array, d[0], to be the x, and the second element to be the y.

All you have to do after that, is to pass the output of the generator to the d attribute of the path you create. Thus, your code should look like this:

```
var fda = d3.select("#fun-drawing-area");
data = [
    [  0, 150], [ 25,  50], [ 50, 150], [ 75,  50], [100, 150],
    [125,  50], [150, 150], [175,  50], [200, 150]
];

var gen = d3.svg.line().x(function(d){
    return d[0];
}).y(function(d){
    return d[1];
});

var lineGraph = fda.append("path")
                    .attr("d", gen(data))
                    .attr("stroke", "black")
                    .attr("stroke-width", 2)
                    .attr("fill", "#EEE");
```

Note that the y takes the value of 150 when x is divisible by 50, and y is 50 otherwise. So, you can simplify your code by writing a slightly different data array and generator, like this:

```
data = [0, 25, 50, 75, 100, 125, 150, 175, 200];
var gen = d3.svg.line().x(function(d){
    return d;
}).y(function(d){
    if (d % 50 == 0){
        return 150;
    } else {
        return 50;
    }
}).interpolate("step");
```

It might be a good idea to use the scale functions from the previous chapter inside the generators to make sure the resulting chart fits into the SVG area regardless of the data used. In addition to the x() and y() methods of the generator, we usually use another method called interpolate. It specifies how the points are being connected.

In the previous code we used a step interpolation. Nevertheless, there are different other interpolations offered by the library. Running the above code will create one of the shapes in Figure 6-2, depending on which interpolation options we use with our path generator.

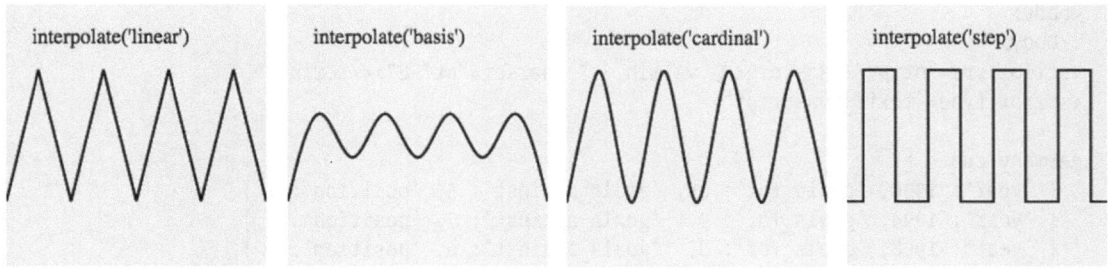

Figure 6-2. *The effect of the different interpolate values for path generators*

Using Area Charts

Area charts are similar to line charts, except that for each value of x, you have two corresponding values for y to express, which will result in a closed area being drawn. This means it is more suitable for expressing bivariate data, especially when you need to show the differences between those two variables. Bear with me, we will clarify with an example now.

Suppose you want to plot the goals the German football team scored and received in the consecutive world cup championships between 1990 and 2014. It is clear that not only do you want to show the goals, for and against, but also the differences between the two. And an area chart is good at representing this, as the upper and lower boundaries of the area will highlight the goal differences.

The data you are going to use is represented in the form of an array of objects, each object shows the goals scored for and against Germany in a certain year, and the final position of the team by the end of the tournament. Here is an example of the data:

```
germany_wc = [
  { 'year': 1990, 'goals_for': 15, 'goals_against': 5, 'position': 1 },
  { 'year': 1994, 'goals_for': 9, 'goals_against': 7, 'position': 5 },
  ..
];
```

Instead of the d3.svg.line() generator, you are going to use d3.svg.area() this time. It has an x() method like the line generator, but two methods for the y-value, y0() and y1(). The years will be represented horizontally, on the x axis, and the goals for and against will be represented using y0 and y1, respectively. To make things easier, you will use linear scales, similar to the ones you used in the previous chapter, to make sure the values fit well in the drawing area. Here is the code for the entire page, including the data you have:

```
<html>
  <head>
    <title>Germany World Cup Goals</title>
    <style>
      .area {
        fill: #7F0OFF;
        stroke: #BBB;
      }
    </style>
  </head>
```

```
<body>
</body>
<script src="http://d3js.org/d3.v3.min.js" charset="utf-8"></script>
<script type="text/javascript">

germany_cup = [
  { 'year': 1990, 'goals_for': 15, 'goals_against': 5, 'position': 1 },
  { 'year': 1994, 'goals_for': 9,  'goals_against': 7, 'position': 5 },
  { 'year': 1998, 'goals_for': 8,  'goals_against': 6, 'position': 7 },
  { 'year': 2002, 'goals_for': 14, 'goals_against': 3, 'position': 2 },
  { 'year': 2006, 'goals_for': 14, 'goals_against': 6, 'position': 3 },
  { 'year': 2010, 'goals_for': 16, 'goals_against': 5, 'position': 3 },
  { 'year': 2014, 'goals_for': 18, 'goals_against': 4, 'position': 1 }
];
</script>

<script type="text/javascript">

// The Width and Height of our SVG area
var w = 400; h = 300;

// Margin around our chart.
var margin = 20;

// Let the JavaScript append the SVG area into our page body.
var svg_area = d3.select("body")
                .append("svg")
                .attr('width', w)
                .attr('height', w);

var xScale = d3.scale
              .linear()
              // It is better to programmatically calculate
              // the domain values from the data.
              // Here, we do it manually for simplicity.
              .domain([1988, 2016])
              .range([margin, w-margin]);

var yScale = d3.scale
              .linear()

              // Again, the domain values from the data
              // are calculated manually for simplicity.
              .domain([0, 20])
              .range([h-margin, margin]);

var gen = d3.svg.area()
              .x(function(d){
                return xScale(d['year']);
              })
              .y0(function(d){
```

```
                return yScale(d['goals_for']);
                })
              .y1(function(d){
                return yScale(d['goals_against']);
                })
              .interpolate('monotone');

  svg_area.append("path")
          .attr("class", "area")
          .attr("d", gen(germany_cup));

  </script>
<html>
```

In the previous chapter we mentioned that the SVG elements can have CSS classes attached to them for easier styling. That's why we use a CSS class that we call area to give the path fill and stroke colors. Figure 6-3 shows the shape that you will see in your browser once you paste the previous code in your HTML page.

Figure 6-3. *Germany, football world cup history*

Adding Text

What is a bit annoying about the chart in Figure 6-1 is that you cannot tell the tournaments apart; nor can you tell the number of goals scored, and most importantly, what the chart is about if it is taken out of context.

You can start by adding a title and subtitle to the chart. The title goes on the top and the subtitle at the bottom. You can simply use the SVG text element for that, and put your title 20 pixels from the top and horizontally align it to the middle, like this:

```
svg_area.append("text")
        .attr("x", w/2)
        .attr("y", 20)
        .text("Goals For/Against");
```

Well, if you try this code, you will notice something wrong about the horizontal alignment. When you set x to half the area's width, w/2, you are actually setting the beginning of your text to go there. What you actually want to do, is to set the midpoint of your text to be in the middle of the area. There is an attribute for that, and it is called text-anchor. Thus, let's change the code to look like this:

```
svg_area.append("text")
        .style("text-anchor", "middle")
        .attr("x", w/2)
        .attr("y", 20)
        .text("Goals For/Against");
```

For the subtitle, repeat this code for our subtitle but have the phrase "Germany World Cup" positioned 20 pixels from the bottom (see Figure 6-4).

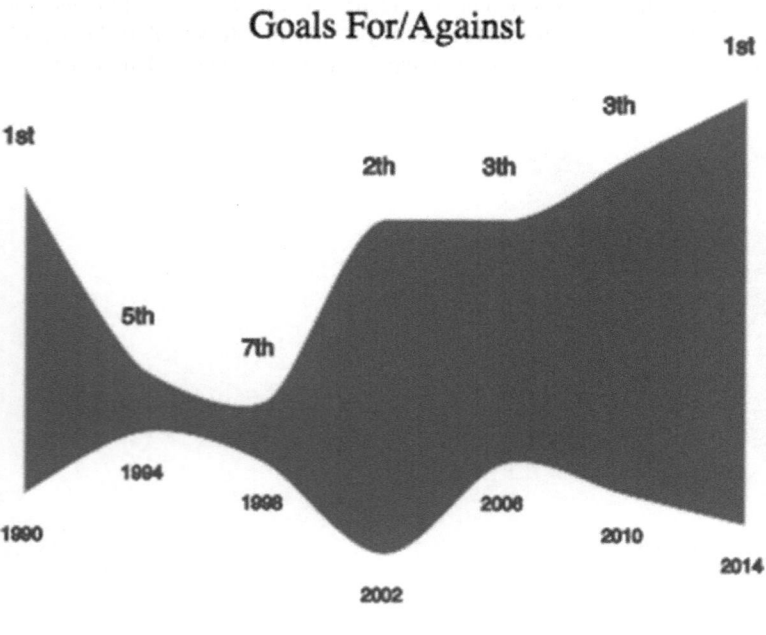

Figure 6-4. *Germany, football world cup history, with labels*

Next, add the tournaments dates and the German final position in each tournament as shown in Figure 6-4. As shown in Figure 6-4, the aforementioned labels go few pixels above and below y0 and y1 values.

To add the years, first start by defining a CSS class to be used for styling the labels as follows:

```
.year-labels {
        font-family: sans-serif;
        font-size: 8px;
        stroke: #555;
}
```

Then use the data binding technique from Chapter 5 to set the labels in accordance to the data points. Also use the scales you defined earlier, then set each label 10 pixels to the left of each point, and 20 pixels below it. Here is the code:

```
svg_area.selectAll(".year-labels")
        .data(germany_cup)
        .enter()
        .append("text")
        .attr("class", "year-labels")
        .attr("x", function(d){
          return xScale(d['year']) - 10;
        })
        .attr("y", function(d){
          return yScale(d['goals_against']) + 20;
        })
        .text(function(d){
          return "" + d['year'] + "";
        });
```

Surely you can do the same for the team's position in each tournament. Don't forget to use a separate CSS class for that, or else you will be overriding your previous data binding.

JavaScript's `this` keyword

Before explaining how to add an axis to the graph, we need to briefly explain some JavaScript concepts. In JavaScript, functions are objects. When inside a function, the keyword this refers to the context of the function, and the value of this is determined by the way the function is invoked.

Nevertheless, JavaScript gives you ways to dictate what value should be assigned to this within a function. This is done using one of two methods, call() and apply():

```
myfunction = function(){ return this; }

// Normally, the value of this here is set to the global object.
// Unless you are running in strict mode, but you can ignore that for now.
myfunction();

// Since we used apply to change the functions's context and overwrite the value this refers to,
// the value of this now is set to the given object, {'name': 'some object'}
myfunction.apply({'name': 'some object'});
```

The call() method is almost identical to apply(). The only difference is in the way additional parameters are passed to myfunction(). In the case of apply() the parameters will be passed as an array; myfunction.apply({'name': 'some object'}, [parameter1, parameter2, ..]), whereas in the case of call(), the following syntax is used, myfunction.call({'name': 'some object'}, parameter1, parameter2, ..).

Adding an Axis

It is still not clear in Figure 6-4 how many goals are scored, so maybe adding a vertical axis can be helpful here. Setting an axis requires two steps. First, you define the axis using d3.svg.axis(), then you call the defined axis to be rendered in your area. Here is a minimal code for generating your y-axis:

```
var yAxis = d3.svg.axis()
              .scale(yScale)
              .orient("right");
svg_area.call(yAxis);
```

Note that the axis needs to know what scale to use to adjust itself to the drawing area. You can use the same yScale you are already using here for all vertical data. The orient() method defines where the numbers should be put, to the left, to the right, or maybe beneath the axis if it is a horizontal one.

Similar to scales, axis are functions, too. In other words, yAxis() is a function. To add the axis to the drawing area, you are supposed to call yAxis() and set its context to svg_area. Nevertheless, d3 selectors—svg_area here—provides a shorthand method for this task, call(). In the last line of the code, the selectors call() methods is called with yAxis as its parameter. Internally, this results in yAxis being invoked as follows, yAxis.apply(svg_area, [the selector's original arguments]).

Finally, you can now see the axis rendered in your SVG area (see Figure 6-5).

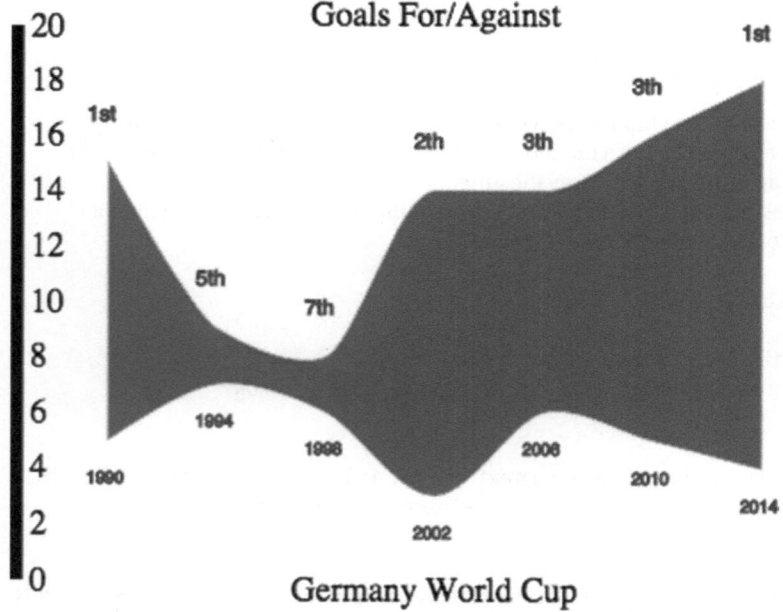

Figure 6-5. *Germany, football world cup history, with labels and y-axis*

To set the precision for your axis, define the number of ticks you want as follows:

```
var yAxis = d3.svg.axis()
              .scale(yScale)
              .orient("right")
                 .ticks(10);
```

At this point, the axis still is a bit raw; wouldn't it look nicer if it were placed a bit more to the right so that the graph resembles the one shown in Figure 6-6?

Figure 6-6. *Germany, football world cup history, with labels and the y-axis on the right*

The best cure for appearances is CSS. Let's define a bunch CSS classes to style the axis with:

```
.axis path,
.axis line {
  fill: none;
  stroke: #BBB;
  shape-rendering: crispEdges;
}
.axis text {
  font-family: sans-serif;
  font-size: 10px;
  stroke: #333;
}
```

To be able to move the axis, you need to put it inside a group. Probably you still remember how to create groups from the previous chapter. Then you will use the transform to move the axis to the right, right before the margin, that is, with a distance equals to the width of your drawing area minus the margin. Here is the code:

```
svg_area.append("g")
    .attr("transform", "translate(" + (w - margin) + ",0)")
    .attr("class", "y axis")
    .call(yAxis);
```

Notice how we defined a CSS class for our axis line and text, and we set it in the code above using the attribute method.

Connecting the Dots with SVG Diagonal

Another shape that you can find in the SVG toolbox is the diagonal. It draws a path connecting two points using Bézier curve, which is commonly used in computer graphics to draw smooth curves that can be scaled indefinitely. You are going to see it in action in a moment, and surely you will find those curves more appealing than thin and angular lines.

For the following example, you are going to create a scatter plot, where each dot represents one Linux distribution. The x-axis has the years where each distribution had its first release, the y-axis shows their popularity, via the amount of visits each one received in the last six months on distrowatch.com. Additionally, as some of these distributions are based on other ones, we need to show this in the form of links between them, hence, the need for the diagonals. Figure 6-7 shows the final chart.

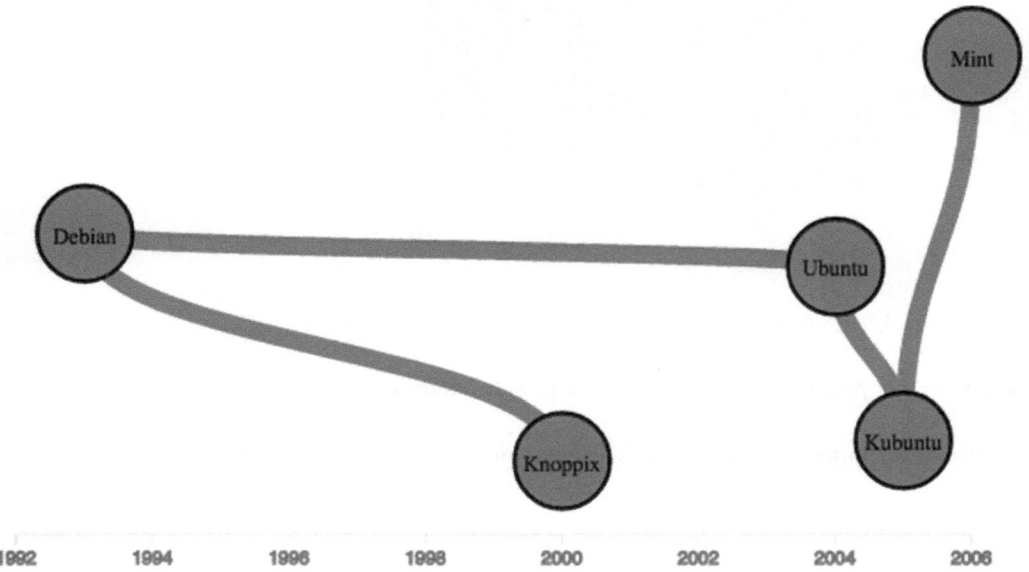

Figure 6-7. *History of some Linux Distributions*

The chart in Figure 6-7 shows two sets of data. The first set, let's call it distros, contains the names of the Linux distributions, the years they were created and the visits they got. The second set, relations, will show the relationships between those distributions, and which of them is based on the other. The "from" and "to" fields contain references to elements in the distros array. For example, the first element of relations, {'from': 0, 'to': 1}, means that item 0, the distro Debian, is what item 1, Ubuntu, is based on. Here is the code for the data:

```
distros = [
    { 'name': 'Debian', 'year': 1993, 'visits': 1820},
    { 'name': 'Ubuntu', 'year': 2004, 'visits': 1588},
    { 'name': 'Kubuntu', 'year': 2005, 'visits': 363},
    { 'name': 'Mint', 'year': 2006, 'visits': 3069},
    { 'name': 'Knoppix', 'year': 2000,'visits': 219},
];
```

```
relations = [
   {'from': 0, 'to': 1},
   {'from': 1, 'to': 2},
   {'from': 2, 'to': 3},
   {'from': 0, 'to': 4},
];
```

Start, again, with a drawing area and x and y scales as follows:

```
// Width and Height of our SVG area
var w = 600; h = 300;
// Margin around our chart
var margin = 40;

var darea = d3.select("body")
                   .append("svg")
                   .attr('width', w)
                   .attr('height', w);
```

D3 provides min() and max() function so you can easily tell the minimum and maximum values within an array. You need these to be able to dynamically set the domains of our x and y scales as follows:

```
var years_range = function(data){
    y1 = d3.min(data, function(o){ return o.year});
    y2 = d3.max(data, function(o){ return o.year});
    return [y1-1, y2]
}

var visits_range = function(data){
    v1 = d3.min(data, function(o){ return o.visits});
    v2 = d3.max(data, function(o){ return o.visits});
    return [v1, v2]
}

var xScale = d3.scale.linear()
                   .domain(years_range(distros))
                   .range([margin, w-margin]);

var yScale = d3.scale.linear()
                   .domain(visits_range(distros))
                   .range([h-margin, margin]);
```

Next, continue with the easy part, the scatter plot. Remember the four red dots you drew in the previous chapter? You're basically doing the same here, where the cx values will be set using the years field and the cy values will be the visits. Here is the code for the scatter plot:

```
darea.selectAll(".distrodot")
      .data(distros)
      .enter()
      .append("circle")
      .attr("class", "distrodot")
```

```
 .attr("cx", function (d, i) {
    return xScale(d.year);
 })
 .attr("cy", function (d, i) {
    return yScale(d.visits);
 })
 .attr("r", "26")
 .attr("stroke", "#000000")
 .attr("stroke-width", "2px")
 .attr("fill", "#5599FF");
```

Start by selecting a CSS class, distrodot. This class doesn't even exist in your CSS, but your code will still work if you select it and set it to your circles in a moment. Actually, selectAll("circle") is valid, too, however, as a best practice, it is always better to select your components by their more specific class rather than their shape. When you have more than one component, all using the same shape, selecting them by their shapes may confuse the D3 bindings. It is also more semantically correct to refer to things by what they mean and not just how they look like. In lines 2 to 5, you basically do the data binding, creating circles and setting the CSS class to them. You then assign their cx and cy values, using the data from the distros array. In the end, you give all your circles a fixed radius, and add some styling to them. In practical life, you might prefer to move the styling from here and write it in your CSS file under the distrodot class.

■ **Note** The main difference between scatter plots and bubble charts, is that the former has a fixed radius for its circles, thus it can only show two variables, via the positions of the dots in the x and y directions. The latter is able to show one additional variable by having variable radii for its circles. To draw a bubble chart in the future then, all you need to change in this code, is to set the radius, attr("r"), using one additional variable from your data then, in a similar fashion to how we set cx and cy here.

Now, it is time to draw the links between the circles. Like you have done earlier in this chapter, you are going to create a generator, but this time of diagonal type. As you can see, the diagonals are drawn between two points, source and target. Thus, the diagonal generator mainly needs two methods to be defined, source and target, so that it can learn how to extract the x and y values of the source and target points, respectively. First the code for the diagonals, followed by an explanation:

```
var gen = d3.svg.diagonal()
             .source(function(d){

                var x = xScale(distros[d.from].year);
                var y = yScale(distros[d.from].visits);
                return {'x': x, 'y': y};
             })
             .target(function(d){

                var x = xScale(distros[d.to].year);
                var y = yScale(distros[d.to].visits);
                return {'x': x, 'y': y};
             });
```

```
darea.selectAll("path")
    .data(relations)
    .enter()
    .append("path")
    .attr("d", gen)
    .attr("stroke", "#FF5599")
    .attr("stroke-width", "10px")
    .attr("fill", "none");
```

The second part of the code should be clear now, you select all paths, bind your selection to the relations data array you defined earlier, append the paths, set our d to the generator defined few lines earlier, and finally do some styling to your paths. Next, have a look at the generator. It will be called for each element of the relations array, and that element will be passed to both the source and target methods as d. So, for the first element, {'from': 0, 'to': 1}, d.from will be 0 and d.to will be 1, that is, the source is 0 and the target is 1. The problem, is that you still have no clue what are the x and y values of these sources and targets. So, you need now to visit the distros array, get the years and visits from there and scale them using xScale and yScale, respectively, to get the x and y values. You then return these values in the form of {'x': x, 'y': y}, which is the diagonal's default way of getting these values, otherwise, we would have needed to set one additional method called projection. No need for that for now.

We will skip the code needed to create the axis and write the text labels this time; surely, you know how to write an axis by now.

We started by drawing the scatter plot, then we added the diagonals. The problem with that is that the diagonals will be drawn on top of the circles and will look as shown in Figure 6-8.

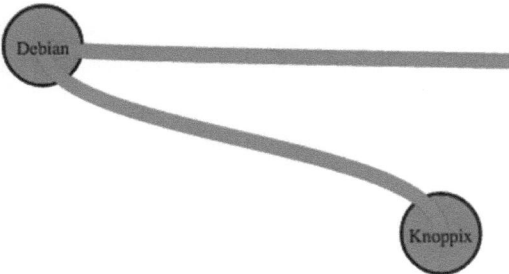

Figure 6-8. *Diagonals on top of the circles*

If you too find this ugly, then all you have to do is to switch this order. Start with the code snippet for the diagonals, then have that for the scatter plot later on in your code.

In general, SVG does not have a notion of z-index, thus, you always have to make sure the order of the drawings matches how you want them to appear on top of each other.

Using Arcs

Using the Arc generator is easy. You define its innerRadius, outerRadius, startAngle and endAngle, and your arc is ready. The following code generates an arc whose start angle is 0 and its end angle is π, while its inner and outer radii are 40 and 60 pixels. Note that D3 uses Radian angles, which means that a complete circle goes from 0 to 2π, rather than 0 to 360 degrees:

```
var arc = d3.svg.arc()
            .innerRadius(40)
            .outerRadius(60)
            .startAngle(0)
            .endAngle(Math.PI);
```

Obviously, things get more interesting when you tie your shapes to data. So, let's represent the GDP data from the previous chapter into the shape shown in Figure 6-9.

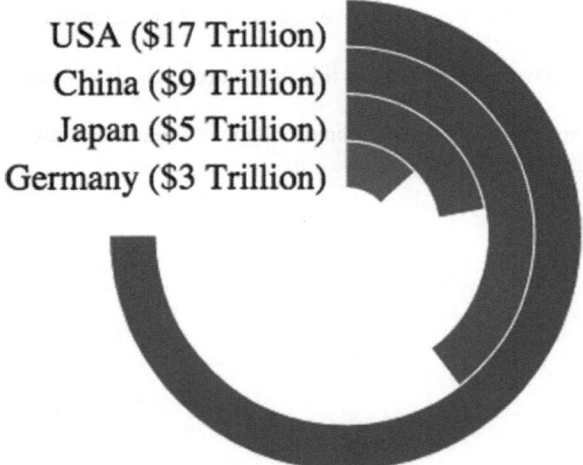

Figure 6-9. *Bending bars into arcs*

First, the data you want to represent:

```
var gdp = [

    { 'country': 'Germany', 'color': '#2ca02c',  'value': 3 },
    { 'country': 'Japan', 'color': '#9467bd',  'value': 5 },
    { 'country': 'China', 'color': '#d62728',  'value': 9 },
    { 'country': 'USA', 'color': '#1f77b4',  'value': 17 },
];
```

Then you set the drawing area as follows:

```
var w = 400,
    h = 300;

var svg = d3.select('body').append('svg')
    .attr('width', w)
    .attr('height', h);
```

The angles for a full circle goes from 0 to 2π. You are drawing three quarters of a circle here, thus, 0 to 1.5π. You used d3.max() to find the maximum GDP value and use it for the scale's domain:

```
var max_gdp = d3.max(gdp, function(o){ return o.value});
var angleScale = d3.scale
                    .linear()
                    .domain([0,max_gdp])
                    .range([0, 1.5*Math.PI]);
```

Next, set the arc generator. The angles depend on the data. All four arcs have a start angle of 0, while their end angle is function of the GDP value. We use the angleScale() we just created here. For the inner and outer radius, we are going to show you a better way to calculate these in the next chapter instead of the clumsy calculations here:

```
var arc = d3.svg.arc()
            .innerRadius(function(d, i){
              return (i+1)*25;
            })
            .outerRadius(function(d, i){
              return (i+2)*25;
            })
            .startAngle(function(d){
              return angleScale(0);
            })
            .endAngle(function(d){
              return angleScale(d.value);
            });
```

This time you are going to group your drawing and text together so you can use them as a single unit. Here is the remaining code you need to draw the chart:

```
// Create a group and append it to the drawing area.

var g = svg.append("g")

// Rather than adding shapes to the drawing area,
// this time they are added to the newly created group, g.
g.selectAll("path")
 .data(gdp)
 .enter()
 .append("path")
 .attr("d", arc)
```

```
   .attr("fill", function(d,i){
      return d.color;
   })
   .attr("stroke", "#FFF")
   .attr("stroke-width", "1px");

// Text is appended to the group too.
g.selectAll("text")
 .data(gdp)
 .enter()
 .append("text")
 .text(function(d){
      return d.country + " ($" +  d.value + " Trillion)";
   })
 .attr("x", function(d,i){
      return -10;
   })
 .attr("y", function(d,i){
      return -(i+1)*25;
   })
.attr("dy", -8)
 .style("text-anchor", "end")
 .style("font-size", "19px");

// Moving the entire group, including the shapes appended to it using SVG transformation.
g.attr("transform", "translate("+w/2+","+h/2+")");
```

■ **Note**   The x and y attributes are for absolute positions, while dx and dy attributes can be used to shift an object in relation to its x and y coordinates. Here dy is used to vertically adjust the text.

Bar charts are used for comparisons while pie charts are more suitable for composition. The shape in Figure 6-9 is aesthetically as circular as a pie chart, yet is good for comparing values.

Summary

In this chapter, you learned how to draw paths—first without the need for generators, as you already had the path data strings for them. Then you learned how to create them with generators. Remember that sometimes, you might actually have the "d" string with you. You will normally find them there in SVG files generated by vector graphics software, additionally, you may easily find the map of your country in SVG format on Wikipedia. Then, all you need is to give this path data to D3 to draw your map and start playing with it.

You have also learned how path generators can help you draw more complex shapes, such as line charts, area charts, and diagonal charts, which might be suitable to draw your family tree. There are other generators such as arc, which can be useful in drawing pie charts and sunburst diagrams. There is also chord generator, which is useful for creating chord diagrams.

If you still need to experience more, why not try creating a pie or donut chart using the arc generator. Nevertheless, don't worry if you find the creation of pie charts using the arc generator boring. In the next chapter you are going to see an easier way for that, using layouts.

CHAPTER 7

Transforming Data with Layouts

In this chapter you will be introduced to layouts. D3 layouts are usually where most of the magic happens, as they can transform your data in different ways for you to be visualize later on. Layouts will be used here to create pie charts, treemaps, and stacked charts; in addition to nontraditional visualizations using the partition and packing layouts.

Pie Chart Layout

Pie and donut charts are probably the most hated charts within the data visualization community. In his book, "The Visual Display of Quantitative Information," Edward Tufte wrote that "a table is nearly always better than a dumb pie chart." Problem is that they are overused. Nevertheless, you most probably need to use pie and donut charts sometimes.

As mentioned in the previous chapter, you can use arc generators to create pie and donut charts. However, using arc generators only, without the use of layouts, makes the creation of these two charts a boring and a non scalable process. Paul Graham of Y Combinator advised startups to "do things that don't scale," and once their business model is sound, they shall find ways to automate stuff and make them scalable. I'd like to tweak his advice here and tell you to try creating your charts the most boring and least flexible way first, and once you learn how things work, use more advance techniques. We, thus, are going create the most basic donut chart now. It is divided into two equal sectors, each in a different color, as shown in Figure 7-1.

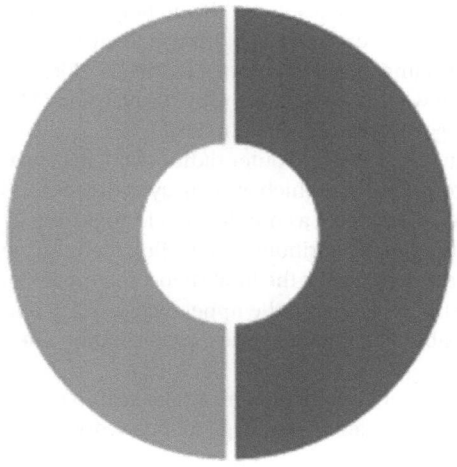

Figure 7-1. *The most basic donut chart*

© Tarek Amr and Rayna Stamboliyska 2016
T. Amr and R. Stamboliyska, *Practical D3.js*, DOI 10.1007/978-1-4842-1928-7_7

To draw the path shown in Figure 7-1, you have to use the arc generator. It has four main methods: outerRadius(), innerRadius(), startAngle(), and endAngle(). The outerRadius() specifies the size of the circle, while the innerRadius() specify size of the hole you want to dig into that circle. The innerRadius() here is what differentiate between pie and donut charts; pie charts have an inner radius of zero. Figure 7-1 has two sectors, each has its own startAngle and endAngle. Here is the code for the chart in Figure 7-1:

```
var w= 200, h = 200;
var svg = d3.select('body').append('svg')
    .attr('width', w)
    .attr('height', h);

var colors = d3.scale.category10();

var arc = d3.svg.arc()
            .innerRadius(30)
            .outerRadius(80)
            .startAngle(function(d){ return d['start']; })
            .endAngle(function(d){ return d['end']; });

svg.selectAll("path")
    .data([
        {'start': 0, 'end': Math.PI},
        {'start': Math.PI, 'end': 2*Math.PI}
    ])
    .enter()
    .append("path")
    .attr("d," arc)
    .attr("fill," function(d,i){
        return colors(i);
    })
    .attr("stroke," "#FFFFFF")
    .attr("stroke-width," "3px")
    .attr("transform," "translate(" + w/2 + ,"" + h/2 + ")");
```

As usual, we started by setting the drawing area, called svg, and then we set its width and height to 200 pixels. One new scale that we are seeing for the first time here is d3.scale.category10(), this will to give us a nice set of colors, that we can use later on. As you can tell from its name, it has 10 colors, #1f77b4, #ff7f0e, #2ca02c, and so on. So, now if you enter colors(0) in the console, it will return #1f77b4. Obviously, colors(1) will return #ff7f0e, and so on. You can also try .category20(), .category20b() and .category20c().

The arc generator gives all the arcs, or sectors, an inner radius of 30 and and outer radius of 80. Because each arc has different start and end angles, we set these values from the data, which is an array of object, each has its start and end attributes. D3 uses Radian angles, which means that a complete circle goes from 0 to 2π, rather than 0 to 360 degrees. Surely you are an expert in setting paths attributes and styling them, so we won't bore you by explaining this part. The very last part of the code transforms the final shape and moves it to the centre of the drawing area, or else the "donut" would have had its centre in the upper left corner of our drawing area, and consequently, most of it would have been invisible. Try removing the transformation line to see what we mean.

Now, have one more look at the data used in this pie chart; we specify start and end angles within each element. Let's say, we want to draw another chart to show what percentages of people go to their work by car versus bus and those who like to walk. Our data might then be as follows:

```
var transportation = [
    { 'mean': 'Car' , 'value': 30 },
    { 'mean': 'Bus' , 'value': 60 },
    { 'mean': 'Walk', 'value': 10 }
];
```

The car sector should be represented by an arc whose area is 30 percent of the circle. In other words, set its startAngle to zero and its endAngle 0.3 * 2π. Setting the bus sector is a little bit more challenging. Its start angle should start where the previous sector ends. So, its startAngle will be 0.3 * 2π, and its end angle will be 0.3 * 2π + 0.6 * 2π. And for the walk sector, the startAngle should be 0.3 * 2π + 0.6 * 2π, and the endAngle will be 0.3 * 2π + 0.6 * 2π + 0.1 * 2π, or just 2π.

As you can see, we have two issues here. The easy issue is how can we map the 30 to 0.3 * 2π, and map 60 to 0.6 * 2π, and so on. This is the easy issue; we can just use a scale like this one:

```
var pieScale = d3.scale.linear().domain([0, 100]).range([0, 2 * Math.PI]);
```

The second issue is the hard one. The start and end angles for each sector of the chart, do not only depend on their corresponding element, but they also depend on the previous elements in the array. Is there a solution for this issue, then? Yes, and it is called layouts. In fact, the pie layout solves both issues for us.

In the previous chapter, we have seen path generators that help us convert data items into path strings. Layouts on the other hand, as explained by the D3 manual, "typically operate across a collection of data as a whole, rather than individually." They see the data as a whole, and converts individual items while keeping an eye on the other items in the data array.

A very basic pie layout, is defined as follows:

```
myPie = d3.layout.pie();
```

As you have seen in the previous chapters with scales and axis, what pie layout returns is a function that you can apply to your data. Now, if you call myPie() and give it an array of numbers, it will return an array of objects each with its corresponding startAngle(), endAngle(), and some other attributes such as the original data you passed to it. After defining your pie layout, you can now try writing myPie([5,3,2]), myPie([4,2,3,1]) or myPie([3,3]) in the console of your browser's developers tools and see what you will get:

```
myPie([3,3]);
// Gives you the following output
// [
//   {
//     data: 3,
//     endAngle: 3.141592653589793,
//     startAngle: 0,
//     value: 3,
//   }, {
//     data: 3,
//     endAngle: 6.283185307179586,
//     startAngle: 3.141592653589793,
//     value: 3,
//   }
// ]
```

As you can see, the layout inspects the the data as a whole, and decides what are the start and end angles for each item accordingly.

Obviously, your input data can be more complex than an array of numbers. A value() method gets you covered on this, where you can define how the layout extracts values form your data. Don't want your chart to be in the form of a whole circle, you can use its startAngle() and endAngle() methods to define the span of your chart. Additionally, you can sort your data on the fly using sort(), and have some spacing between your sectors using padAngle(). Notice that padAngle() is only supported in versions 3.5 and up.

Now, you are all set to draw the following chart within the same drawing area, svg, and using the same transportation dataset and color scale we defined earlier.

Figure 7-2. *Plotting means of transportation in semidonut chart*

As shown in Figure 7-2, we decided to draw a semicircle this time—the start and end angles for the layout span between -0.5 π and 0.5 π. Here is the code needed to draw the chart:

```
// Define the pie layout.
var pie = d3.layout.pie()
            .startAngle(-0.5*Math.PI)
            .endAngle(0.5*Math.PI)
            .padAngle(0.04)
            .sort(null)
            .value(function(d){
              return d.value;
            });

// Define an arc generator.
var arc = d3.svg.arc()
            .innerRadius(40)
            .outerRadius(150)
            .startAngle(function(d){
              return d.startAngle;
             })
            .endAngle(function(d){
              return d.endAngle;
             });
```

```
// Use the layout and generator in drawing the char.
svg.selectAll("path")
    .data(pie(transportation))
    .enter()
    .append("path")
    .attr("d," arc)
    .attr("fill," function(d,i){
      return colors(i);
    })
    .attr("transform," "translate("+w/2+,""+h/2+")");
```

The steps involved should be familiar by now: You start first by defining both the pie layout and the arc generator. The pie layout spans between -0.5 π and 0.5 π, it has a padding of 0.04 between the different sectors. You do not want to sort the data, thus sort is set to null. Finally, you tell it how to extract the values from the transportation dataset using the value function. The arc generator sets the inner and outer radii for all arcs to 40 and 150, respectively. Because the generator is going to deal with our data after it has been processed by the layout, therefore, each item in the dataset already have new fields added to it by the layout, including startAngle() and endAngle(). The startAngle() and endAngle() methods of the generator it able to use these new fields now. Notice in third part of the code, the defined layout is applied to the data before giving it to the data method of the path.

Nothing stops us from having varying inner and outer radii for each arc. Do you feel like being artistic today? You can tweak the generator a little bit as follows to get the result in Figure 7-3:

```
var arc = d3.svg.arc()
            .innerRadius(function(d,i){ return 30 + 20 * i;})
            .outerRadius(function(d,i){ return 120 + 20 * i;})
            .startAngle(function(d){
              return d.startAngle;
            })
            .endAngle(function(d){
              return d.endAngle;
            });
```

Figure 7-3. *Plotting means of transportation in a slightly chaotic semidonut chart*

Treemap Layout

Treemap charts are commonly used to represent hierarchies, where you also need to show the comparative values of each item. You probably have seen these types of charts in softwares that shows you which folders occupy the biggest chunks of your hard disk. It is usually chosen for this task, since you want to show which folders are nested inside which ones, while also showing their sizes. You may also see tree maps being used to plot governmental budgets, where each department can have multiple subdepartments, and their budgets contribute to the total budget of their parent department.

To show how the treemap chart work, we are going to plot the expenditure budget of New York City in 2015, shown in Figure 7-4.

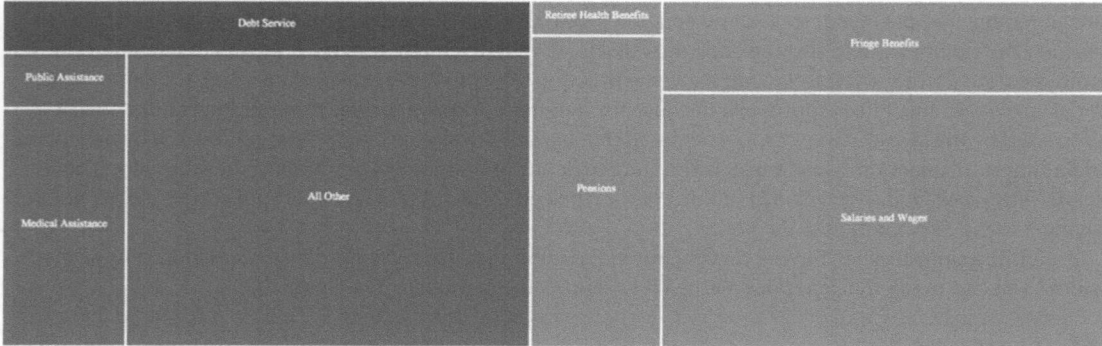

Figure 7-4. *NYC Expenditure plotted in Treemap Chart*

The data used by the treemap layout is usually in the form of a root object, containing nested objects inside it, and only leaf objects, objects with no children, have values. In other words, NYC expenditure should be formatted as follows:

```
var nybudget = {
    'name': 'NYC Budget 2015'   , 'children': [
        {'name': 'Personal Services', 'children': [
            {'name': 'Salaries and Wages', 'value': 24023},
            {'name': 'Pensions', 'value': 8621},
            {'name': 'Fringe Benefits', 'value': 8635},
            {'name': 'Retiree Health Benefits', 'value': 955},
          ]
        },
        {'name': 'Other Services', 'children': [
            {'name': 'Medical Assistance', 'value': 6275},
            {'name': 'Public Assistance', 'value': 1472},
            {'name': 'All Other ', 'value': 25149},
          ]
        },
        {'name': 'Debt Service', 'value': 5971},
      ]
};
```

The root node here is "NYC Budget 2015," it has three child nodes: Personal Services, Other Services, and Debt Service. Personal Services and Other Services have their own four (or three) child nodes as well. The treemap layout is smart enough to calculate the sum of the values of the child nodes and assign them to their parents, that way we only need to set values to leaf nodes. Having the data ready, drawing the treemap can't be any easier. Here is the code needed:

```
var w = 800, h = 250;
var svg = d3.select('body')
        .append('svg')
        .attr('width', w)
        .attr('height', h);
var colors = d3.scale.category10();

var tm = d3.layout.treemap().size([w, h]);

svg.selectAll("rect")
   .data(tm(nybudget))
   .enter()
   .append("rect")
   .attr("x," function(d,i){ return d.x; })
   .attr("y," function(d,i){ return d.y; })
   .attr("width," function(d,i){ return d.dx; })
   .attr("height," function(d,i){ return d.dy; })
   .attr("fill," function(d,i){
      if (d.parent) {
        return colors(d.parent.name);
      }
   })
   .attr("stroke," "#FFF")
   .attr("stroke-width," 2);
```

The treemap layout is part of the D3 family of hierarchical layouts, they all assume data to be formatted as above. Thus, the only information you need to give to the layout, when defining it, is the width and height of the drawing area. If you are using different attributes to define your children and values, then you might need to tell the layout how to get this data using children() and value() methods respectively. Other members of the hierarchical layouts family are Cluster, Pack, Partition and Tree.

As you have seen in the pie layout, once the layout is defined, you can use the returned function to alter your data, tm(nybudget). When applied to the data, the treemap layout converts it into an array of object. We, then, use the x, y, dx, and dy attributes of the returned objects to define each rectangle's x, y, width and height, respectively. In addition to these 4 values, the returned objects also have value (the original value of that node), depth (how deep is it in the hierarchy), parent (pointer to its parent), children (pointer to an array of its children). Here we are coloring children of each parent via same color of their parent.

To add text to the leaf nodes, you can use the following code:

```
svg.selectAll("text")
   .data(tm(nybudget))
   .enter()
   .append("text")
   .attr("x", function(d,i){ return (d.x + 0.5*d.dx); })
   .attr("y", function(d,i){ return (d.y + 0.5*d.dy); })
   .text(function(d,i){
```

```
  // If it has children, don't write its name
    return d.children? "" : d.name ;
  })
.style("text-anchor", "middle")
.attr("font-size", "8")
.style("fill", "#FFF");
```

Although tree maps are usually represented in the form of rectangles, the layout gives you the freedom to use any shapes you want. One shape we haven't introduced yet is the ellipse. It's very similar to a circle, yet, it has two radii, cx and cy. To modify the tree map and get the the ellipses chart shown in Figure 7-5, replace the rects with ellipses.

```
svg.selectAll("ellipse")
  .data(tm(nybudget))
  .enter()
  .append("ellipse")
  .attr("cx", function(d,i){ return (d.x + 0.5 * d.dx); })
  .attr("cy", function(d,i){ return (d.y + 0.5 * d.dy); })
  .attr("rx", function(d,i){ return 0.5*d.dx; })
  .attr("ry", function(d,i){ return 0.5*d.dy; })
  .attr("fill", function(d,i){
    if (d.children) {
      return '#FFF';
    } else {
      return colors(d.parent.name);;
    }
  })
  .attr("stroke", "#FFF")
  .attr("stroke-width", 2);
```

Voilá!

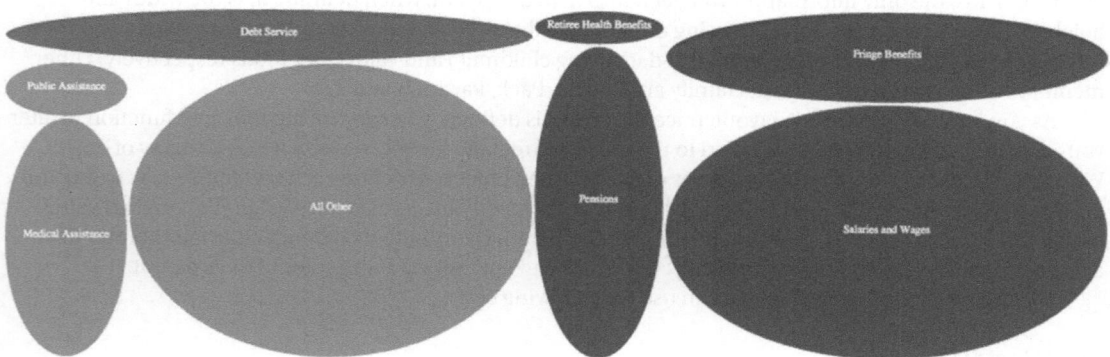

Figure 7-5. *NYC Expenditure plotted in a treemap chart, using ellipses*

Pack Layout

Granted, our choice to introduce the ellipses in the previous example won't get high marks from designers. The Pack Layout yields a better chart (see Figure 7-6), with the same data we already have, since it is also member of the hierarchal layouts family. As the family name implies, the pack layout is also used to represent hierarchies, however, unlike the treemap the emphasis here is on the parent-child relationships between the items shown rather than on the size of each item.

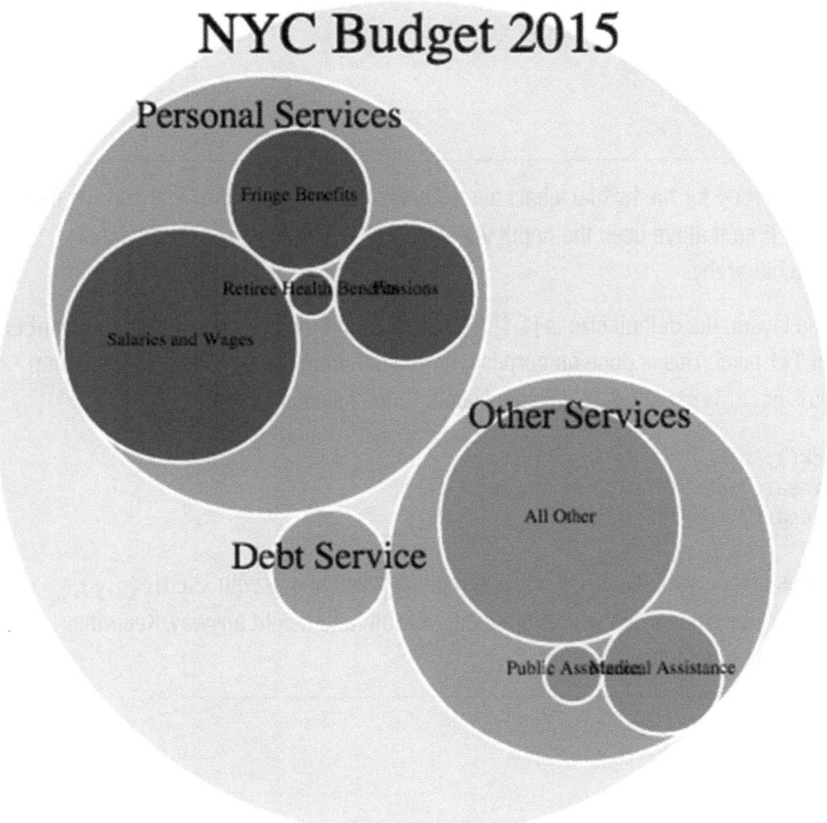

Figure 7-6. *NYC Expenditure plotted in using Pack Layout*

Here are the changes you need to make to the previous code to define the new layout using circles. Feel free to come up with better ideas for the fill part to change the colors of the nodes.

```
var w = 400, h = 400;
var pack = d3.layout.pack().size([w, h]);
svg.selectAll("circle")
    .data(pack(nybudget))
    .enter()
    .append("circle")
    .attr("cx", function(d,i){ return d.x; })
    .attr("cy", function(d,i){ return d.y; })
```

```
.attr("r", function(d,i){ return d.r; })
.attr("fill", function(d,i){
    if (d.depth == 0) {
      return '#EEE';
    } else if (d.depth == 1) {
      return '#BBB';
    } else {
      return colors(d.parent.name);;
    }
})
.attr("stroke", "#FFF")
.attr("stroke-width", 2);
```

■ **Note** We omitted the code needed for the textual labels here. You should be able to add that code at this point without our guidance. Just note that we used the depth variable to have various sizes for the labels depending on their depth in the hierarchy.

If you do not set the size of the layout, the default size is [1,1]. This means that the layout assumes you want to draw everything in an area of 1x1 pixel. This is done on purpose, so you can then use your own scale to map everything to it; i.e. d3.layout.pack().size([w, h]) is equivalent to the following code:

```
var pack = d3.layout.pack();
var xScale = d3.scale.linear().domain([0,1]).range([0,w]);
var yScale = d3.scale.linear().domain([0,1]).range([0,h]);
```

After you replace all occurrences of d.x with xScale(d.x), and replace those of d.y with xScale(d.y), and use any of the new scales for d.r since since we have the same width and height anyway. Keep this information in mind, we are going to need it in a moment.

Partition Layout

Nothing says that we should use the x and y values a layout added to our data to set the x and y values of our shape. Knowing this, in addition to what we just said about using Scales in combination with layouts, will help you draw the sunburst diagram in Figure 7-7 using the partition layout.

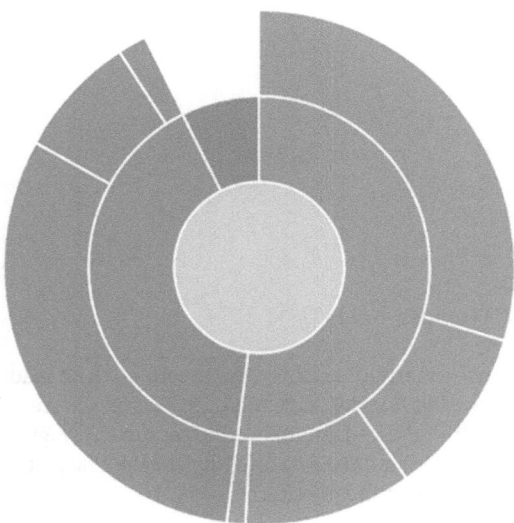

Figure 7-7. *NYC Expenditure plotted in using Partition Layout*

We are going to use two scales, one for distances and one for angles, as follows:

```
var partition = d3.layout.partition();
var radiusScale = d3.scale.linear().domain([0,1]).range([0,0.5*Math.min(w,h)]);
var angleScale = d3.scale.linear().domain([0,1]).range([0,2*Math.PI]);
```

Here is the rest of the code, followed by the explanation.

```
// Create an arc generator, using the defined scales.
var arc = d3.svg.arc()

            .innerRadius(function(d){
              return radiusScale(d.y);
            })
            .outerRadius(function(d){
              return radiusScale(d.y+d.dy);
            })
            .startAngle(function(d){
              return angleScale(d.x);
            })
            .endAngle(function(d){
              return angleScale(d.x+d.dx);
            });

// Draw the arcs using the arc generator,
// in combination with the partition layout
svg.selectAll("path")
   .data(partition(nybudget))
   .enter()
   .append("path")
```

```
.attr("d", arc)
.attr("fill", function(d,i){
   if (d.depth < 2){
     return colors(d.name);
   } else {
     return colors(d.parent.name);
   }
})
.attr("stroke", "#FFFFFF")
.attr("stroke-width", "2px")
.attr("transform", "translate("+(margin+w/2)+","+(margin+h/2)+")");
```

We need an arc generator to draw the arcs. Its parameters—innerRadius, outerRadius, etc—will be read from the data after it is being processed by the layout. Hence, we use d.x, d.y, d.dx and d.dy; dx and d.y are used for startAngle and innerRadius respectively, while d.x+d.dx and d.y+d.dy are used to set the endAngle and outerRadius. Notice, how we are using the scales we just created, radiusScale and angleScale. The rest of the code where paths are created is almost identical to the one used for the pie chart.

■ **Note** that the parent-child relationships in Figure 7-7 is represented in layers. Inner circles represent parents, and the outer circles represent their children; sub-department here. This layered representation of the data helps the reader of your chart explore it one layer at a time. Additionally, its pie-chart-like structure helps them see the size of each child node in comparison to its parent, which is not possible in Figure 7-6, for example.

Changing the initial range of the radiusScale into anything greater than zero and less than 0.5*Math. min(w,h) will convert the pie-like chart into a donut-like one. Similarly, changing the range of the angleScale to other values can convert the circular shape into a semicircular one. They can range between -0.5 π and 0.5 π, or maybe between 0.25 between 0.25 π and 0.75 π. See Figure 7-8 for some examples.

Figure 7-8. *The effect of scale parameters on shape created using Partition Layout*

Stacking Stuff in Layers

Next is the stack layout. You have already seen how to create bar charts, line charts and area charts, but what if we want to use these charts to represent more than one variable?

One way is to have the variables represented via overlapping areas, as in Figure 7-9. Make the areas a little bit transparent so readers can tell each from the other.

USA Energy Consumption by Source (1949–2014)

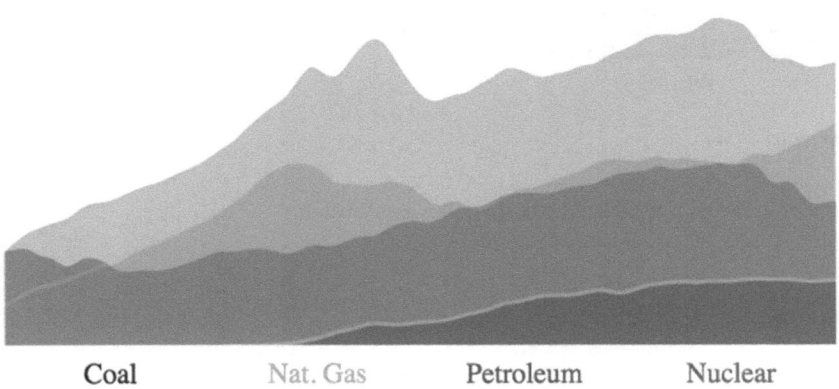

Coal Nat. Gas Petroleum Nuclear

Figure 7-9. *Chart of overlapping areas*

This is useful in comparing variables. The consumption of petroleum is way more than anything else, and is not declining. Natural gas and coal are more or less the same, while electricity from nuclear energy is the least. However, it is not easy to tell whether the overall energy consumption, regardless of its source, is increasing or decreasing, and what is the rate of that increase. This is an example of where it is helpful to stack the areas on top of each other. Obviously, there is another issue; as colors are overlapping and it may be hard to tell which is which, however, this can be fixed by decreasing their opacity even more or using a line chart instead of the area chart.

Figure 7-10 represent the same data, yet via stacking our areas on top of each other. The trends of the overall consumption is better represented now. So how do you draw this chart? Take a look at the areas in Figure 7-10: the dark area representing the coal has its y0 values as zeros, and its y1 values vary according to the consumption of coal. It gets a bit trickier with the natural gas. Its y0 should be equal to the y1 of the coal, and its y1 should be the summation of its values as well as the values for the coal. See, we are having a typical problem where layouts is needed to process the data as a whole and calculates the dependencies between the variables for us.

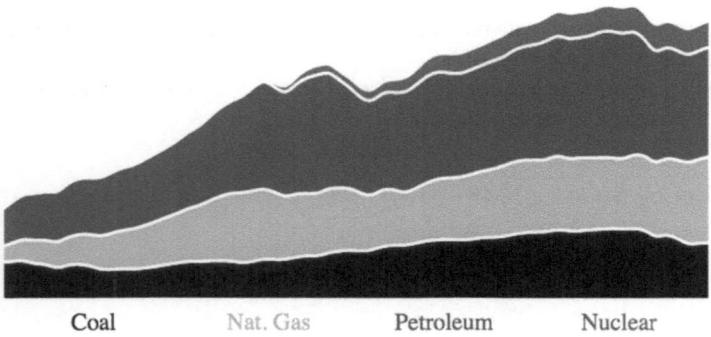

USA Energy Consumption by Source (1949–2014)

Coal   Nat. Gas   Petroleum   Nuclear

Figure 7-10. *A stacked area chart*

For the stack layout to work, it needs our data to be in the following format:

```
var energy = [
  {
    "name": "Coal",
    "values": [
      { "x": 1949, "y":  11.980905},
      { "x": 1950, "y": 12.347109},
        ..etc.
    ]
  },
  {
    "name": "Nat. Gas",
    "values": [
      { "x": 1949, "y":  5.145142},
      { "x": 1950, "y": 5.968371},
        ..etc.
    ]
  },
  ..etc.
];
```

The data is in the form of an array of objects, one object per variable. Each object, in turn, has another array of objects, one per each data point. When given to the stack layout, it will alter the values and add y0 there, which tells where is the lower boundary of the area for the corresponding x.

```
var energy = [
  {
    "name": "Coal",
    "values": [
      { "x": 1949, "y":  11.980905, "y0": 0},
      { "x": 1950, "y": 12.347109, "y0": 0},
        ..etc.
    ]
```

```
  },
  {
    "name": "Nat. Gas",
    "values": [
      { "x": 1949, "y":  5.145142, "y0": 11.980905},
      { "x": 1950, "y": 5.968371, "y0": 12.347109},
        ..etc.
    ]
  },
  ..etc.
];
```

A basic stack layout can be defined and used as follows:

```
var stack = d3.layout.stack().values(function(d){ return d.values; });
var energy_stack = stack(energy);
```

Here is the code for calculating the ranges for x and y and setting their scales accordingly.

```
var w= 690, h = 380;
var h_margin = 20, v_margin = 55;

max_y = d3.max(
  // the y0 for the last element, has the sum of all previous y's
  // thus, we need to add it to its corresponding y, and find max.
  energy_stack[energy_stack.length - 1]["values"],
  function(d){ return d.y0 + d.y; }
)

x_range = energy_stack[0]["values"].filter(function(e,i,a){
    return (i == 0 || i == (a.length - 1)) ? true : false ;
}).map(function(d){
  return d["x"]
});

var x = d3.scale.linear().range([h_margin, w-h_margin]).domain(x_range);
var y = d3.scale.linear().range([h-v_margin, v_margin]).domain([0, max_y]);
```

We will get to data manipulations and arrays handling, a la d3.max(), in chapter 9. Just embrace the charm of method chaining and functional programming for now.

Finally, all is left to do is use an area generator and append the paths, one per each element of the energy stack array:

```
var area = d3.svg.area()
    .interpolate('basis')
    .x(function(d, i) { return x(d.x); })
    .y0(function(d) { return y(d.y0); })
    .y1(function(d) { return y(d.y0 + d.y); });

svg.selectAll(".layer")
      .data(energy_stack)
```

```
  .enter()
  .append("path")
  .attr("class", "layer")
  .attr("d", function(d){
    return area(d["values"]);
  })
  .style("fill", function(d, i){
      // A preset color scale, not shown here
    return colors(i)
  })
  // Note that you can set opacity to shapes.
  // That was more useful in figure 7-9 than here.
  .style("opacity", 0.8)
  .attr("stroke", "#FFF")
  .attr("stroke-width", 3);
```

That's it. Adding the title and labels should be a piece of cake by now. Nevertheless, this is a good opportunity to introduce you to a new scale. Have a look at the labels at the bottom. There are four of them and they are evenly distributed across the horizontal access. For that, we'd use an ordinal scale this time. It works as follows. You assign the scale a domain; an array of n elements. Then, set its rangePoints() to some range. As a result, it will divide the given range into (n-1) parts as in the example below:

```
s = d3.scale.ordinal().domain([0,1,2,3,4]).rangePoints([50,60])
// s(0) will give us 50
// s(1) will give us 52.5
// s(2) will give us 55
// s(3) will give us 57.5
// s(4) will give us 60
```

In Figure 7-10, we initially set the rangePoints between 0 and the width of our drawing area, w. It didn't look that nice, so we tried to keep some margin, and let the range go between 0.15*w and 0.85*w. To dynamically create the array used in the scale's domain from the data; we did the following:

```
energy_stack.map(function(d,i){ return i; });
// returns [0, 1, 2, 3]
```

Stacking Stuff in Circles

As in the partition layouts, nothing prevents us from using the data given to us by the layout however we want. Knowing this, in addition to one new shape we haven't seen yet, radial areas, we can change our code a little bit:

```
// First scale for angles, to be used in the radial area.
var a = d3.scale.linear().domain(x_range)
                         .range([-0.80*Math.PI, 0.80*Math.PI]);
// Second scale is for radii, also used in the radial area.
var r = d3.scale.linear().domain([0, max_y])
                         .range([0, 0.7*h]);
```

```
// Define colors, and the stack layout.
// Then use the layout to transform the weekly_visits data.
var colors = d3.scale.category20c();
var stack = d3.layout.stack()
              .offset('silhouette')
              .values(function(d){  return d.values; });
weekly_visits_stack = stack(weekly_visits);

// Unlike the previous area generator,
// radial area has angles and radii instead of x and y values.
var area = d3.svg.area.radial()
    .interpolate('cardinal')
    .angle(function(d, i){ return a(d.x); })
    .innerRadius(function(d){ return r(d.y0); })
    .outerRadius(function(d){ return r(d.y0 + d.y); });

svg.selectAll("path")
      .data(weekly_visits_stack)
      .enter()
      .append("path")
      .attr("d", function(d){
        return area(d["values"]);
      })
      .style("fill", function(d, i){
        return colors(i);
      })
      .style("opacity", 0.70)
      .on("mouseover", function(d) {
          d3.select(this).style("opacity", 0.95);
       })
      .on("mouseout", function(d) {
          d3.select(this).style("opacity", 0.70);
       })
      .attr("transform", "translate("+(0.5*w)+","+(0.8*h)+")");
```

Running the code should give us the shape in Figure 7-11. The data used to create the shape represents the number of visits to a certain site by day of the week. The actual data, weekly_visits, is not shown here for brevity, yet, it should be formatted as in the energy_stack data in the previous section. Showing your data in a circular form like this can be useful when representing continuous and repetitive events like days of the week.

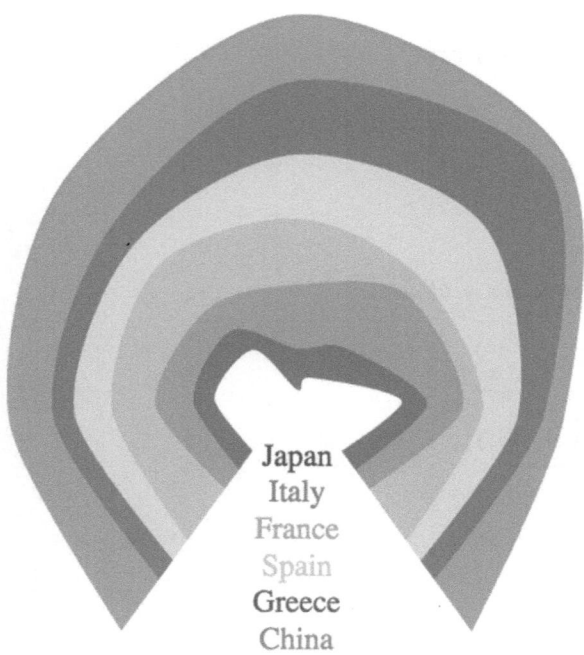

Figure 7-11. *Stacked radial area chart that looks like a Looney Tunes ending, kind of*

The x_range, max_y are also calculated as in the previous section. Furthermore, the code for plotting the text labels is skipped for brevity. We used an ordinal scale as before, where its rangePoints span between 0.2*r(max_y) and 0.6*r(max_y).

Summary

In this chapter you were introduced to layouts. Layouts are D3's way of altering your data and preparing it for different kinds of visualizations, and it is where most of the magic happens. In the next chapter, we are going to continue discovering more layouts, and see how to create our own layouts.

CHAPTER 8

■ ■ ■

Using Advanced Layouts

In this chapter you will be introduced to more advanced layouts. First, you will learn how to create flexible force-directed graphs using the force layout in D3. You will learn the layout's different settings and how they can be used to alter your force-directed graphs. Then you will learn to create your own layouts and use them in your code.

Using the Force Layout (to Move Objects)

I like how, software developer, Jim Vallandingham describes the force layout as "a lazy way to move nodes."[1] In a scatter plot, you have a number of nodes, each represents two variables, thus, you decide to let the x and y positions of each node represent those two variables. By contrast, in the force layout, you have nodes, but this time you specify the forces of attraction and repulsion acting on these nodes, and the layout positions your nodes accordingly. It's physics, my dear.

Like all other layouts, the force layout is used to manipulate data. It does not dictate or interfere in how this data will be visualized. Nevertheless, the force layout is slightly different from the layouts we have discussed so far. Unlike the other layouts, it does not manipulate the data given to it all at once, but rather on stages, i.e. ticks. To clarify, here is some pseudo-code contrasting the differences between the other layouts and the force layout; first some pseudo code for the Pack layout:

```
original_data;
pack = d3.layout.pack();
modified_data = pack(original_data);

nodes = svg.selectAll("circle")
        .data(modified_data)
        .enter().append("circle")
        .attr("cx", function(d,i){ return d.x; })
        .attr("cy", function(d,i){ return d.y; })
        .attr("r", function(d,i){ return d.r; })
```

---

[1]Using and Abusing the Force, https://www.youtube.com/watch?v=Mucmb33711A

© Tarek Amr and Rayna Stamboliyska 2016
T. Amr and R. Stamboliyska, *Practical D3.js*, DOI 10.1007/978-1-4842-1928-7_8

Now, have a look at the following pseudo code for the force layout. After setting the force layout, we pass the data to its node method. Although, it is going to inject x and y values for each element of our data so we can use them in our drawing, we should not expect those values to be available to us right away. That's why when we drew the circles, we just set their radii, omitting their positions for now. Also notice that we are using the original_data still, and not expecting any modified data from the force layout yet. The force layout, however, has an event called tick. Because the data manipulation happens on steps, the tick event is dispatched with each of these steps. In the code here, we tell the force layout to execute some code that sets the nodes cx and cy values with each tick. In more programmatic terms, we are registering a callback function to be called with every tick event. Finally, we have to start the force layout:

```
original_data;
var force = d3.layout.force();
force.nodes(original_data);

nodes = svg.selectAll("circle")
           .data(original_data)
           .enter().append("circle")
           .attr('r', '40');

force.on('tick', function() {
    nodes.attr('cx', function(d) { return d.x; })
           .attr('cy', function(d) { return d.y; });
});
force.start();
```

Now, let's draw the colored circles shown in Figure 8-1 using the force layout.

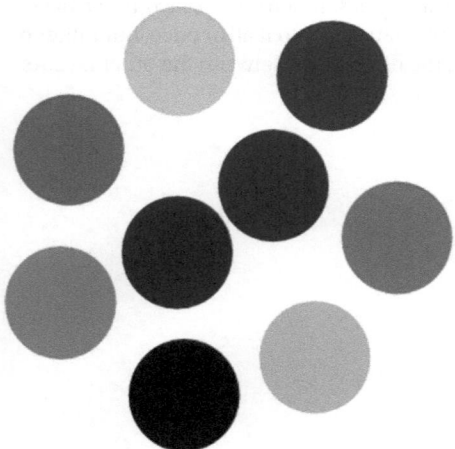

Figure 8-1. *Nine colored circles floating on the screen*

First, set the data and the drawing area as you usually do:

```
var colored_balls_data = [
  {'color': '#000044'}, {'color': '#004444'}, {'color': '#444444'},
  {'color': '#444488'}, {'color': '#448888'}, {'color': '#888888'},
  {'color': '#8888CC'}, {'color': '#88CCCC'}, {'color': '#CCCCCC'},
];

var w= 450, h = 350;
var svg = d3.select('body').append('svg')
            .attr('width', w).attr('height', h);
```

No need to set any x or y parameters for each node, the layout will set them for you when it starts. Next, set the layout and pass the data to it:

```
var force = d3.layout.force()
    .size([w, h])
    .charge(-850)
    .gravity(0.25)
    .nodes(colored_balls_data);
```

The two forces specified here are *charge* and *gravity*. The charge dictates whether the nodes should be attracted to or repelled from each other. A negative charge means they will be repulsive, while a positive value lets them get attracted to each other. The gravity, by contrast, simulates a virtual spring connecting each node to the centre of the drawing area, that is, w/2 and h/2. If not specified, the default charge is –30 and the default gravity is 0.1.

Why do we need to set those two forces, charge and gravity? If you set the two aforementioned forces to 0, all nodes will take the initial random position given to them after the layout is started. In other words, they will be randomly scattered within your drawing area. Not too bad, though, nothing guarantees that none of them might not step on each other's feet. Additionally, you cannot be sure that none of them will be drawn outside the drawing area.

If you keep no gravity and use the default value of charge. All nodes will be repulsive to each other. This means that few nodes will stay in the drawing areas while the rest will be kicked out, thanks to the repulsion. Conversely, if you use a positive charge, nodes will get attracted to each other, and you will end up with clusters where number of nodes are drawn on top of each other.

Having no charge at all, and relying only on gravity will bring all nodes to the centre of the drawing area, in an anti-big-bang fashion. Figure 8-2 shows the aforementioned cases visually.

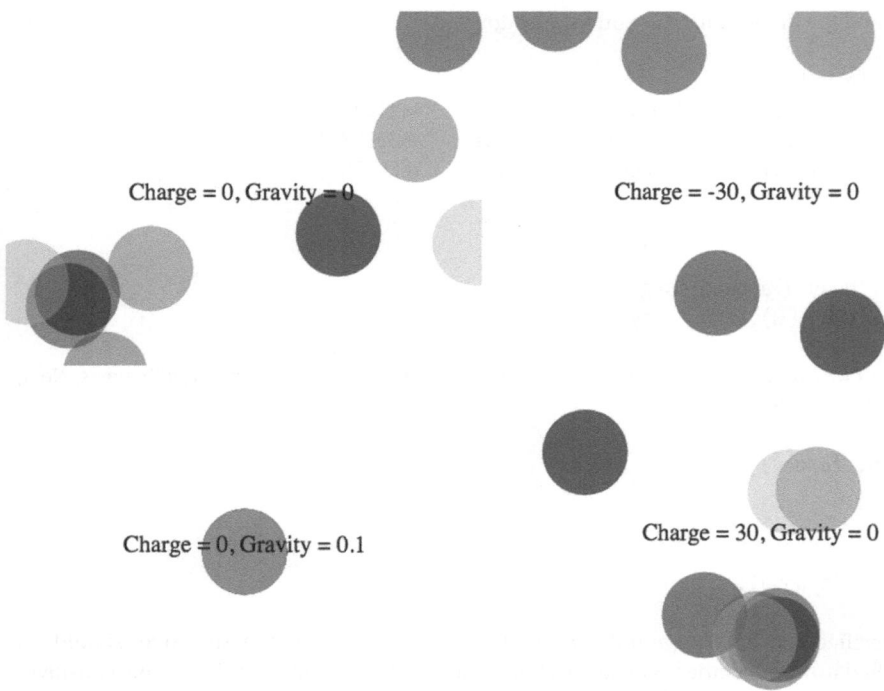

Charge = 0, Gravity = 0

Charge = -30, Gravity = 0

Charge = 0, Gravity = 0.1

Charge = 30, Gravity = 0

Figure 8-2. *The effect of different values of charge and gravity*

The force layout is already set and the original data has been passed to it. Now draw the nodes as usual from the original data, while ignoring their positions for now.

```
var nodes = svg.selectAll('circle')
    .data(colored_balls_data)
    .enter()
    .append('circle')
    .style('fill', function(d,i){ return d.color; });
```

Finally, set the nodes position with each tick and start the force layout in the end:

```
force.on('tick', function() {
    nodes.attr('cx', function(d) { return d.x; })
        .attr('cy', function(d) { return d.y; })
        .attr('r', '40');
});
force.start();
```

Refresh the page and you will see the nodes roaming in your drawing areas till they slowly reach their final positions. Cool, huh?

Which Add-ons Do News Outlets Use?

Websites use different add-ons for tracking users, serving advertisements and offering other functionalities such as social media sharing and commenting. I used a Chrome extension called Ghostery to list the add-ons used by the *Guardian*, the *New York Times*, *Die Zeit*, the *BBC* and *Volkskrant*.

This time you not only want to plot nodes; you also want to plot the relationships between those nodes: which add-on is used by which news website. In other words, you want to plot a bipartite graph, where each of its node can either represent a news website or an add-on, and the links between the nodes represent which add-ons are used by each site. In addition to nodes, the force layout has links, too.

The data for the nodes and the links can be as follows:

```
var nodes = [
        {'type': 'newspaper', 'name': 'Zeit'},
        {'type': 'newspaper', 'name': 'BBC'},
        {'type': 'newspaper', 'name': 'The Guardian'},
        ..
        {'type': 'plugin', 'name': 'Flashtalking'},
        {'type': 'plugin', 'name': 'Integral Ad Science'},
        ..
];
var links = [
        {'source': 0, 'target': 6},
        {'source': 0, 'target': 7},
        {'source': 0, 'target': 16},
        ..
];
```

As shown in the previous section, the format of the nodes array is up to you. The force layout is going to inject some values for each node, such as x, y, and so on. The source and target properties of each link are reference to elements of the nodes array; for example, the element {'source': 0, 'target': 6} means that the first node has link connecting it to the 7th node.

■ **Note** Here's how you can scrap the list of add-ons from the Ghostery extension: open the console of Chrome DevTools inside the Ghostery's interface, and then run the following JavaScript/jQuery code:

```
(function(){
  var addons = [];
  $('.app-div .app-info-container .app-text .app-name')
    .each(function(){ addons.push( $(this).html() ) });
  return addons;
})();
```

To combine combine the scrapped data and transform it into the nodes and links above, you write a script to do the transformation. A Python script is included included in the accompanying CD-ROM.

***Figure 8-3.** A bipartite graph for five news websites and the add-ons they use*

The initialisation of the force layout is not that different from what we described in the previous section. In addition to nodes, you also pass the layout your links array. Among the data the layout injects into the nodes is weight. The weight reflects the number of links each node has. Thus, to keep nodes with many links apart from each other, you let their charge be a function of the weight of each node rather than have constant repulsion charges:

```
var force = d3.layout.force()
    .size([w, h])
    .charge(function(d){
      return - 150*d.weight;
     })
    .gravity(0.35);

force.nodes(nodes);
force.links(links);
```

For the links, use the diagonal generator you used in Chapter 6. Unlike in the previous section, this time you are going to use text for the nodes rather than circles; so you start by drawing the links first so that they do not appear on top of the text:

```
var gen = d3.svg.diagonal();
var link = svg.selectAll("path")
              .data(force.links())
              .enter()
              .append("path")
              .attr("stroke", '#aec7e8')
              .attr("stroke-width", "2px")
              .attr("fill", "none")
              .style("opacity", 0.35);

var node = svg.selectAll('text')
              .data(force.nodes())
              .enter()
              .append('text')
              .text(function(d){
                return d.name;
              })
              .style("text-anchor", "middle")
              .attr('font-size', function(d){
                return (d.type == 'newspaper')? 28 : 14;
              })
              .style("fill", function(d,i){
                return (d.type == 'newspaper')? '#1f77b4' : '#ff7f0e';
              })
              .style("opacity",function(d){
                return (d.type == 'newspaper')? 0.99 : 0.60;
              })
              .call(force.drag);

force.on('tick', function() {
    node.attr('x', function(d) {
            return d.x;
        })
        .attr('y', function(d) {
            return d.y;
        });
    link.attr("d", gen);
});

force.start();
```

The format of the links array is compatible with the diagonal generator, hence, you do not need to set the generator's source and target method as described in Chapter 6. Then, you bind the force.links() array to the paths you create using the generator. You postponed the d attribute of the paths while creating them, as you are going to set it later on with each tick. Similarly, you bind the force.nodes() array to the text nodes, and you postpone the assignment of their x and y values to be done with each tick, too. This way, you let the force layout move your links and nodes around with each tick till they settle down. The .call(force. drag) method enables you to interact with the graph by dragging the nodes and moving them around. Finally, you start the force layout.

You can try different values for charge and gravity. For example, try keeping the charges constant or variable for each node and see the effect of these changes on your graph. Additionally, there is another constraint you can put on links, which is links distance. Its default value is 20, but you can change that to, say, 60 percent of the drawing area's width. If you set the force layout as follows you are going to get the graph in Figure 8-4:

```
var force = d3.layout.force()
    .size([w, h])
    .charge(function(d){
      return (d.type == 'newspaper')? -880 : -80;
      })
    .linkDistance(0.6*w);
    .gravity(0.4);
```

Figure 8-4. *A bipartite graph with links distances being set*

Try dragging the text with your mouse and see how the chart behaves.

A Closer Look at Gravity

We mentioned earlier that gravity, in D3's sense, is what brings the element towards the centre of your drawing area. The D3 documentation explains it as follows, "Near the centre of the layout, the gravitational strength is almost zero, avoiding any local distortion of the layout; as nodes get pushed farther away from the centre, the gravitational strength becomes stronger in linear proportion to the distance."

Still, I haven't shown yet how it is actually implemented. I always advise you to read the source code of the libraries you use, and this is what you are going to do in a moment. But first, a note about a parameter we haven't mentioned yet: alpha.

Surely, you noticed when running any of the previous charts, that all your objects move around your screen trying to reach their final destination. They start moving quickly, then they start to decelerate and move slower and slower till they settle down once they reach their final position. This deceleration happens, thanks to the cooling parameter, alpha.

By default, alpha starts as 0.1, and then it decreases with each tick, till it goes below 0.005 and then things should stop completely. The aforementioned forces such as gravity and charge take the alpha into their considerations with each tick. Here is some code to clarify:

```
if ((alpha *= .99) < .005) {
        event.end({type: "end", alpha: 0});
        return true;
}
```

For each tick, d3 re-calculates alpha; multiplies it by 0.99. Then it checks whether it went below its threshold value; 0.005. If so, it calls event.end() with the following object, {type: "end", alpha: 0}. If the value of alpha is still above 0.005, it applies the different forces on our links and nodes.

The focus here is on gravity. The gravitational parameter is multiplied by the current value of alpha for this tick. Their combined value (k) is what is going to be used to attract the nodes towards the centre of the drawing area:

```
// Set k = alpha * gravity, and check it is not zero
if (k = alpha * gravity) {
        // x = w/2, i.e. centre of the drawing area
        x = size[0] / 2;
        // y = h/2, i.e. centre of the drawing area
        y = size[1] / 2;
        // For each node we set their x and y values as follows
        i = -1;
        if (k) while (++i < n) {
                o = nodes[i];
                // Move nodes towards the centre by a factor of k.
                o.x = o.x + (x - o.x)*k;
                o.y = o.y + (y - o.y)*k;
        }
}
/* Some code is omitted here */
// Then tick event is called, given an object with the new value of alpha
event.tick({type: "tick", alpha: alpha});
```

■ **Note** If a node is already at the center, o.x will be the equal to x, and o.y will be equal to y. Thus, x - o.x = y - o.y = zero, and it will not move, which is the desired behavior of the gravitational force according to the documentation. Conversely, a node that is far from the center will move toward the centre with speed proportion to its distance from the center.

Time to Defy Gravity

Just like astronauts, we are all set to defy gravity. In the next chart we are going to plot the FIFA world cup winners. Each of them will be represented by a bubble whose size is proportional to the number of times they achieved the trophy. The European countries will be represented in blue bubbles, while the Latin American ones will be shown in orange bubbles (see Figure 8-5).

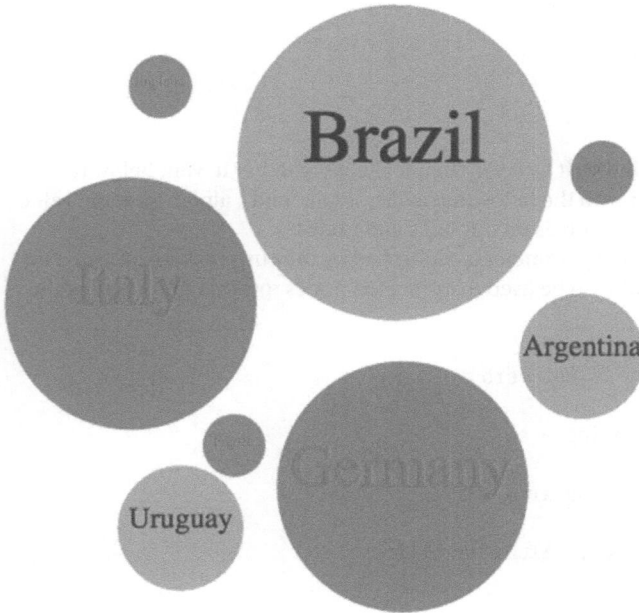

Figure 8-5. *Fifa World Cup winners*

You might be wondering now if a normal force layout with the default centre of gravity can do the trick. Well, there is a catch. When you click on any of the bubbles, you want the European countries; Germany, Italy, England, France and Spain, to cluster around some point to the right, while Brazil, Uruguay and Argentina go the the left (see Figure 8-6).

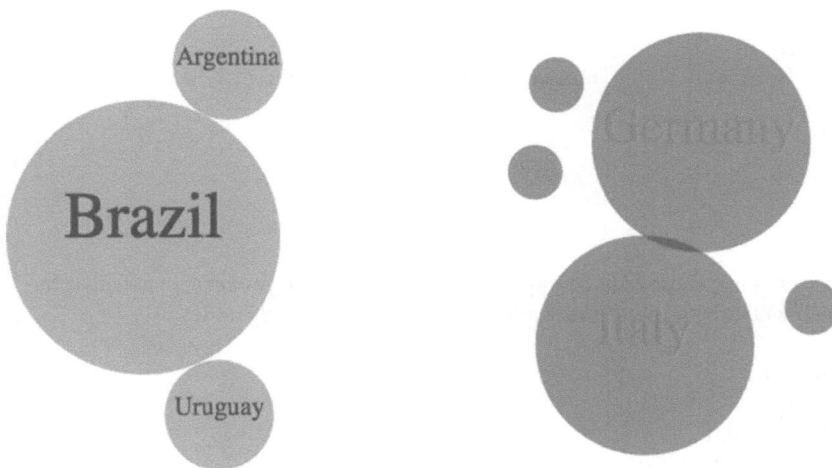

Figure 8-6. *Fifa World Cup winners, by continent*

You need to set the default gravity to zero this time, and implement your own gravity with its varying central points. One click makes its central point (0.5*w, 0.5*h). One more click and you have two central points instead, (0.35*w, 0.5*h) and (0.65*w, 0.5*h) for Americas and Europe, respectively.

Here is the data:

```
var cup_winners = [
  {'country': 'Brazil', 'wins': 5, 'continent': 'Americas'},
  {'country': 'Germany', 'wins': 4, 'continent': 'Europe'},
  {'country': 'Italy', 'wins': 4, 'continent': 'Europe'},
  {'country': 'Argentina', 'wins': 2, 'continent': 'Americas'},
  {'country': 'Uruguay', 'wins': 2, 'continent': 'Americas'},
  {'country': 'France', 'wins': 1, 'continent': 'Europe'},
  {'country': 'England', 'wins': 1, 'continent': 'Europe'},
  {'country': 'Spain', 'wins': 1, 'continent': 'Europe'},
];
```

For this example, you need a JavaScript object. JavaScript objects are how the language enables you to write object-oriented code. This object can have two modes, *single* and *double*. When the mode is *single*, its focus method should return one focal point regardless of the continent a country is in. That focal point is just the midpoint of your drawing area. When the mode is switched to *double*, the focus method will give you one of two focal points depending on the continent. Have a look at the object in question:

```
var cup_chart = {
  mode: 'single',
  toggle_mode: function(){
    this.mode = (this.mode == 'single')? 'double' : 'single';
  },
```

```
    focus: function(continent){
      if (this.mode == 'double'){
        return (continent == 'Americas')? {'x': 0.35*w ,'y': 0.5*h} : {'x': 0.65*w ,'y': 0.5*h};
      } else {
        return {'x': 0.5*w ,'y': 0.5*h}
      }
    }
};
```

The drawing area will be set as in the previous examples, same for the force layout except for the value of the gravitational force which will be set to zero. You don't have links this time, only nodes:

```
var force = d3.layout.force()
              .size([w, h])
              .charge(function(d){
                  return -120*d.wins*d.wins;
              })
              .gravity(0);

force.nodes(cup_winners);
```

Next comes the code for creating the bubbles and their text. For brevity, we've omitted the parts of the code setting their style. The fill style is set here to #ff7f0e for Americas, and to #1f77b4 otherwise:

```
var node_shape = svg.selectAll('circle')
      .data(force.nodes())
      .enter()
      .append('circle')
      .attr('r', function(d){
        return 19*d.wins;
      })
      .on('click', function(){
        cup_chart.toggle_mode();
        // restarting the layout with each click
        force.start();
      });

var node_text = svg.selectAll('text')
      .data(force.nodes())
      .enter()
      .append('text')
      .text(function(d){
        return d.country;
      });
```

For the bubbles, you are registering a callback function to be executed on the click event. There you first toggle the chart's mode, and then you force the force (that's not a typo) to restart.

So far, you have no gravity. You need to implement it within each tick, by imitating the internal d3 code shown earlier. The tick callback function is handed an object containing the current value of alpha. Thus, you can easily get that value and multiply it by whatever gravitational force you set. A gravitational force of 0.2 did work for me well this time. You can try changing that and see the effect. Then, you need to loop over each item of the data, cup_winners, and change their x and y values in a similar fashion to what d3 internally does. After that, you need to move the circles and text around accordingly:

```
force.on('tick', function(e) {

    var gravity = 0.2;
    var k = gravity * e.alpha;

    cup_winners.forEach(function(o, i) {
        o.x = o.x + (cup_chart.focus(o.continent).x - o.x) * k;
        o.y = o.y + (cup_chart.focus(o.continent).y - o.y) * k;
    });

    node_shape.attr('cx', function(d) {
            return d.x;
        })
        .attr('cy', function(d) {
            return d.y;
        });

    node_text.attr('x', function(d) {
            return d.x;
        })
        .attr('y', function(d) {
            return d.y;
        });

});
```

Finally, don't forget to start your force layout after you are done. This will draw the initial chart:

```
force.start();
```

───

■ **Note** After creating the force layout and starting it, you should be able to restart it again whenever someone clicks on one of the bubbles. Restarting the layout is what makes the nodes move to their new destinations, guided by the gravity. Restarting the layout is handled by the callback function registered for each circle using the .on('click', ...) method.

───

Creating Your Own Layouts

One rant you might hear sometimes about d3, is that you need to reinvent the wheel every time you create a basic bar chart or scatter plot. The truth is that you can encapsulate the code for these charts in your own layout and re-use it whenever you need it. In this section we are going to create a custom layout, and use it like we used the built-in layouts earlier. First, however, we need to discuss some JavaScript concepts. These concepts will help you have a d3-like interface for your new layout. If you are an experienced JavaScript guru, feel free to quickly skim through these subsections.

Method Chaining

In object-oriented programming, you tend to have objects with attributes, and methods for setting those attributes. Throughout your code, you need to edit those attributes. D3 is not any different here. You might have an object representing a shape on your screen, and you need to set its width or height or any of its styling attributes as well. Take the following rectangle object as an example:

```
var rectangle = d3.select("rect");
```

Rather than writing the following four lines of code:

```
rectangle.attr("y", 0);
rectangle.attr("x", 0);
rectangle.attr("width", 100);
rectangle.attr("height", "20");
```

Method chaining allows you to do the same task using a more concise code as follows:

```
rectangle.attr("y", 0).attr("x", 0).attr("width", 100).attr("height", "20");
```

If you think about it, the attr() method belongs to the rectangle object. Thus, if you let it return the same object after it is done setting the values given to it, you can use the same object over and over again. Let's try to simulate that for a new object, say car:

```
var car = {
  wheels: 4,
  color: 'red'
};
```

Time to add a method to the car object for setting its attributes:

```
car.attr = function(key, value){
  switch(key) {
    case 'wheels':
        // set car's wheels
        this.wheels = value;
        break;
    case 'color':
        // set car's color
        this.color = value;
        break;
```

```
    default:
        // Let's catch undefined attribute
        console.log('Unknown attributes!')
    }
    // return the car object back
    // that's the essence of method chaining
    return this;
};
```

Now, you can write the following code. The first time we call attr('wheel', 6), it returns the car object, which you use to call its attr() once more:

```
car.attr('wheels', 6).attr('color', ' blue');
```

In d3, methods are both setters and getters. In other words, you want car.attr('wheels', 6) to set the number of wheels to 6, while car.attr('wheels') returns the current number of wheels. Thus, tweak your method as follows:

```
car.attr = function(key, value){
  switch(key) {
    case 'wheels':
        if (arguments.length < 2){
          // get car's wheels
          return this.wheels;
        }
        // set car's wheels
        this.wheels = value;
        break;
    case 'color':
        if (arguments.length < 2){
          // get car's color
          return this.color;
        }
        // set car's color
        this.color = value;
        break;
    default:
        // Unknown attribute
        console.log('Unknown attributes!')
    }
    // return the car object back
    return this;
};
```

consequently, we can use it as follows:

```
car.attr('wheels');       // returns 4
car.attr('wheels', 6);    // sets wheels to 6, and returns car object
car.attr('wheels');       // returns 6
car.attr('color');        // returns 'red'
```

Do you think something like, `car.attr('wheels').attr('color')`, is going to work or not? As you can see in the definition of the car object, the `.attr()` methods returns a reference to the object, only when it is used as a setter. When used as a getter it returns the value of the attribute in question. In this case, the first call to `.attr()` is used as a getter and should return the number of wheels, which doesn't have an `.attr()` method of its own. Thus, the line above is going to give you an error.

Nested Functions and Closure

In JavaScript, functions are first-class citizens. A function can take another function as an argument, and it also can return another function. In the next example, you are going to create one function, `outer`, and let it create another function, `inner`, and return it:

```
var outer = function(x){
  var sub_total = x;
  var inner = function(y){
    return sub_total + y;
  }
  return inner;
};

var sub = outer(100);    // assigns inner to sub
sub(50);                 // returns 150 (100+50)
```

■ **Note**   that the `inner` function has access to the variables defined by the `outer` function, that is, `sub_total`. That behaviour is what is called *closure* in functional programming.

Array Map and Reduce Methods

The `map()` method when called on an array, given some callback function, it will apply that function to each element of that array, and return the new array back:

```
var myarray = [1,2,3,4];
var transform = function(d,i,a){ return d + 20; }
myarray.map(transform); // returns [21, 22, 23, 24]
```

The callback function is given three arguments; the current item it is dealing with (we called it d here), the index of that item in the array (i) and the whole array (a).

The reduce method, by contrast, works as follows. To get the sum of all elements of an array, you use the following code:

```
var myarray = [1,2,3,4];
var transform = function(x, y){ return x+y; }
myarray.reduce(transform); // returns 10, calculated as follows: (((1+2)+3)+4)
```

"Meatballs" Layout

You are all set now to create a custom layout. For this example, rather than bars, you want to represent your data as a series of circles (or "meatballs") whose sizes represent the values of the data (see Figure 8-7).

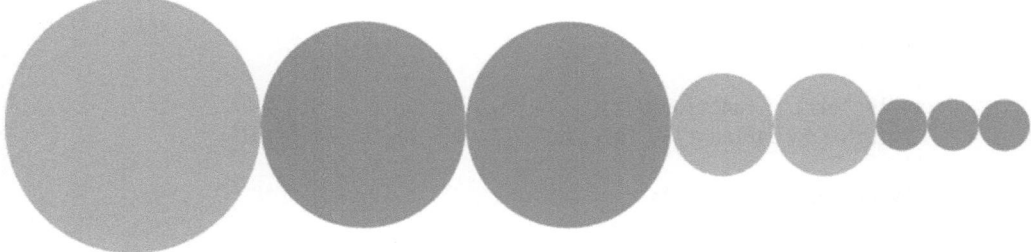

Figure 8-7. *Fifa World Cup winners, using our new meatballs layout*

Start by deciding how you want to use the layout, then go on and create the internal code for the layout. Using the same cup_winners data you used earlier in this chapter. Thankfully, the data is already sorted by the number of wins, otherwise, you are going to learn in the next chapter how to sort data. Now, you can use the newly created layout as follows:

```
var w = 640, h = 420;

var svg = d3.select('body').append('svg')
    .style("background", "#FFF")
    .attr('width', w)
    .attr('height', h);
// Setting the meatballs layout.
// Since our data elements look like this:
// {'country': 'Italy', 'wins': 4, .. }
// We need to tell the layout to extract values from the wins attribute
// We finally let the layout know the width and height of our drawing area
var meatballs = mylayout.meatballs()
    .value(function(d){
        return d.wins;
    })
    .size([w, h]);

// We then apply the layout to our data
// It will attach x, y and r values to each data item
var transformed_data = meatballs.cook(cup_winners);

// Use the transformed data to draw the circles
var node = svg.selectAll('circle')
                .data(transformed_data)
                .enter()
                .append('circle')
```

```
             .attr('cx', function(d){
               return d.x;
              })
             .attr('cy', function(d){
               return d.y;
              })
             .attr('r', function(d){
               return d.r;
              })
             .style("fill", function(d,i){
               return (d.continent == 'Americas')? '#ff7f0e' : '#1f77b4';
              })
             .style("opacity", 0.55);
```

Obviously, before using the previous code, you need to write the actual layout code. In case you are going to write a number of layouts, you need to package them altogether. Thus, you create a namespace object, call it mylayout, and put your meatballs and any other future layouts inside it:

```
var mylayout = {};
```

Then you define the meatballs function. This is somehow like a construction function that does the initial housekeeping of defining some default variables, and create an object attaching methods to it. First the code for the function, then the explanation:

```
mylayout.meatballs = function(){

    // define balls object, we will assign all methods to it
    var balls = {};
    // default method for extracting values from array items
    var value = function(d){
        return d.value
    };
    // like in d3, default size is 1x1 px
    var size = [1,1];

    balls.cook = function(data){
        // calculate the sum of all array items
        var sum = data.map(function(d, i){
            return value(d);
        }).reduce(function(a,b){
            return a+b;
        });
        // offset each circle after all previous ones
        var offset = 0;
        // transform given data;
        // add x, y and r to each item of it
        // then return the transformed data back
        return data.map(function(d, i) {
            r = 0.5* value(d) * size[0] / sum;
```

```
            d.r = r;
            d.x = offset + r;
            d.y = size[1]/2;
            offset += 2 * r;
            return d;
        });
    }

    // layout size getter and setter
    balls.size = function(x){
        if (!arguments.length) return size;
        size = x;
        // for method chaining in case of setter
        return balls;
    }

    // layout value extraction function getter and setter
    balls.value = function(x){
        if (!arguments.length) return value;
        value = x;
        // for method chaining in case of setter
        return balls;
    }

    // return balls object
    return balls;
}
```

That is one hell of a long function. When you call mylayout.meatballs(), it will set its initial variables (balls, value and size). The value() function is used to extract values from the data array given to the layout. By default, it extracts the value attribute from each array item, however, users can override that as you have done earlier. Size defaults to [1,1] for width and height respectively. The balls object is initially defined as a empty object, though, right after that, you go on an attach some methods to it (cook, size and value). The methods size() and value() are getters and setters for the size and value attributes, respectively. Note how we check the number of parameters given to decide whether they should behave as getters or setters. If no parameters are given, they return the current value of the corresponding attribute, otherwise, you set the corresponding attributes using the given value and return the balls object back to allow further method chaining. The cook method is what is used to transform a given data, decide the corresponding x, y, and r values to each item of it. In our case here, x and y determine the central point of each circle, while r determines its radius.

All methods are attached to the newly created object, balls. That's why the meatballs method returns that object back to us when done. Thus, you can easily chain all your method calls from there. Note that you were able to write something like this earlier—mylayout.meatballs(). value(...).size(...)—thanks to that.

Obviously, that's not the only way to define a layout. You can now check the d3's source code and see how the layouts you used in this chapter and the previous one are actually created. The internal code for the force layout is conceptually different from the stack layout, yet both of them from outside follow the same convention for a consistent user interface. Hat tip to Mike Bostock, for designing such a good interface.

Mixing Layouts

Figure 8-7 looks like a bit of a mess: it has no labels and no one can tell which ball represents which country. Yet, it's relatively easy to improve upon the chart, not by adding textual labels, but by painting the balls according to the colors of each team's jersey (see Figure 8-8). Here's how: Each team will get a donut. Donuts will have four sectors. The top and bottom sectors, each occupy 40 percent of the whole circle; while each of the remaining two sectors occupy 10 percent. In other words, all the donuts will have the same data array, [4,1,4,1].

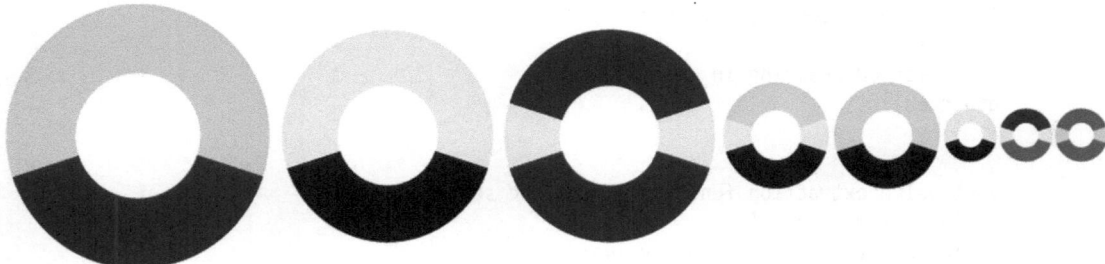

Figure 8-8. *Fifa World Cup winners, using colorful meatballs*

First, change the cup_winners array and add the colors for each country in the form of subarray of colors as follows:

```
var cup_winners = [
  {
    'country': 'Brazil', 'wins': 5,
    'colors': ['#fdd835','#fdd835','#0d47a1','#fdd835']
  },
  {
    'country': 'Germany', 'wins': 4,
    'colors': ['#eeeeee','#eeeeee', '#212121', '#eeeeee']
  },
  {
    'country': 'Italy', 'wins': 4,
    'colors': ['#0d47a1', '#eeeeee', '#0d47a1', '#eeeeee']
  },
  {
    'country': 'Argentina', 'wins': 2,
    'colors': ['#b3e5fc','#eeeeee','#212121','#eeeeee']
  },
  ..
];
```

For brevity, we omitted the remaining four items of the array, Uruguay, England, France and Spain. Don't forget to add them to your code and set their color arrays accordingly. The next step is to define two layouts, the meatballs and the pie layout as follows:

```
var meatballs = d3.layout.meatballs()
    .value(function(d){ return d.wins; })
    .size([w, h]);

var pie = d3.layout.pie()
    // moving the start angle a bit to the left
    .startAngle(-0.4*Math.PI)
    // making sure we have a full circle still
    .endAngle(1.6*Math.PI)
    // do not re-order sectors
    .sort(null);
```

As you have seen in the previous chapter, you also need an arc generator to create the donuts. We will explain in a moment why all arcs have inner and outer radii less than 1:

```
var arc = d3.svg.arc()
            .innerRadius(0.45)
            .outerRadius(0.95);
```

To draw the actual chart, we are going to transform the data using the meatballs cook() method. Then we will loop through the transformed data. For each item, we are going to create a donut chart. Then we are going to move the donuts to the points determined by the meatballs layout. We also scale them using the radii determined by the outer layout, that is, meatballs.

Note that before getting to this point, we had no clue how big each donut should be, thus, we set the initial arc to have a unit radius and postponed its scaling to be done by the transformation function later. To keep some margin between the donuts, we set the ouster radius a little bit less than 1, 0.95. Try changing this to other values between 0 and 1 and see the effect on your donuts. You can also set the inner radius to 0 and convert your donut into a pie.

The data array given to the pie layout, [4,1,4,1] is to create the four colored sectors for each country. We color each sector using the corresponding color in subarray: colors[i]:

```
meatballs.cook(cup_winners).forEach(function(d,i){
    // Each donut will have its own CSS class.
    // Let's call them after the country names.
    var cssclass = d.country;
    // Grab the array of colors in a variable,
    // so we can use it few lines later.
    var colors = d.colors;

    svg.selectAll(cssclass)
        .data(pie([4,1,4,1]))
        .enter()
        .append('path')
```

```
      .attr('class', cssclass)
      .attr("d", arc)
      .attr("fill", function(d,i){
        return colors[i];
       })
      .attr("transform", "translate("+ d.x +","+ d.y +") scale(" + d.r + ")");

});
Fascinating; isn't it?
```

Summary

In this chapter you learned about the force layout. You have seen how to tweak its gravity and charges, and how to replace the default central point of gravity with your own. Jim Vallandingham has a nice video about abusing the force layout, he also tried replacing the default charge with a collision detection algorithm. We advise you to watch his video, you can find a link to it in the footnotes of this chapter. Finally, you explored the world of creating our own layouts and mixing multiple layouts together.

CHAPTER 9

Working with Data

In this chapter you are going to learn how to load data from external websites. More specifically, you learn how to transform the data between different formats and do some slicing and dicing to the data before visualizing it.

Using Third-Party Data

Up to now, we provided our own data to visualize. In real life, we may also want to visualize data published by other people. Governments and many web applications nowadays publish their data via public APIs, and we may need to get this data on the fly by accessing those APIs, thus our visualizations are updated in real time, whenever the publisher pushed more data or updates the numbers.

Data publishers can provide their data in a plethora of formats such as JSON (JavaScript Object Notation), CSV (comma-separated values), XLS (Microsoft Excel file format), or PDF. JSON and CSV are the easiest formats to deal with, for two reasons: they both are open formats, which means that developers can easily create libraries to process them; and they are machine readable. Excel files are machine readable but not open, while PDF files are not machine readable, which makes them the hardest ones to deal with.

In the next section you are going to learn how to load external data in CSV format, do some basic manipulation to it before putting it into a bar chart.

Charting the Global Gender Gap

The Global Gender Gap Index was first introduced by the World Economic Forum in 2006 as a framework measuring the gap between men and women. The index has four categories (subindexes): Economic participation and opportunity, educational attainment, health and survival, and political empowerment. One hundred forty-two countries were covered in the report of 2014. The report is originally published in a number of PDF files, but thanks to data journalist Alice Corona, a machine-readable version of it is now online.

It is always good if data publishers release their data in machine-readable formats. Unfortunately, it is not always the case, that's why—as explained in Chapter 4—data cleaning and data scraping skills are important for those who analyse and visualize data.

T. Amr and R. Stamboliyska, *Practical D3.js*, DOI 10.1007/978-1-4842-1928-7_9

D3 provides a method for loading external CSV data. It works as follows. You give it the URL for the data you want to load, in addition to two optional functions; let's call them access() and callback(). The access() is called for each data row. This way you can manipulate those rows of data before the next step. The callback is how you tell D3 to go fetch the data for you, and call you back whenever it has it. In other words, it is an asynchronous method. Don't worry, the next brief example should make it all clearer.

Let's say we have the following CSV table, which is published on the imaginary web link, http://website.com/data.csv. The first line specifies the names of the columns. Let's call that line header. The following four lines are the data rows. In our case here, we have three columns, "Country," "Overall – Rank," and "Overall – Score." For the Bahamas, its overall rank is 35 and its overall score is 0.7269, while Côte d'Ivoire is ranked 136 with an overall score of 0.5874:

```
Country,Overall - Rank,Overall - Score
Bahamas,35,0.7269
Côte d'Ivoire,136,0.5874
Egypt,129,0.6064
Syria,139,0.5775
```

Now, execute the following code:

```
var url = 'https://raw.githubusercontent.com/ali-ce/datasets/master/Global-Gender-Gap-
Index-2014/Country%20Main%20Indices.csv';
var access = function(d){
  return {
    country: d['Country'],
    // The second parameter for parseInt, specifies the numeral system to be used for conversion.
    // In old browsers, the default was 8 (octal system), and it's 10 (decimal system) in
    newer browsers.
    rank: parseInt(d['Overall - Rank'], 10),
  };
}
var callback = function(error, rows) {
  if (error){
    console.log(error.responseText);
    return;
  }
  console.log(rows);
}
d3.csv(url, access, callback);
```

The access function will be called for each data row. The rows will be given to it in the form of a hash map as follows: {'Country': 'Bahamas' , 'Overall - Rank': '35' , 'Overall - Score': '0.7269'}. Note how column names are used as keys, while all values are converted to strings. In the example, we omit the overall scores, and convert the ranks from strings to integers. The callback function will be given the rows after they have been manipulated by access. Thus, they will only have county and rank as a string and integer, respectively. Therefore, we are going to have the following array if objects (maps) logged onto our console, [{'country': 'Bahamas' , 'rank': 35}, {'country': 'Côte d'Ivoire' , 'rank': 136}, ...]

Now it's time to draw the actual data for the Global Gender Gap Index. We are going to plot the high-income countries only. Countries will be colored according the the regions to which they belong. Figure 9-1 shows the result.

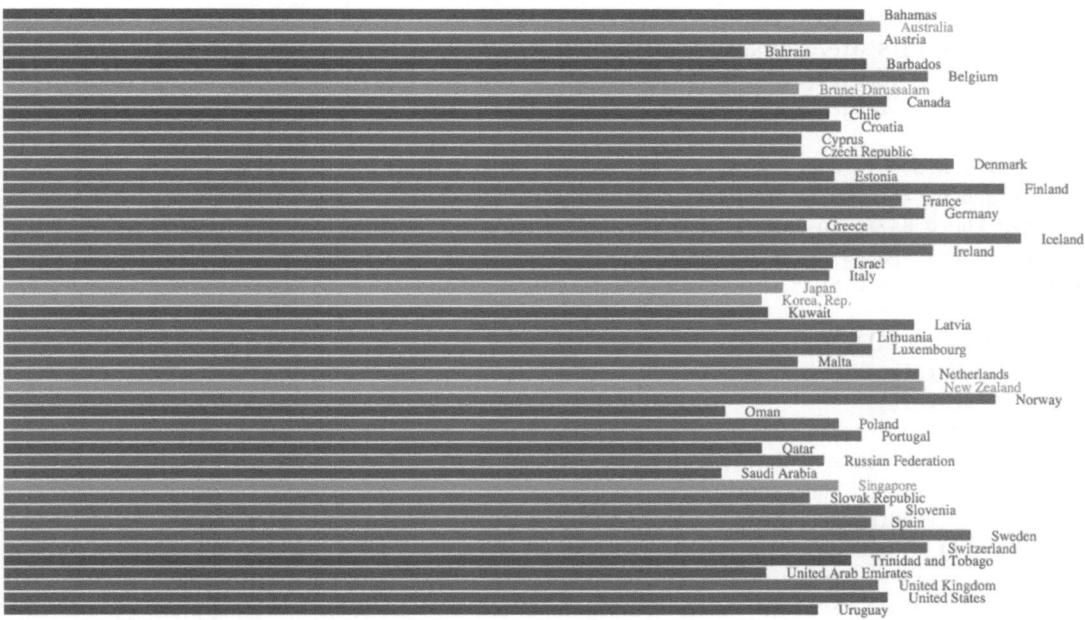

Figure 9-1. *The Global Gender Gap Index (High Income Countries)*

First, define the drawing area and color palette. Additionally, define a variable, url, to hold the link to the cleaned version of our data.

```
var w = 1200, h = 620, margin = 20;
var svg = d3.select('body').append('svg')
            .attr('width', w).attr('height', h);

var colors = d3.scale.category10();

var url = 'https://raw.githubusercontent.com/ali-ce/datasets/master/Global-Gender-Gap-
Index-2014/Country%20Main%20Indices.csv'
```

The rest of the code is shown here. As we said earlier, d3.csv() is asynchronous. When called it returns immediately, then when the HTTP request is done and the data is available it invokes the callback method. To make the code more readable, we are going to put all the logic for drawing the bars into a draw() function. The callback method should call the draw method and passes the obtained data to it. Further explanations will come right after the code here:

```
var draw = function(rows){

  // Scores are between 0 and 1, hence xScale
  var xScale = d3.scale.linear()
                .domain([0, 1])
                .range([margin, w-margin]);
```

```
  // We want our bars to occupy the whole vertical area
  var yScale = d3.scale.ordinal()
                  .domain(rows.map(function(d,i){ return i; }))
                  .rangePoints([margin, h-margin]);

  // A bar's width is equal to the hight without the margin,
  // divided by the number of rows in our data.
  // Then the 0.85 is to make it a little bit less,
  // so we have spaces between bars.
  var bars_widths = 0.85 * (h - 2*margin) / rows.length;

  bar = svg.selectAll('bar')
          .data(rows)
          .enter()
          .append('rect')
          .attr('class', 'bar')
          .attr('x', function(d,i){
             return xScale(0);
           })
          .attr('y', function(d,i){
             return yScale(i);
           })
          .attr('width', function(d,i){
             return xScale(d.score) - xScale(0);
           })
          .attr('height', function(d,i){
             return bars_widths;
           })
          .attr("fill", function(d,i){
             return colors(d.region);
           });

}


d3.csv(url, function(d){
  return {
    country: d['Country'],
    // We convert income group from '1 (High Income)' to '1'
    income: d['Income Group'].split(' ')[0],
    region: d['Region'],
    // Scores are between 0 and 1.
    score: d['Overall - Score'],
  };
}, function(error, rows) {
  // In case of error, print error message and exit
  if (error) {
    console.log(error.responseText);
    return;
  }
  // We call the draw function defined earlier.
  // We use filter to plot high income countries only.
```

```
draw(
  rows.filter(function(d,i){
    return (d.income == '1');
  })
);
});
```

We will explain the d3.csv() part first. The first function is for manipulating the data. It returns four columns only—"country," "income," "region," and "score"—and omits all other columns. We also changed the column names from "Income Group" and "Overall – Score" to just "income" and "score," respectively. Values for income are converted from something such as '1 (High Income)' to just '1.' The second function takes the resulting data, rows. Filter out anything with income not equal to '1,' then calls the drawing function with the remaining data rows.

The filter function works as follows. It is applied to an array and is given a callback function. The callback function is called for each element of the array. If you return true in your callback function the element is kept in the array; if false is returned, the element is removed, or filtered out of the new array returned array by filter, that is, [1, 2, 3, 4].filter(function(d){ return (d==2)? false: true;}); should return [1, 3, 4].

The draw() function is not any different from how you used to draw things in the previous chapters. We added some comments to the code, and omitted the part for adding the country labels for brevity.

Sorting the data by score, as shown in Figure 9-2, may make it clearer if some regions have higher scores than others. In this case, we just need to sort data before calling the draw function as in the following code snippet:

```
draw(
  rows.filter(function(d,i){
    return (d.income == '1');
  }).sort(function(a,b){
    return (a.score == b.score)? 0 : ((a.score > b.score)? -1 : 1);
  })
);
```

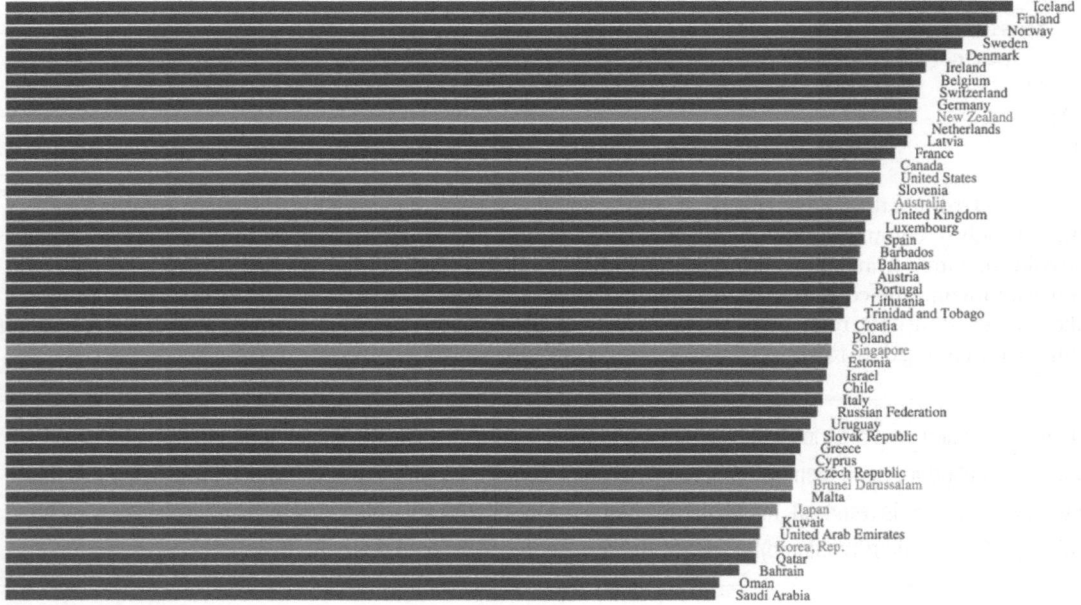

Figure 9-2. *The Global Gender Gap Index (High Income Countries, sorted by score)*

Rather than sorting the data, you can also sort your d3 selections. Do not sort the data this time, and add the following code into your draw() function and see what will happen. Notice, how the durations of the transitions varies among bars, so they appear as if they are moving one after the other. And do not forget to sort your labels if you have them, too:

```
bar.on('click',function(){
  bar.sort(function(a,b){
    return (a.score == b.score)? 0 : ((a.score > b.score)? 1 : -1);
  })
  .transition()
  .duration(function(d,i){ return 80 * i;  })
  .attr('y', function(d,i){
    return yScale(i);
  });
});
```

To give you the ability to decide how you want to sort your selections, the sort() method takes a function with two parameters. While comparing each pair of elements, sort will call your function passing the pair of elements being compared as your function's parameters. If you return '-1' (or any negative value), then you want 'a' to come before 'b'. If a positive value is returned, then 'a' should come after 'b'; otherwise, 'a' and 'b' are considered equal and the order is arbitrary. In the example here, we compared the scores of the elements, and returned '-1', '0' or '1' accordingly.

Charting the Top Music Tracks

Last.fm tracks what music people listen to. This makes it interesting to use their API to determine which musicians are popular at the moment. In the next chart we are going to plot the top 50 tracks in a scatter plot (see Figure 9-3). The x-axis shows the number of individual users listening to each track, while the y-axis shows the total number of times it has been played. We are going to give tracks by the same musician the same color.

Top Tracks by Last.fm

Listing the top 50 tracks

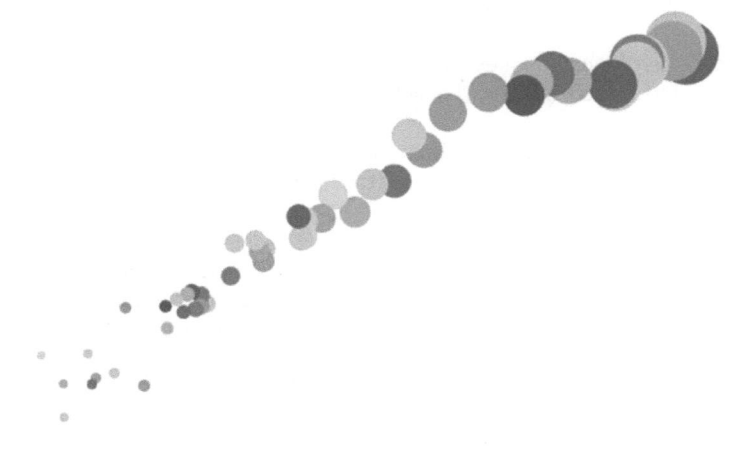

Figure 9-3. *Last.fm top 50 tracks*

To make things more interactive, we also added a slider at the bottom. One can use that slider to say, "I only want to plot a subset of those top 50 tracks, and push the remaining dots out of the drawing area." The following snippet specifies the body of the HTML page:

```
<body>
  <h1>Top Tracks by Last.fm</h1>
  <h3 id='top_label'></h3>
  <div id='svg-container'></div><br/>
  <input type="range" id="slider" style="width: 660;"
      min="0" max="10" value="10" step="1"
      onchange="filter(this.value)" />
</body>
```

Initially, the top_label will have "Listing top 50 tracks." When you reduce the number of tracks shown using the slider, the label should be changed accordingly. Additionally, when you hover on one of the dots, the label should show the tracks name as well as the musician behind it. The svg-container is where we are going to add out SVG tag in, that is, our drawing area. The slider's id is slider. Once data is loaded, its maximum value will be set to the number of tracks retrieved, that is, 50. We are going to use the filter() function whenever the slider is changed.

Now, let's move to the JavaScript code. First, as always, you need to set the drawing area and other variables:

```
var w = 660, h = 450, margin = 80;
var nodes = null, labels = null;
var all_tracks = [];
var colors = d3.scale.category20();

var svg = d3.select('#svg-container').append('svg')
            .attr('width', w).attr('height', h);

// Last.fm API, You'll need to use your own key instead.
var url = 'http://ws.audioscrobbler.com/2.0/?method=chart.gettoptracks&api_key=YOUR-OWN-KEY-
HERE&format=json'
// If you don't want to create a key, you can replace the above line with this
// var url = 'https://raw.githubusercontent.com/gr33ndata/d3book/master/ch9/data/lastfm.
json'
```

To load JSON files, use d3.json(). Like in d3.csv() earlier in this chapter, you need to define a callback function to be called once the data is available. In this example, you first load the tracks returned and assign them to the tracks variable. Next, sort tracks by number of listeners, and then call the draw() function, which we will define shortly. For brevity, we omitted error handling this time:

```
// Load the JSON data from Last.fm, and draw them!
d3.json(url, function(error, data){
  var tracks = data.tracks.track;
  tracks = tracks.sort(function(a,b){
    var a = parseInt(a.listeners, 10);
    var b = parseInt(b.listeners, 10);
    return (a == b)? 0 : ( (a > b)? -1 : 1 );
  })
  draw(tracks);
});
```

So far we have used two functions, draw() and filter(), though we haven't defined them yet. The former is to assign the retrieved tracks to the global variable all_tracks, plot the dots into the drawing area, move the slider according to the number of tracks retrieved, and set the labels. We are using global variables here. It's not a best practice, but we don't want to complicate the code here. The latter function, filter(), is invoked by the slider, with the number of tracks, n, a user wants to see. It takes the first *n* items of the all_tracks array, move them a bit, so they occupy the whole drawing area and push the remaining tracks out. This is simply done by changing the x and y scales, so they only incorporate the subset of tracks we want to display. It's clear now that we need a way to change the scales according to the number of tracks we want to plot, thus we are going to define a third function set_scales() to do that task for us. It will be used by both draw() and filter().

Before jumping to the code, we need to quickly tell you about a helpful d3 method called extent. When applied onto an array, it returns the minimum and maximum values of that array:

```
d3.extent([3,4,1,6,12,5,8]); // returns [1, 12]
```

Extent can also be given a way to extract the values from the array's items.

```
var people = [{'name': 'Tarek', 'age': 35}, {'name': 'Amr', 'age': 63}];
d3.extent(people, function(d){return d.name }); // returns ["Amr", "Tarek"]
d3.extent(people, function(d){return d.age }); // returns [35, 63]
```

And here are the three remaining functions, which are all we need to make the chart interactive:

```
// Change scale according to number of tracks to be shown.
var set_scales = function(tracks){

  var xDomain = d3.extent(tracks, function(d){
    return parseInt(d.listeners, 10);
  });

  var yDomain = d3.extent(tracks, function(d){
    return parseInt(d.playcount, 10);
  });

  return {
    'xScale': d3.scale.log().base(10).domain(xDomain)
                .range([margin, w-margin]),
    'yScale': d3.scale.log().base(10).domain(yDomain)
                .range([h-margin, margin])
  }
} // End of set_scales()

// Draw and set everything once we get the data.
var draw = function(tracks){

  // Define x and y scales,

  // based on the number of available tracks.
  var scales = set_scales(tracks);
  var xScale = scales.xScale;
  var yScale = scales.yScale;

  nodes = svg.selectAll('node')
          .data(tracks).enter()
          .append('circle').attr('class', 'node')
          .attr('cx', function(d,i){ return xScale(d.listeners); })
          .attr('cy', function(d,i){ return yScale(d.playcount); })
          .attr('r', function(d,i){ return 25*Math.pow(0.96, i); })
          .attr("fill", function(d,i){ return colors(d.artist.name); })
```

```
        .on('mouseover', function(d,i){
            // Set label to track/atrist names upon hover.
            d3.select('#top_label')
               .text('' + d.name + ' by ' + d.artist.name);
        })
        .on('mouseout', function(d,i){
            // Set label back to number of tracks we have.
            d3.select('#top_label')
               .text('Listing top ' + tracks.length + ' tracks')
        });

   all_tracks = tracks;

   // Set labels to number of tracks retrieved.
   d3.select('#top_label')
     .text('Listing top ' + tracks.length + ' tracks');

   // Move slider to show all 50 tracks.
   d3.select('#slider').attr('max', tracks.length).attr('value', tracks.length);

} // End of draw()

// Move dots when slider is changed.
var filter = function(n){

   // We only want top n tracks,
   var tracks = all_tracks.slice(0, n);
   // Define x and y scales accordingly
   var scales = set_scales(tracks);
   var xScale = scales.xScale;
   var yScale = scales.yScale;

   // Change the top label according to the new value of n.
   d3.select('#top_label').text('Listing top ' + tracks.length + ' tracks');

   // Move nodes to their new positions.
   nodes.transition()
        .duration(2000)
        .attr('cx', function(d,i){ return xScale(d.listeners); })
        .attr('cy', function(d,i){ return yScale(d.playcount); })
        .style("opacity",function(d, i){ return (i>n)? 0 : 1; });

} // End of filter()
```

In addition to CSV and JSON, d3 has d3.text(), d3.xml(), d3.html() and d3.tsv() for retrieving text files, XML, HTML and TSV (tabulation-separated values) data, respectively. They all work more or less the same way, thus, it should be easy for you to use them whenever you need to deal with such kinds of data.

Combining Data from Multiple Sources

We have already demonstrated how to load data from external sources. Sometimes you might need to combine data from multiple sources on the fly. Calling d3.json() or d3.csv() multiple times sounds like a good idea here; however there is a catch: they all work in an asynchronous manner. This means that you cannot be sure which data will be available to you first, and which one will be there next. Maybe, you want to wait for all your data to be available at once in order to combine them, and the asynchronous calls might complicate that for you.

Mike Bostock, the author of d3.js, created another helper library called Queue. It gives you the ability to specify the URLs for the data you want to get; it grabs the data asynchronously and calls back when done:

```
<script src="https://d3js.org/d3-queue.v2.min.js"></script>
<script type="text/javascript">

queue()
    .defer(d3.json, "http://urlone.com/data1.json")
    .defer(d3.json, "http://urltwo.com/data2.json")
    .await(function(error, d1, d2) {
      if (error) return console.warn(error);
      console.log(d1, d2);
    });
</script>
```

As you can see, in defer() you first specify that you want to use "d3.json" to load the data, then the URL for your data. The await() method is called when the data is available, the first parameter contains error messages in case of error, followed by the data loaded. We called our data variables d1 and d2 here.

■ **Note**   Queue will be included in D3 in version 4.

Open Data Around the World

The Global Open Data Index—published by Open Knowledge Foundation—provides a snapshot of the global state of open data. Countries are given score based on how open their governmental data is. These scores go from zero to 100%. For the next example, we will plot these scores on a map as shown in Figure 9-4, where each country is represented by a circle, its size represents the score. We are going to combine the data from the Global Open Data Index with another data file containing the latitude and longitude of each country, so that the circles are arranged according to the countries' geographical locations. D3 provides us with more advanced ways for plotting geographical data, but we are not going to cover them in this book. Let's stick to this simple method for now.

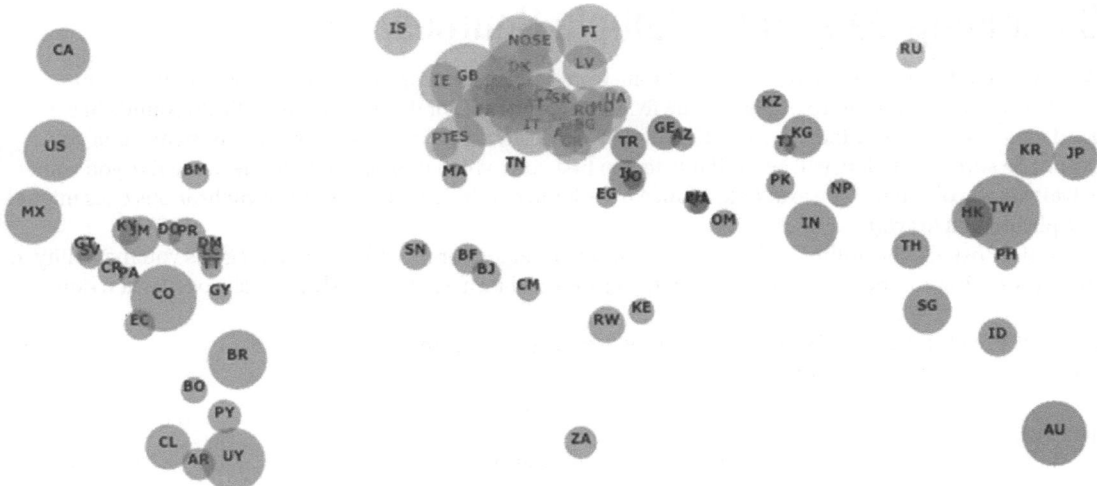

Figure 9-4. *Global Open Data Index*

To get the chart in Figure 9-4, start by setting your variables and drawing area. Don't forget to include the queue library before this code:

```
var w = 900, h = 450;

var odi_url = "http://index.okfn.org/api/places.json";
var geo_url = "https://gist.githubusercontent.com/sindresorhus/1341699/raw/84704529d9ee4965d
f2cddc55e5f2bc3dc686950/countrycode-latlong-array.json";

var svg = d3.select('body').append('svg').attr('width', w).attr('height', h);
```

Next, specify the scales.

```
// Circles for each region will be in different color
var colors = d3.scale.category10();

// Longitude goes from -180 to 180
var xScale = d3.scale.linear().domain([-180, 180]).range([0, w]);

// Latitude goes from -90 to 90
var yScale = d3.scale.linear().domain([90, -90]).range([0, h]);

// Circles radii are function of score
var rScale = d3.scale.linear().domain([0, 100]) .range([0, 28]);
```

Use the queue() method to grab the data for both the Index and the coordinates. Once done, pass the data to the drawing function:

```
queue().defer(d3.json, odi_url).defer(d3.json, geo_url)
        .await(function(error, odi, geo) {
            if (error) return console.warn(error);
```

```
      draw(odi, geo);
    });

var draw = function(odi, geo){

  // Add coordinates to Index data
  odi.forEach(function(d, i){
      try {
        d.lat = geo[d.id][0];
        d.lng = geo[d.id][1];
      }
      catch(err) {
        d.lat = d.lng = null;
      }
  });

  // Ignore countries we could not get coordinates for.
  // Also declutter the drawing by ignoring countries with low score
  odi = odi.filter(function(d, i){
    if (d.lng == null) {
      return false;
    } if (d.score < 20) {
      return false;
    } else {
      return true;
    }
  });

  // Draw a circle for each country
  svg.selectAll("circle")
    .data(odi)
    .enter()
    .append("circle")
    .attr("cx", function(d,i){
      return xScale(d.lng);
    })
    .attr("cy", function(d,i){
      return yScale(d.lat);
    })
    .style("r", function(d,i){
      return rScale(d.score);
    })
    .style("fill", function(d,i){
      return colors(d.continent);
    })
    .style("opacity",function(d){
      return 0.45;
    });

  // Similarly, add country labels yourself

}
```

Some countries are overlapping with each other. Maybe force layout can be helpful here, by giving the circles some charges to keep them apart, while using the latitudes and longitudes as centres of gravity for each circle then.

Summary

In this chapter you have learned how to load external data. Although, data can be available in different formats, from CSV to JSON to text, C3 provides ways for loading each format. You have also seen how to load data from multiple sources asynchronously, and process them once they are all available and ready. Throughout, you have also learnt how to reorder data, and use filters to only plot parts of your data while ignoring other parts you don't want to show.

In the previous chapters you also leaned how to use layouts to manipulate the data you want to present, and prepare it for the various visualization forms. You also know, by now, how to create different shapes with D3. Additionally, you have seen how to use other D3 facilities such as scales and transitions. You should treat all of those D3 components as building blocks now. Whenever you need to represent some data in a visual form, you can mix and match these blocks to come up with a visualization that perfectly represents your data, even if this requires you to come up with some visualizations no one has created before.

In the end, as they say in the fields of industrial design and architecture, "form follows function." Choosing how to deliver your message via data visualization is a combination of art and science. You always have to think, what form of visualization will make your findings clearer? You also have to think of the media you use. Animations are good for online materials and on TV, but will not work in a printed newspaper or a book. You should always look for inspirations wherever you can, and feel free to try new things when possible.

Index

T. Amr and R. Stamboliyska, *Practical D3.js*, DOI 10.1007/978-1-4842-1928-7

Q, R

Quantitative and Ordinal Scales, 83
Quantitative Linear Scales, 83

S

Scalable Vector Graphics (SVG)
    bar chart, 76
    CSS class, 98
    cx values, 103
    cy values, 103
    D3 (*see* Data-Driven Documents (D3))
    data binding, 99
    data values, 92
    definition, 75
    diagonal generator, 104
    diagonals, 105
    HTML file, 75
    HTML page, 92
    Linux distributions, 102
    max() function, 103
    min() function, 103
    path, 91
    scales, 103
    text-anchor attribute, 98

Stack layout
    code implementation, 123
    overlapping areas chart, 121
    stacked area chart, 122
    stacked radial area
        chart, 126
startAngle() method, 110

T

Text-anchor attribute, 98
Treemap Layout
    code implementation, 115
    cx function, 116
    cy function, 116
    NYC Budget 2015, 115

U

United Nations High Commissariat for Refugees
    (UNHCR), 45

V, W, X, Y, Z

value() method, 112, 115

Get the eBook for only $5!

Why limit yourself?

Now you can take the weightless companion with you wherever you go and access your content on your PC, phone, tablet, or reader.

Since you've purchased this print book, we're happy to offer you the eBook in all 3 formats for just $5.

Convenient and fully searchable, the PDF version enables you to easily find and copy code—or perform examples by quickly toggling between instructions and applications. The MOBI format is ideal for your Kindle, while the ePUB can be utilized on a variety of mobile devices.

To learn more, go to www.apress.com/companion or contact support@apress.com.